PERFECT MURDER, VIOLENCE, AND DESECRATION, AT THE ASYLUM

BOOK I OF THE DANNY MCGRAW DETECTIVE SERIES

A NOVEL BY CARL DOUGLASS

Neurosurgeon Turned Author
Writes With Gripping Realism

PUBLICATION
CONSULTANTS
We Believe In The Power Of Authors

8370 Eleusis Drive, Anchorage, Alaska 99502-4630
books@publicationconsultants.com—www.publicationconsultants.com

ISBN Number: 978-1-59433-005-6
eBook ISBN Number: 978-1-59433-208-1

Library of Congress Number: 2024948604

Manufactured in the United States of America

DISCLAIMER

This is strictly a book of fiction; all characters and events are the products of the author's twisted mind and any resemblance to people living or dead, crimes, or other miscarriages, would be no more than coincidental and certainly unintentional.

CONTENTS

Contents

PART III: JACOB ROTH WHITESIDES

PART IV: DANNY MCGRAW & JACOB WHITESIDES

PART I

JACOB WHITESIDES

CHAPTER 1

Between St. Louis Street and Soto Street along Brooklyn Avenue, Boyle Heights, Los Angeles, California, July 30, 1940

JULY 30 THAT YEAR WAS something of an important day in Boyle Heights. Fourteen new Jewish children were born in the subdivision in the Mt. Sinai Hospital—now located on in the new building on Bonnie Beach Place. It was an all-time record for the growing Jewish community. It was greeted as a happy indicator of the successful and safe growth of the Jewish community in California, and a welcome harbinger of the future.

Jacob Abramson Whitesides and Rebecca Whitesides welcomed a new eight-pound-two-ounce boy into the world and quickly gave him the name of Jacob Roth Whitesides—the middle name being a nod to Rebecca's prestigious father, the Rabbi Roth. The *Brit Milah* [Bris] was scheduled on his eighth day of life even though that would occur on Shabat. Given that he was the first child–the first son, of the prominent couple–a fairly major celebration was planned, and everyone who was anyone was invited. That included community leaders of the predominately Yiddish speaking Jewish elite, their close neighbors, business associates from the Hispanic, Japanese, Russian, Armenian, Mexican, Turkish, Italian, and African American families, the elected leaders of the Boyal Heights Socialist and Communist parties, and the ranking members of the members of the *Arbeter Ring* [Workers Circle]. It gratified the proud new parents that there was more than enough of the congregation to form a *minyan* [the congregational quorum of 10 is required in order to recite certain prayers, according to Jewish law].

The excited and congratulatory party met in the ballroom of the Boyle Hotel: a fine hotel adjacent to the new streetcar lines on First Street, an area known as the Cummings Block. The elegant hotel opened to the public in 1889, the Queen Anne style building featured decorative brickwork, cast iron columns, and a corner turret with an open balcony and quickly became a hub of social and political activity in the neighborhood. Although the hotel had a fine dining room and excellent chefs and kitchen help, the manager agreed to have the after-bris luncheon catered by Canter's Brothers Delicatessen because the principals of the Jewish community and the parents kept kosher. For the gentiles, a feast was put together by young women from the Russian Molokan community, a Christian sect.

The *mohel* performing the circumcision bris itself was Senior Rabbi Eretz Guzik of the Sinai Temple–a Conservative synagogue located at on Wilshire Boulevard, Westwood, Los Angeles. The Sinai Temple congregation was the oldest and largest congregation in the greater Los Angeles area. Rabbi Guzik was quick and proficient. No females were permitted in this enclave of orthodox and kosher fastidious Jewry. There were mohels from among many physicians, rabbis, cantors, and nurse-midwives. Senior Rabbi Guzik was considered to be the best trained in the Jewish laws concerning circumcision, as well as in modern surgical hygiene.

He was also the most sought after; so, his agreement to do the circumcision factored as a decided plus in the start of the new boy-child and his family's lives. The baby boy was given a sugar nipple soaked in whiskey to suck on, then went into a dreamless sleep. The *mohel* recited a blessing acknowledging that the *mitzvah* [commandment] of circumcision is about to be fulfilled. The bris surgery itself seemed to be almost an afterthought because Rabbi Guzik was so deft, quick, and bloodless. Little Jacob made only a momentary whimper.

A gentile nanny took over care of the sleeping baby while the adults enjoyed a beautiful lunch. During the lunch, there was a lecture on the progress of Judaism in the United States, and the questionable status of the faith in Germany, by Upton Sinclair. Afterwards, a local Yiddish band played lively klezmer music. The men offered handkerchiefs to their women, who held them while they danced about the polished ballroom floor working up a healthy sweat. They rested from the ardors of the dance for a light lunch including the obligatory bread for saying *HaMotzi* [the blessing over bread], and wine for the *Kiddush* [the blessing over wine]. Local baker's union kosher bakers made the finest bagels and the green grocers union provided the best quality lox, cream cheese, and chopped onions. Immediately after lunch, Senior Rabbi Guzik officiated in the baby naming ceremony.

The satiated congregants listened to Arlene Feingold play Beethoven's *Für Elise* in a piano recital, and to an soprano operatic solo—Puccini's *Nessun dorma*– by Judith bat Sofer, the music teacher in the schul.

And, thus, Jacob Roth Whitesides, was set on his preordained course of a Jewish life: religious observance, kosher habits, strict Jewish schooling, and eventually an acceptable profession for a man. In order—doctor, lawyer, engineer, professor of rabbi. He would marry in the faith, have children until his wife was no longer to do her part, and to settle into his role as a generous provider and patriarch of a large and religious progeny.

CHAPTER 2

A boy's life in Boyle Heights, 1930-1950

ORIGINALLY MARKETED AS AN UPSCALE development with pictur-esque views, beautiful parks, and a convenient location, Boyle Heights was home to approximately 2,000 residents by 1890, most of whom were affluent, white Protestants who lived on large estates in the western-most portion of the neighborhood. In an 1889 article, the *Los Angeles Times* described it as a "delightful suburb", and "here the choicest residence sites are located." The *Times* continued its laudatory description citing its "magnificent views" and a "climate that cannot be improved upon. That turgid text was featured alongside sketches of their large estates and "princely mansions", concluding with the flourish that, "the Heights was the Nob Hill of the City of Angels."

For the Whitesides, that was largely true. Almost nowhere else in the West were Jews able to live as unmolested in an unprejudiced community as provided in the progressively growing and progressively diversifying Boyle Heights. Although–for the most part–the different ethnic factions were accepting of the differences of the peoples in the subdivision, they were all fairly standoffish from each other. They kept to their own religious centers, shops, construction and repair people, doctors, hospitals, and political preferences. Intermarriage did not happen early on; and only later did newcomers begin to court and marry people not like them, and then, only with grudging acceptance in the isolated communities who lived in close physical proximity with each other.

The Jewish Whitesides kept kosher and spent most of their time with people of like religious practices. Their children went to the Breed Street Shul [actually more of a synagogue], and filled their lives with klezmer and classical music, innumerable bar mitzvahs, weddings, brises, and funeral services, that took place in the Breed Street Shul and the synagogues that dotted the area. But as the European immigrants who made up the majority of the community began to establish themselves and become wealthier, they moved west. And that loosened the tight hold of local Judaism on their lives.

The Whitesides determined to help save their haven. The talk in Europe was ominous. That man Hitler was a real Jew hater. He wrote a nasty little book, *Mein Kampf*, which just reeked of antisemitic hatred and worse; was talking pogroms, exclusions, thefts—including of the Jews' dignity and right to live. That stupid little desert town, Las Vegas, would not let Jews stay anyplace in the whole town except one hotel off the Strip–the King David Hotel, named after the world renowned location by Dan Hotels in Jerusalem. It was squeeze in between Treasure Island and the Mirage. They were lumped with the Blacks who could not walk into a hotel, play a slot, or get a drink. In Boyle Heights, they were safe; and he was not at all sure that he or his family could be safe anyplace else. Even Los Angeles had segregation for Blacks, Hispanics, Japanese, and Jews. All of those got along in Boyle Heights and supported one another.

Jacob Abramson took pleasure in taking his very bright namesake son to shul five days a week, and to Shabat services every Saturday night with the men of the Bikur Cholim Society—[visiting the sick]. It was a way of giving back; but, more importantly, a way to keep the community together in helping itself. Young Jacob was introverted, had few friends, and never seemed to be able to learn anything athletic. But, he took to the mission of the society with genuine enthusiasm, and more than that, to the men and their ideas.

The effort reflected the Jewish value of *bikur cholim* ("visiting the sick")–a traditional *halakhic* (Jewish religious law) principle that deems alleviating the suffering of the ill and offering prayers on their behalf to be an important *mitzvah* [commandment or good deed]. In 1920, the group established the *Bikur Cholim* Society and purchased a small home in Boyle Heights to provide round-the-clock care for the neighborhood's "incurables."

"*Tattele*," he asked his father, "why do Jews so often work together instead of on their own?"

"*Meine Zun*, it is because we have always been weak when we were alone. We do not have it in our souls to fight back. And that is a very poor quality of our community. Now, we are becoming different. We are to work together, collectively. And we are not going to be zo willing to take the guff coming from the goyim. The Bikur Cholim Society is getting together tonight to take care of a real problem in our community. Watch and learn tonight, *meine lieber zun*. I vant you to know that I *kvell* in your successes in the skul. I am proud of you. I look for great things from you, my boy. You will be a fine *mentsch* one day. "

The origins of Mt. Sinai Hospital — part of today's Cedars-Sinai Medical Center — can be traced to the 1918 pandemic, The origins of Mt. Sinai Hospital—one part of today's Cedars-Sinai Medical Center—can be traced to the influenza epidemic of 1918-1919 when a group of Jewish Angelenos provided kindness and comfort to the sick.

By the end of the decade, the Bikur Cholim Society moved into a large building on Bonnie Beach Place. They raised enough funds to purchase a lot on the corner of Breed Street and Michigan Avenue, just a half block from the neighborhood's largest synagogue, the Breed Street Shul for the Congregation Talmud Torah). Jacob, Sr. commissioned architect S. Charles Lee–known for his movie theaters–to design a 12,000 square foot facility on site—Bonnie Beach Place. When it came into service as the Mt. Sinai Home for Chronic Invalids, the facility had a kosher kitchen and chapel, a small prayer room, and a space for observant Jewish patients to receive care. The Mt. Sinai Home provided a space for observant Jewish patients to receive decent care.

The Bikur Cholim Society meetings took on a progressively more serious left-wing tone and intention during the period when young Jacob attended. He had never heard the term "brain-washing"; but, for all intents and purposes, that is what it was.

Three nights a week, the boy—pre-bar Mitzvah—sat with his father and listened to the expressions of unequal treatment in the factories, harassment at the voting polls, discrimination in stores, shops, and for services outside their haven of Boyle Heights. He and his siblings heard the same persuading conversations at home and at school. By age thirteen–when he was to become a man–he was a thoroughly persuaded young and serious socialist.

With the ever increasing demographic diversity in the subdivision, Jacob lived in an enclave of anti-capitalism: Criticism of capitalism comes from various political and philosophical approaches, including anarchist, socialist, Marxist, religious, and nationalist, viewpoints.

The head of the bakers' minyan told Jacob, "Capitalism is inherently exploitative, alienating, unstable, unsustainable, and creates massive inequality, commodifies people, and is anti-democratic and leads to an erosion of human rights and national sovereignty while it incentivizes imperialist expansion and war, and that it benefits a small minority at the expense of the majority of the population."

Despite the man's paucity of formal education, he was well-schooled in his socialistic studies; and Jacob was influenced. That influence was enhanced because of the fact that he was doing an apprenticeship in the bakery trade with the speaker. His father insisted that the job was only temporary, and Jacob was lucky to have any job during the lean and mean Depression times.

Benyamin ben Cohen–a humble bank teller and an anarchist–told him, "I oppose government privilege that protects capitalist, banking, and land interests and the accumulation or acquisition of property, and the forms of coercion that led to it. I believe it is poor economic policy because it hampers competition and keeps wealth in the hands of the few."

Jehosephat Abulafia–a Sephardic Jew from Herzegovina–was living in Boyle Heights while he did an apprenticeship to become a rabbi in the Bonnie Beach Place shul, said, "There is little moral difference between chattel slavery and renting one's self to an owner or "wage slavery". Young man, be ever mindful of the big four monopolies–land, money, tariffs, and patents, that have emerged under capitalism, and hold common men down and foster inequality.

"The badness of inequality in terms of waste and domination is that it leads to waste because resources that would be better off in the hands of the poor are put in the hands of people who don't need them. Inequality leads to domination because when some people are much richer than others, they can manipulate the basic institutions of society so that things keep going their way."

A guest speaker from UCLA, Professor Hyman Shabashewitz, from Warsaw, Poland to avoid the seemingly inevitable onslaught of Nazism, argued that "the case for socialism rests on widely shared premises and values. Different socialists will give different answers to these questions, advocating for worker cooperatives, small communes, national ownership, or something else. It is my personal contention that different sorts of goods should be socialized in different ways; and some goods, like foods, shouldn't be socialized at all. The services of medical care should be entirely socialized and treated like a public utility. Socialism is the only hope for freedom, fairness, and democracy.

"Capitalism requires the intervention of some invisible and inexplicable hand. But think about the range of conditions or types of markets under which the invisible hand fails to work, even in theory; such as dealing with monopolies and cartels, unequal or even hidden information between buyer and seller, negative externalities, tragedies of the commons, public goods, planned obsolescence, rent-seeking, cronyism, markets that manufacture the preferences they satisfy. All of them are inculcate evils of capitalism and unavoidable.

"In socialist societies, most markets fall under at least one of those categories. We can always try to regulate our way towards better markets; but in capitalist societies, regulators tend to work for the businesses they are supposed to regulate. I argue that We the People should use our minds and energies to think of other ways of getting people the goods they need.

"Anyone who has worked at a medium-to large-sized business knows that lots of jobs that do exist shouldn't. This is because managers solve problems by hiring new managers. To some extent, it's because once you create a job, it can be hard to get rid of. That regularly leads to duplication, waste, and abuse in government and in companies. Studies show that most people think that their own jobs shouldn't exist. Think of advertisers, debt traders and collectors, secretaries and assistants for people who don't need secretaries or assistants, and people with political science degrees.

"But think seriously about the most important jobs that you could possibly do, especially with a good, state supported education like researching clean meat, risk research, low-cost overseas public health interventions. Think of different—nonprofit oriented funding for research, treatment, and prevention of diseases of poverty like malaria versus diseases of affluence like hypertension. That is because they appear–in the short term, not to be profitable, or because they run contrary to the interests of the very wealthy.

"Consider those vital but seriously underpaid professions: social workers, home attendants, janitors, police officers, firemen, corrections officers, farm workers, warehouse workers, childcare providers, teachers, and the like. Think what life could and should be like."

Jacob was swayed and very interested. But it was not until his twelfth birthday that he became converted. And that was to Communism.

CHAPTER 3

Preparation for the Bar Mitzvah, Boyle Heights and other locations in California, 1940-1943

A LOW-GRADE FERVOR FOR SOCIALISM and Communism was spreading through Boyle Heights, and not just among the Jewish community. Most of the rest of Southern California was going Republican and leaning heavily towards the right. When young Jacob Whitesides was approaching his crucial thirteenth birthday, considerable attention was drawn to him; first, in the Jewish community where he was becoming recognized as something of a Talmudic scholar, even by the elders. That made his parents–especially his father–proud. Second, in the shul, his teachers had become convinced that the boy had learned all they had to teach; and he should be placed in a Jewish leaning, but full academic, school.

Third, he was noticed by a cohort of young Jewish activists raised in the Yiddish-speaking immigrant milieu of Los Angeles who had come of age in the YCL [Young Communist League] in the thirties, including Dorothy Ruth Healey (née Dorothy Mroczek), who was working on a book manuscript entitled, *Yiddish*, and Rebecca Ben Dobbs (née Ben Shalvi) called the "Cinderella of the sweatshops", and others who were becoming prominent leaders of the California Communist Party by the 1940s.

Jacob and Rebecca Whitesides spared no expense, put their hearts on their sleeves, and announced the upcoming Bar Mitzvah of their son, Jacob Roth Whitesides, for August 2nd, a Monday. The crème de la crème of Boyle Heights gentry, the important figures in Los Angeles Jewry, the rank-and-file members of the union movement in Los Angeles County, the ranking figures in the Socialist and Communist parties, and any and all friends they had ever made to attend. They promised a live band, the presence of a renowned rabbi, and a party like the county had never seen before. The RSVPs began pouring in until it became clear that they were going to have to rent a large hall to accommodate the crowd of well-wishers, even if they were no more than curiosity seekers. The only thing left was to bring all of that to pass—no mean task—they were to discover.

To further their efforts, Jacob and his parents responded in the affirmative to an invitation they received from a Los Angeles Jewish organization.

> "Please join the UC Davis Jewish Studies program for the New Directions in Jewish Studies lecture series, which features research by scholars working outside the tenure track. Our next talk is "California Reds: Young Jewish Communists in the 1930s and early 1940s".
> Eva Kaye Rabinowitz, Director, Jewish Studies Program at UC Davis 1 Shields Ave, Davis, California, Rosenthal Building.

The Whitesides family and Senior Rabbi Eretz Guzik went together to the highly touted lecture to celebrate Jacob's twelfth birthday. They motored into Los Angeles in the rabbi's forest green 1939 Lincoln town car with white sidewall tires. He was fortunate to have purchased his automobile early that year, because he would not have been able to get one for another eight years. Early in the 1940s, carmakers were forced to build tanks and airplanes for the war effort. In 1941, it also became clear that production of passenger cars would need to be cut to save materials for defense purposes. As far as cars were concerned, World War II shut down the industry.

Assistant Professor Rabinowitz introduced the speaker:

"It is my honor to introduce Rosa Louise McCauley Parks as tonight's guest speaker. Mrs. Parks became is an NAACP activist and has participated in several high-profile civil rights campaigns. She is an up-and-coming star in our drive for equality. We expect great things from her. Mrs. Parks:"

Rosa Parks spoke in a clear, soft voice unlike the strident activists who were better known on the Negro Equality circuit. She waited until the assembled crowd was silent before starting her talk.

"During the recent past 1930s, and even now in the 1940s, a series of severe dust storms swept across the mid-west states of Oklahoma, Arkansas, Kansas, and Texas. The storms, years of drought, and the Great Depression, devastated the lives of residents living in those Dust Bowl states. Three hundred thousand of the stricken people packed up their belongings and drove to California. Here in Los Angeles, we speak of "The Dust Bowl, California, and the Politics of Hard Times.

"Let us examine the cultural, social, and political, impact the Dust Bowl migrants has had on California. The photographs of Dorothea Lange, songs and lyrics of Woody Guthrie, and storytelling genius of John Steinbeck, bring to the fore the era and people with their dramatic and poignant styles. Two California governors and their administrations grappled with the influx of the hundreds of thousands who flooded the state throughout the 1930s. The great Dust Bowl migration transformed and reshaped California for years to come.

Or Dust Bowl migrants forced California to examine its attitude toward farm work, laborers, newcomers, and Negroes to the state. The Okies changed the composition of California farm labor. They displaced the Mexican workers who had dominated the work force for nearly two decades. They lowered the standard of living for farm workers and delayed their unionization efforts. Steinbeck, Lange, and Guthrie created an image of the migrant that could not be ignored. They exposed an unfair agricultural system that had gone unnoticed for years. As the nation moves every closer to the brink of war in the 1940s, the public outcry caused by the *Grapes of Wrath*, Lange's photographs, and Guthrie's Dust Bowl ballads has dwindled. The Okies found jobs in the defense industry and are becoming assimilated into society throughout the war decade. Adverse conditions still persist for farm workers but are better than life in the Dust Bowl.

"Dust Bowl migrants forced California to examine its attitude toward farm work, laborers, and newcomers to the state. And, it appears that polite society is beginning to recognize the rights of Blacks and Jews; both are sets of discriminated against peoples. Many of the struggles in which Communists have played a leading role in the 1920s had ended in defeat. But Communists– strengthened by both the world movement of which they were a part and a political structure that united them–kept on coming and learning from the defeats. And as they moved forward, Blacks and Jews have moved with them.

"Many working people on factories and farms—as well as professional people, journalists, teachers, writers, and artists, Blacks, Whites, Jews, and Asians—who participated in these struggles learned to respect Communists for both their words and their deeds, for their courage and commitment.

"Although capitalist media, following the lead of Secretary of Commerce and later President Herbert Hoover, proclaimed the 1920s "a new era" of permanent prosperity where corporations would de-emphasize short term profits to produce better and cheaper products, workers would "democratize" capitalism by owning stocks and bonds, and the "small number" of poor would be generously cared for by private charity, this capitalist phony utopia collapsed in the great stock market crash of October, 1929.

"Communists and the CPUSA leadership took collective initiative to fight the Depression while the capitalist class was both panicking and calling upon government to do nothing and let the "free market" restore prosperity. The Capitalist predictions that the Depression would be over in weeks turned into months, and months into years. Uniting with the Communists, we Blacks carry banners reading, "**Black and white—Unite and fight!**" Our campaigns are for a national anti-lynching law, an end to "legal" segregation and disenfranchisement in the South, and for the elimination of racist policies and practices throughout society. For a new and better America!

"Over the next four years, unemployment rose to more than a third of the workforce; wages for the employed were slashed, and 25 percent of all people with bank accounts lost their savings. A Communist society would have improved all of that, and it is time that we made serious changes in this country. It is to be noted that Communism has to be wanted universally in order for Capitalism to make way for socialism and then eventually work towards Communism. It is an understatement that that will take a lot of sweat, tears, and work.

"Our current working lives of poverty and wage labor are limiting so many of us that it is truly depressing. A Communist life where everyone has equal opportunity according to their ability and need makes way for endless possibilities for anyone to reach their full potential. If that's not convincing enough, then I don't know what is. I, for one, am going to do something about it. Thanks for hearing me out."

Young Jacob Whitesides mixed and mingled with the intelligentsia of Los Angeles and from around the nation that night. He was like a dampened sponge soaking it all up. Even at the tender age of twelve, he was on the brink of signing on as a card-carrying communist. And his parents were supportive. Father Jacob thought that perhaps this movement—and his son's involvement in it would be the answer to his concerns of where Jacob was going to make his name and reputation.

Jacob Sr. and Mother Rebecca, took pains to seek out a desirable and acceptable Bar Mitzvah teacher. It took weeks and considerable research. Finally, they chose a young professor and Rabbi/Senior Jewish Educator Jesse Lasky, who led a Hillel 818 synagogue in Northridge, California. It was no secret to them or any Jew or Communist in the state that his and other similar organizations were used to insinuate trusted party members in places of strategic importance and from these vantage points they managed to recruit, indoctrinate, and carry on the party program, to the best of their ability. They admired him for that and saw him as a stepping-stone for their bright and believing son.

Hillel 818 was a collaboration of Jewish community leaders of Hillel at California State University, Northridge, and Hillel at Pierce and Valley Colleges. Hillels were the face of Jewish life on the campuses, represent Jewish campus life in the San Fernando Valley. In Northridge and at UCLA had infiltrated by a small number of radicals and gained control of the student paper, took on bright young socialistic Jews, and perpetuated the Party's viewpoint without a filter.

Rabbi Lasky was a brilliant Jewish scholar and eminently qualified to tutor the young aspiring Bar Mitzvah. He was also a dedicated working Communist who was very good at insinuating the Party Line into his instructions to Jacob. The boy was fully ready for both indoctrinations and had a curious mind ready to be filled with convincing arguments for both.

The influential rabbi drilled the fundamentals of the *Torah* and the Mitzvah into Jacob's head.

He started by explaining that, "The Lubavitcher Rebbe writes that in preparation for accepting 'the yoke of *mitzvot*,' ie. the bar mitzvah boy should spend time studying the fundamentals of Judaism, including the laws regulating daily life."

Lasky taught his willing acolyte that preparing to read from the *Torah* or chant the *haftarah* is time consuming and not nearly as important as the other studies or as the doing of good things [such as working in Communist charities]. He convinced Jacob that it was preferable to spend his precious time on the more important subjects which Rabbi Lasky chose for Jacob.

In the Whitesides' synagogue, the *Torah* was publicly read on Shabbat, Monday, and Thursday, mornings, holidays, and fast days. congregants are called up for an *aliyah*: the honor of reciting one of the blessings over the *Torah*. Rabbi Lasky made arrangements in advance for Jacob to have his day in the spotlight to read the *Torah* and on the same day to give his speech, for which Rabbi Lasky tutored him with considerable care and finesse.

Jacob became *Bar Mitzvah* [Hebrew for "son of commandment"] on his 13th birthday by the Hebrew calendar—6 Av 5703 [Following Shabbat, Birth after sunset, Saturday, August 7, 1943, by the Gregorian calendar of 1582. His date of birth was recorded as 6 Av 5690/July 30, 1930]. Being traditional, it was rather complicated. Once Jewish children reach that age, they are said to "become" *b'nai mitzvah*—undergoing the coming-of-age ritual in Judaism, at which point they begin to be held accountable for their own actions. Jacob's father first set the boy's first *Torah* reading for the late-afternoon Shabbat service [when traditionally the beginning of the *Torah* portion for the next Shabbat is read]. Then the whole family celebrated the end of Shabbat with the *Havdalah* ceremony [that distinguishes between the end of Shabbat time and the beginning of everyday time], and then the tired Whitesides moved into a Saturday-night party.

According to Jewish law, before children reach a certain age, the parents are responsible for their child's actions. At 5-years-of-age one should study the Scriptures, at 10 years for the *Mishnah*, and at 13 for the commandments. Young Jacob was about to become a man in the eyes of the synagogue congregation and his family—to be accountable. In the traditional Whitesides family, Father Jacob offered thanks to G-d that he is no longer punished for his child's sins. After the formal ceremonies in the Synagogue Israelita Casa de Dios—the first and oldest synagogue in California–young Jacob was now to be permitted to join a prayer quorum, to count him for the purpose of determining whether there is—in fact–a prayer quorum. If necessary and agreed upon, Jacob could now even lead prayer and other religious services in the family and the community. After becoming Bar Mitzvah, Jacob was going to be held responsible for knowing Jewish ritual law, tradition, and ethics, and rewarded with the legal ability to participate in all areas of Jewish community life to the same extent as adults.

CHAPTER 4

Formally becoming Bar Mitsvah ["For today, I am a man!"] in the Synagogue Israelita Casa de Dios.

ON AUGUST 7, 1943, IN view of his family, the congregants of the synagogue, God, and the Communist Party, Jacob Roth Whitesides, became Bar Mitsvah with all the privileges and responsibilities connected thereto. From that date, he was obligated to wear tefillin on a daily basis, participate in synagogue services, and take his place in the Jewish community as a man on equal footing as other men. Because of his superior intelligence and reading ability, Jacob was called to the *Torah*, even to lead the services that day. He was asked to deliver a speech or otherwise to solidify his newfound status. He was presented with his own *tefillin*, a proud gift from his paternal grandparents. *Tefillin* are black leather boxes containing parchments inscribed with the Shema and other biblical passages. The *Torah* commands adult Jewish men to bind the *tefillin* onto the head and upper arm with leather straps in fulfillment of the verse, "You shall bind them as a sign upon your hand, and they should be for a reminder between your eyes." [Deuteronomy 6:8]. *Tefillin* are worn thereafter during weekday morning prayers.

He had studied the thoughts for and the presentation of his speech *ad nauseum* with his parents and his Mitsvah teacher, Rabbi Lasky, until he did not have to glance at his notes throughout its presentation.

The speech was long, given in the way of Talmudic scholars of legal argumentation. He even made mention of the itinerant preacher and claimant to the messiahship [attributed to Moses Maimonides (1135-1204), physician and philosopher, was the greatest Jewish thinker of the Middle Ages.] who made reference to an itinerant Jewish imposter who claimed to be the Messiah, who was described ~300 CE, early in the Common Era. He reminded the congregation that the preacher, Jehosaphat/Joshua was first acknowledged by Judaism in the extant manuscripts of the book *Antiquities of the Jews*, written by the first-century Jewish historian Flavius Josephus ~CE 93–94, containing two references to Jesus of Nazareth and one reference to John the Baptist. Jacob quickly noted that most Jewish references like the contemporary to Flavius named Rabbi Eliezer, referred to "Black Magic" along with any references to the historic Jesus.

Jacob finished the part of this speech which mentioned Jesus with a quote from the *Talmud*,

"In the *Talmud*, we read, 'On the eve of Passover they hanged Yeshu (of Nazareth) and the herald went before him for forty days saying (Yeshu of Nazareth) is going to be stoned in that he has practiced sorcery and beguiled and led astray Israel. Let everyone know aught in his defense come and plead for him. But they found naught in his defense and hanged him on the eve of Passover. [*The Babylonian Talmud, Sanhedrin 43a, "Eve of Passover"*]. The *Talmud* is a collection of Jewish writings constituting their religious and civil law. They were completed by AD 500."

Jacob's speech began with a thought from the weekly *Torah* portion, which he wanted to apply in his own life. The speech was also the perfect opportunity to announce the *Mitzvah project* and thank parents, family, and friends. Jacob did that in the full flowery fashion expected of him. The choice of the project was the brain child of Rabbi Lasky and his superiors in the Party headquarters in San Francisco.

"The term *gemilut hasadim* is translated as acts of loving-kindness. The Hebrew dictionary meaning of the root g-m-l that is most supported by Talmudic usage is 'reciprocal acts'. *Gemilut* signals that these are acts done in the context of a relationship with a built-in *notion of benefit* or compensation in return for the act. This immediately differentiates our tradition from those that emphasize the selflessness of service. The *Talmud* supports this, stating that the reward for service is in this world, not in the world to come. *Chesed* appears in the *Torah* to communicate God's kindness and love toward humanity as well as human kindness and love toward each other. *Chesed* emerges as one of the essential ways humans engage with God to sustain creation.

"In the story of Sodom and Gemorrah [*Genesis* 18:17] the 15th century Italian commentator, Seforno, noted that the reason that G-d decides to engage with Abraham in discussion is based on the *chesed* that Abraham showed to the angels who visited him just prior to this in the text [*Genesis* 18:2]. Consequently, Lot and his family are rescued by G-d after Lot has tried to show *chesed*–in the form of hospitality–to his guests. Human *chesed* there results in evoking G-d's *chesed*.

"The *Talmud* further establishes *chesed* as one of the core pillars of human behavior–"The world rests upon three things, *Torah, avodah,* and *gemilut hasadim.*" [*Pirkei Avot* 1:2]. The term *gemilut hasadim* is distinctly post-biblical and occurs for the first time in the *Mishnah*. In the *Babylonian Talmud, Sukkot* 49b, a discussion is related defining *chesed* by contrasting it with the other fundamental Jewish value of *tzedakah*. *Chesed* is laid out as the broader value because it can be done not only with money, but also with one's person.

"It can be given to the rich and the poor, the living and the dead. It furthermore states that, 'the reward for charity depends entirely upon the extent of the kindness in it.' For example, when a person takes the trouble to give a poor person money in a compassionate manner and at a time when the poor person can use it well, he or she has brought *chesed* to the act of *tzedakah*. Thereby, the command to 'love your neighbor as yourself' is fulfilled [*Mishneh Torah*, chapter 14]. By so doing, one ascends to a greater law–engaging people in relationships of understanding. Through acts of *chesed* supported by *tzedakah* is where you treat someone like a human being, *b'tselem elohim* [in the image of God], with the respect they deserve, that person can be restored to the community. He or she can overcome the stigma of poverty, frailty, disease, or loneliness, and can themselves become engaged, empowered actors of chesed.

"The *Talmud* teaches in *Shabbat 127a* that the reward for *gemilut chasadim* is in this world. How can we begin to understand this? Emanuel Levinas teaches that the meaning of suffering is in the opportunity for the other to respond to that suffering, to embrace the sufferer, and–through doing so–bring G-d into the world. The only meaning for suffering is the redemptive power it may have for the person who may bear witness to that suffering; indeed, our responsiveness to suffering may be *our* only means of redemption. When we respond to the other at a time of need, we fulfill our humanity and can find existential meaning in life.

"In addition to being a prominent Jewish value, service is one important answer to the individual's search for meaning and desire for true relationships in life. The Jewish American community has done a fairly decent job of making *tzedakah* a central Jewish value—now it is time to embrace *chesed*. In doing so, we have the opportunity to bridge service and learning and to set a standard for excellent service programs.

"How do we do that? First, we all can support and contribute to trade unions to support poorly paid, overworked, and discriminated against workers. For example, those with Communist assistance include: the International Longshoremen's and Warehousemen's Union, the Marine Cooks and Stewards Union, the United Office and Professional Workers of America, the State, County, and Municipal Workers of America, the United Federal Workers of America, and the California Labor School near to us at 321 Divisadero Street in San Francisco.

"There are charitable and humanitarian organizations fostered by the peoples' Communist party that deserve and need our coordinated Jewish help: the Abraham Lincoln Brigade, American Committee for Protection of Foreign Born, American Committee for the Settlement of Jews in Birbidjan, Inc., American League for Peace and Democracy, American Rescue Ship Mission, American Russian Institute of Southern California, Los Angeles, American Women for Peace, American Youth Congress, California Emergency Defense Committee, Citizens Committee for Harry Bridges, and the Congress of American Revolutionary Writers, to name but a very few. If you wish to get a more complete list, please get hold of me any day except Shabbat.

"My friends, family, brothers and sisters, help in the cause for democracy, equal rights, nondiscrimination, and be part of the movement for the abolition of racism, antisemitism, and discrimination against foreigners. Remember the evils against Sacco and Vanzetti who were executed simply because they held a minority view. Thank you for listening to my Bar Mitzvah project. *Shalom!*"

Jacob and Rebecca beamed with pride; Rabbi Lasky smiled with deep satisfaction for his part in his acolyte's conversion; the congregation gave the new Bar Mitzvah an unprecedented standing ovation in the synagogue's main sanctuary. As ego uplifting as the response to his Bar Mitzvah speech was–particularly the presentation of his Bar Mitzvah project–it would one day come to haunt the young man and to change the direction of his life.

CHAPTER 5

Crossing the House UnAmerican Activities Committee, 1953-1960

JACOB ROTH WHITESIDES LIVED UP to his family's pride and expectations. He graduated top of his lower school class in the old Eastern European brick *heder* [religious elementary school] built in 1916 to replicate educational institutions in the old country. There had formulated the belief among many Jewish families born and educated in America that it was no longer necessary to send their children to public school to acculturate them as Americans. Those parents—including the Whitesides–wanted a Jewish educational system for their children to imbue them with Jewish thought and values. Unlike the old country, girls were to study equally with boys.

The attitude towards life and learning and therefore the curriculum was decidedly different from the Los Angeles regular school district. The parents and teachers determined that a ten-year-old needed to know how to write an ironclad contract that would stand up in court, how to be a witness on a contract, and how to make sure you're not ripping anyone off with this contract. By that stage in life, it was deemed essential to learn how to get married [the proper Jewish way], how to get divorced, how much you are going to have to pay out if you opt for divorce, and why the whole divorce thing is not a good idea. Of course, it was also of prime importance for the youngsters to learn the laws of collateral, liens on property, leases, loans, and the responsibilities of both parties in all these cases. They also put in some time on reading, writing, and arithmetic.

The founders of the American Yiddish schools were radical political activists who had come to America with the great waves of Jewish immigrants from Russia at the beginning of the 20th century. Their aims were ambitious: To continue the radical secular movement in the new land. For that reason, they determined to raise a new generation of Jews who would merge Jewishness with socialism, while at the same time becoming genuine Americans. That was going to require some near contortionist machinations to accomplish.

Religious subjects had an old and fixed place in the Jewish curriculum, while secular and nationalist themes were to be a product of more modern times. From the ages of 10-15 the young Jewish students had to learn the fine points of their religion's rituals: like how to do a kosher slaughter of an animal or fowl, how to check its inner organs to ensure it is not *treif* [food unfit to eat, non-Kosher], and how to salt it to remove its blood. The curriculum included the laws of circumcision, offerings in the Temple, tithes to the *kohanim* and levites, and the myriad of rules about ritual impurity, so that when one provided those tithes, the recipients who received it will actually be able to eat it.

The children's reading and writing had popular titles including: *Snow, Snow, The Old Tree, A Comparison between How a Miner Lives in Russia and How a Miner Lives in the United States, The Struggle of the Miner, In a Time of Strike,* Henrik Ibsen's *Spring, The First of May, The Fiddle. The School, Our Bazaar. A Crisis in the Land. Nicaragua, My Doll, My Kitten, My Little Sister, My Dream, The Shoe-Shiner, A Worker's Luck, The Squirrel, What School Accomplished for Me, Our Literature,* and *My Little Bird.*

There was a place in the daily grind of school work to include, Socialism: Utopian and Scientific [Frederick Engels' pamphlet provided a popular account of the origin of socialist ideas and the Marxist view of history, *The Mass Strike, What is to be Done?* [1903 pamphlet by Lenin], Permanent Revolution, [Leon Trotsky's theory of how the working-class struggle for socialism must develop in countries that were economically backward], *Principles of Communism, (On the Topic of Free Trade), Critique of the Gotha Programme, The Communist Manifesto* by Karl Marx, *Origin of the family, Private Property and the State, The Development of Socialism from*

Utopia to Science, Permanent Revolution [Leon Trotsky's kind of revolution that makes no compromise with any single form of class rule, does not stop at the democratic stage, and goes over to socialist measures and to war against reaction from without], and several other works that presumably delighted the enthusiastic children.

High school in Boyle Heights had a generous component of Yiddish, Jewish history and culture, and leftist politics and Zionism, a growing subject and cause. His parents had attended different high schools in the subdivision–Roosevelt and Lincoln—which gave Jacob two slightly different slants on the same subjects. He became the valedictorian of his high school class at Lincoln High School. Third, he was noticed by a cohort of young Jewish activists raised in the Yiddish-speaking immigrant milieu of Los Angeles who were coming of age in the YCL [Young Communist League] in the thirties, including Dorothy Ruth Healey (née Dorothy Mroczek), who was working on a book manuscript entitled, *Yiddish*, and Rebecca Ben Dobbs (née Ben Shalvi) called the "Cinderella of the sweatshops", and others who were becoming prominent leaders of the California Communist Party by the 1940s.

With Kristallnacht in 1938, life-threatening dangers facing European Jewry became all too real. In contrast with other American schools, the Yiddish schools taught students about the Holocaust from the very beginning. In the Yiddish schools, the children were viewed as young Jews, partners in despair, who were not to be shielded–as were other American Jewish children in that period–from the horror and suffering that was endured by their people during the war. The realistic representations of the Holocaust created a stark emotional connection between Yiddish-speaking children in America and Jews in Eastern Europe.

By the time he finished his precollege education, Jacob Whitesides was an expert on Socialism and Communism and–on his own–was tired and bored of the subjects. He was determined to strike out on his own, thought wise; but he did follow tradition by matriculating in pre-med studies at UCLA. During the mid-1940s, tuition remained fairly stable at $81 per year for in-state students and $288 for out-of-state students. Jacob and his family was disgruntled at the high price, but what choice did they have?

Jacob had been required to achieve a scholarship rank in the highest tenth of his graduating class, with a substantial academic preparation, which Father Jacob had insisted upon. Young Jacob had had to file a certificate showing successful vaccination against smallpox within the last seven years. Father Jacob had insisted on the entire family having the immunizations despite the general community's feelings that it was just one more indignity foisted on Judaism by the *goyim*. Some exceptions in the subject requirements for admission were made for men and women who were for at least one year members of the armed forces of the United States.

All new students–graduate and undergraduate—had to appear before the University Medical Examiners and pass a medical and physical examination so that the health of the University community–as well as the individual student–was safeguarded. It was strongly urged that before coming to the University, every student should have his own physician examine him/her for fitness to carry on University work. Prospective students were required to have all defects capable of remedial treatment–such as diseased tonsils, dental cavities, imperfect hearing or eyesight— corrected to prevent possible loss of time from studies.

The 1940 University Bulletin carried serious warnings for students related to their behavior: If he (no mention of she) should be guilty of unbecoming behavior or should neglect his academic duties, the University authorities *will take* such action, as the particular offense requires. "Students who fail to make proper use of the opportunities freely given to them by the University must expect to have their privileges curtailed or withdrawn. There are five degrees of discipline: warning, censure, suspension, dismissal, and expulsion. Expulsion is the most severe academic penalty and is final exclusion of the student from the University."

Housing for out-of-town women students enrolled in the University is available in one of several way–as paying guests in private homes or with relatives; in Mira Hershey Hall, the only University-operated residence hall for undergraduate women; in one of the privately owned residence halls or cooperatives; or as a resident member of one of the many sororities. Mira Hershey Hall, made available by the will of the late Miss Mira Hershey, is the only residence hall operated by the University located on the campus. Accommodations are available for 129 regular students.

Most of the men enrolled in the University lived at their family homes in the community. Living accommodations for out-of-town students are usually arranged for in two ways: as paying guests in private homes and rooming houses or as members, profit, student-managed groups. The University itself does not own or operate any dormitory or residence hall for men. Prices range from $55 to $75 per month for room and board and from $30 to $50 per month for room only. Granted, it was expensive, but the university could not be expected to bear living costs for its hundreds of students and there were a very limited number of scholarships available. There were 85 men's fraternities.

Boyle Heights was a considerable distance from the UCLA campus (18 miles); no one had cars then; and the bus and trolley system required several hours of travel time. It was crucial that the hyper-time conscious young man find lodging somewhere on or near the campus. Segregation was not the law, but it was still very much in existence. Jews and Negroes need not apply. Being a woman was hard enough (women's place was in the home, as the common social dicta went). All the fraternities were closed to Jacob; so, he had to find a shared apartment arrangement with several Negro, Jewish, and Hindu, boys.

He was able to find a fifth-floor walk-up apartment on 1590 East 114th Street in Nickerson Gardens–a 1,066-unit public housing apartment complex in Watts, Los Angeles. Nickerson Gardens was the largest public housing development west of the Mississippi River and the complex occupied the blocks northeast of the corner of Imperial Highway and Central Avenue, and southwest of 111th St and Compton Avenue. It is on the border of both Watts in South Los Angeles and Willowbrook. Nickerson Gardens was already 95% African American when Jacob applied. The complex was operated by HAPLA [Housing Authority of the City of Los Angeles].

The locals in the complex did not care about his race, religion, or ethnicity; they were too poor and were struggling too hard to have time for managing a segregated society.

The rent was $16 a month with a shared outside privy. He considered that to be a successful find since the median monthly gross rent across the United States then was $27 a month. The average income was $1,368. 51%

of all families were poor in 1940; minimum wage was 25 cents an hour; so, with a little supplemental grocery delivery job, Jacob was in good company.

The bus service ran 24 hours a day and on time; so, Jacob could get in a little study time on the way to classes. He considered that he wasted no time of any significance for travel. His hours were very early in the morning and late afternoon; so, he avoided the crowds and the bus and train violent crime that made life miserable for his fellow citizens of Nickerson Gardens.

UCLA was—at the time—on the "Beverly Site"—an undeveloped 383-acre area just west of Beverly Hills—edging out the panoramic hills of the still-empty Palos Verdes Peninsula. Los Angeles, Santa Monica, Beverly Hills, and Venice, raised the $3M bond for purchase of the property. Ground breaking on the new campus in Westwood had taken place in September, 1927; but construction officially began May 7, 1928, on four buildings. The neighboring communities of Westwood Village and Bel Air were developed alongside the university.

Jacob and his neighbors were in the "other America": the unskilled workers, migrant farm workers, the aged, minorities, and all the others who lived in the economic underworld of American life. Residents had struggled to secure housing in Los Angeles extending back to the 19th century, when transient laborers rode the rails west to the city seeking work. Single, often older, White, men comprised most of nonBlack segment of the Compton and Watts population into the 1970s.

Jacob matriculated formally at UCLA by registering in the College of Letters and Sciences, the department which had the pre-med curriculum he had his heart set on. It was a most interesting and difficult time to be starting college. By virtue of his acceptance in the university, Jacob had a draft deferment.

The UCLA student body in those years gained a radical reputation. One of its provosts described UCLA as "the worst hotbed of communism in the US, and the faculty suspended five members of the ASUCLA Associated Students of UCLA]–student government–for "using their offices to assist the revolutionary activities of the National Student League, a Communist organization which has bedeviled the University for some months." The Communist Party inveigled more than 3,000 students to gather in protest in Royce Quad; and a campus police officer–attempting to silence the speakers–was thrown into some bushes. The crowd dispersed before any arrests were made, but the university president reinstated those students. A vigilante group of 150 athletes calling themselves "UCLA Americans pledged to purge the campus of radicals".

The December 7, 1941 airstrike on Pearl Harbor immediately put the campus on a wartime basis. Faculty adjusted the curriculum and academic schedule to assist students entering military service. President Sproul immediately established a University War Council, and with the year an "Engineering, Science and Management War Training" program in industrial sciences was established at UCLA, which trained workers in defense industries. UCLA became responsible for Project 36 of the Manhattan Project, that of purchasing and inspecting equipment for the scientists at Los Alamos. In conjunction with these projects, the UCLA College of Engineering was established in 1943. Male enrollment at UCLA dropped from 5107 before the war to 2407 the year after.

Before the war ended and Jacob Whitesides graduated, veteran students on the G.I. Bill began to trickle in at UCLA creating more competition for the tired young man. He was approaching the time to apply for his clinical years of medical school. Up to that time, UCLA had only two years of medical school—the preclinical subjects. By 1947, veterans accounted for 43% of the total student body.

By dint of his very hard work in academics and in his off-campus work, Jacob got straight As, made a success of his arduous efforts to keep afloat money-wise, and had no social life outside his work. He became almost invisible socially, a status he did not like, and developed a somewhat reclusive approach to life that would cause him regret very soon and for years to come. The curricula of the College of Letters and Science were designed to provide the student with opportunities to broaden his culture and to prepare him for specialized professional studies. These curricula led to the degree of Associate in Arts, normally at the end of the fourth semester, and to the degree of either Bachelor of Arts or Bachelor of Science, normally at the end of the eighth semester. Jacob achieved his BS degree after six semesters with a perfect academic record. German was required of him because of his interest in medicine, and the best work in the world for medicine was being done in Germany.

Although his personal preference would have been to concentrate wholly on the biological sciences and premed courses, the university required a more liberal education to become "well-rounded." To achieve that end, Jacob studied German and became fluent, and found relaxation in learning to play the piano. He considered himself lucky to be chosen to have the eminent and personable Dr. Hilda Straude as his teacher. She taught him to enjoy the piano, the tunes, the history, and the sheer joy of listening and performing. The city had a plethora of venues, ranging from small, intimate, clubs to massive stadiums. Dr. Straude played in them all. She played piano for physical education classes in the UCLA women's gym, appeared in the small clubs like the Troubador and the Roxi, and performed with the Hollywood Bowl Symphony Orchestra which drew its players from among members of the Los Angeles Philharmonic and various film studios orchestras. Jacob took two nights off to see her featured as the solo pianist playing such complicated pieces as Stravinsky's *Trois mouvements de Petrouchka*, Ravel's *Gaspard de la Nuit*, and Listzt's *La Campanella* with flawless professional ease.

During their extended practice sessions, Jacob learned that they shared an almost secret interest. After his third week under her tutelage, he learned that she was a registered member of the California Communist Party and she was delighted to find out that his youth was dominated by Communist parents and their circle of friends in the very Communist friendly suburb of Boyle Heights. He occasionally accompanied Dr. Straude when she lectured to Communist gatherings in his hometown.

During WWII, accelerated 3-year medical school programs were initiated as a novel approach to address physician shortages; government incentives were used to boost the number of 3-year medical schools along with changed laws aiding licensure for graduates. A three-year program and some financial help appealed greatly to Jacob. With his degrees in hand, Jacob applied for medical schools with a fast-track three-year graded curriculum in medicine and surgery: Columbia University College of Physicians and Surgeons, University of Miami, Mercer University School of Medicine in Savannah, The New York University School of Medicine, Duke University School of Medicine, the Perelman School of Medicine at the University of Pennsylvania, and Harvard Medical School.

He was accepted at Columbia, Mercer, and two Canadian schools. A week after receiving his congratulatory letters from the four schools, he got a curt letter from each rescinding the invitation to matriculate.

"We do not accept Jewish students. This is a Christian only school. However–in your case–there is a second reason for us to rescind our invitation. It has come to our attention that you are a known associate of a prominent member of the American Communist Party, Dr. Hilda Straude, who is a person of interest by the HUAC [House Un-American Activities Committee] investigating public and private individuals in active association with the Communist movement which is detrimental to our democracy and to the war effort."

Upon opening the letters, Jacob rushed to the music building to talk to Dr. Straude. She was hurriedly packing her papers into satchels and boxes preparatory to leaving the university, and—presumably—her blossoming musical career.

"Dr. Straude, what is going on? Have you seen letters like these?"

He showed her his letters. She began to cry softly because her association with a promising student was proving to be highly injurious to him.

"Look at this," she said, and showed him an official letter—in fact a summons—ordering her to appear before the HUAC the following week.

A second letter came from the provost of UCLA dismissing her from the faculty because of her Communist affiliation. It was a terse firing in the extreme. She looked haggard.

"I will probably never be able to have a university position again, Jacob."

"And, I will never get into medical school," he said on the verge of tears.

"In your case, I think there is an option. Denounce me and all communists. Keep mum about your family's and your own associations with the party. You are obscure enough that they will not have records that incriminate you. Deny that you are Jewish and stay away for Jews and Jewish institutions until this terrible war is over. Apply to UC Davis Medical School or to an almost unknown school called Texas Tech. My informants tell me that they generally dislike government interference, and are still accepting Jews, but not communists. Leave that out of your interviews. You have no other choice. I'm sorry, but I have to catch a plane to DC; so, I won't be late for the subcommittee meeting. They threaten me with prison if I miss or are even late to the hearing. I am truly sorry for having brought this on you, Jacob. Try and forgive me."

"I am not going to deny my heritage or my Communist background. That would be cowardly."

"This is not the time to be silly, young man," she said sternly, "you must take care of yourself and leave behind those parts of your life. You will never get ahead at all if you speak of me, or about being a Jew, or a communist. Grow up, Jacob. You will do what I say, or you will go down with all the rest of the Jews and communists. This is completely serious. I will go to prison; there is no denying or evading my involvement. You still have a chance!"

CHAPTER 6

Meeting Senator Joe McCarthy, 1953-1960

JACOB ROTH WHITESIDES RECEIVED A subpoena to appear before the SPSI [Senate Permanent Subcommittee on Investigation] on August 1, 1953. Famous Republican Senator, Joseph McCarthy from Wisconsin was the chairman of the subcommittee, and the man's name alone caused hardened men to quake with fear, some even to commit suicide. He was renowned for destroying the careers of men and women in government, religion, the military, show business, the medical and legal professions, and in the sciences. The hearings were to be broadcast live using the relatively new medium of television and were eventually viewed by an estimated 20 million people. Just prior to the hearings, prominent men featured in the hearings were David Schine and Roy Cohn. The two well-known men appeared on the cover of *Time Magazine* a few months before the highly touted hearings, under the banner "McCarthy and His Men". 23-year-old Jacob had developed a nervous tic anticipating his having to answer to the infamous inquisitor.

On the day, Jacob was sworn in by placing his left hand on an ornate and gilded, oversized *King James Version of the Bible* and raising his right hand to the square. By 1953, the anticommunist crusade had taken on a distinct right wing religious quality largely supplied by the popular evangelical preachers. Joseph McCarthy–an intolerant Irish Catholic, made common cause with prominent anticommunists, anti-Semites, segregationists, racist, religious right-wing, fundamentalist, premillennialist theology, evangelicals including southern evangelist Billy James Hargis of

Christian Crusade, Rev. David Noebel, Dr. James D. Bales, Charles Curtis McIntire Jr.—a staunch anti-Catholic–John Gresham Machen—a harsh Presbyterian professor–Bob Jones Jr., and Ian Paisley.

Cold War religion in America also crossed the political divide further separating liberals and democrats from Republicans and the far-right John Birch Society. During the 1952 campaign, Dwight Eisenhower spoke of US foreign policy as "a war of light against darkness, freedom against slavery, Godliness against atheism." The *HUAC* [House UnAmerican Activities Committee] which was created in 1938 to investigate alleged disloyalty and rebel *activities* on the part of private citizens, became considerably more powerful in the fifties. Jacob felt that he was beleaguered from both sides and began to accept the wisdom of his friend, Dr. Hilda Straude, about hiding his Jewish and Communist past.

The hit show on television all over the country and in much of the rest of the world was the video of the Senate Permanent Subcommittee on Investigations starring the darling of the far right and hero of the battle with the Red Scare, Senator Joseph McCarthy. The senator had purchased a new, tailor-made black suit, power red tie, and expertly polished Florsheim wingtip oxfords for the occasion. He was freshly shaved, and his usually straight unruly hair had been cut by the Senate barber and waxed into place. His teeth appeared to have been whitened for the performance. It was no accident that he resembled a thick featured John Wayne, the movie star. The agenda for the day was the beginning of and investigation into conflicting accusations between the United States Army and US Senator Joseph McCarthy and Attorney Roy Cohn.

McCarthy looked at his chief counsel Roy Cohn, who nodded, then the officious McCarthy banged the gavel with a special flourish and brought the hearing to order. His first witness was the unfortunate "representative of the military Communist deep state", Army Private, G. David Schine. Jacob Roth Whitesides was scheduled to be an add-on after the Schine to be swept into the ash bin of history along with the other—more minor—communists, pinkos, com-symps, and "fellow travelers".

McCarthy started immediately into his harsh, almost growling, interrogating pattern—as he had so regularly done in the recent past to Martin Luther King Jr., Cold War liberals, the New Deal and its defenders, and even scholarly liberals in the traditions of the reformation and the renaissance–such as historian Arthur Schlesinger–who had fought against Communism but nonetheless found themselves smeared by the red scare:

Q- State your name, birth date, age, and current occupation and rank.

A- Gerard David Schine, better known as G. David Schine, or David Schine. September 11, 1927. Twenty-six. Seconded from the US Army to serve as special counsel to Committee Chair Senator Joseph R. McCarthy, and Chief Counsel Roy Cohn of the Senate Permanent Subcommittee on Investigation, US Army lieutenant.

Q- Are you now, or have you ever been a member of the Communist Party of America?

A- No.

Q- Are you now, or have you ever been a member of the Abraham Lincoln Battalion, the Workers' Party of Marxist Unification or Spanish: *Partido Obrero de Unificación Marxista, POUM; Catalan: Partit Obrer d'Unificació Marxista*–the Spanish communist party formed during the Second Republic, the FAI [the *Federación Anarquista Ibérica*, a purely anarchist association, with the intention of keeping the CNT focused on the principles of anarchism. Anarchists played a central role in the fight against Francisco Franco during the Spanish Civil War. It is said that Stalin never wanted socialist revolution there and it's pretty clear that communists artificially got more support than their voter base would allow because they had USSR support, the Popular Front. Mind your answer, Mr. Schine. This question is specific, and the punishment for the crime of perjury is a substantial prison term.

A- No.

Q- Do you now, or have you ever, pledged allegiance to the red banners of revolutionary socialism, and the red-and-black banners of revolutionary anarchosyndicalism?

A- No.

Q- Were you a leader or secret fellow traveler behind the so-called Spanish "Republican" lines, the power in the hands of the trade unions and their political organizations like: the million-member UGT [General Confederation of Workers], the PSOE [labor federation of the Socialist Workers Party], or the equally large CNT [General Confederation of Labor], the FAI [clandestine Iberian Anarchist Federation]. The far leftist organization, POUM [the Workers Party of Marxist Unification], whose more radical members and leaders had been rooted in a Trotskyist tradition in earlier years, followed up the more influential socialists and anarchists, the Communist and Socialist Parties which united to form the predominantly Communist-controlled PSUC [Unified Socialist Party of Catalonia], the Popular Front, or the PCE [Communist Party]?

A- No.

Q- I say that you are a liar, Sir. I have a mountain of evidence that incriminates you and your fellow travelers in the United States Army and the Department of State for treason, for sharing of our sacred national secrets with the USSR, and perjury. How do you plead? It is time for you and your gang of commies in the army to confess and bring back power to the God blessed United States of America and away from godless Communism and its little brother, Socialism.

A- Is there a question in all of that, Senator?

Q- Of course there is, you misinformed elite Harvard snob. Are you guilty? Are you ready to come forward and confess at long last?

A- I am not guilty. I am not a communist. I do not know a single communist in the US Army or any other branch of the US military, for that matter. I challenge you before the People of the United States to produce any documentary evidence of Communist affiliation or treason by the military, General George Marshall, or—for that matter—the Department of State. I challenge you, Sir!

At that point, the army's head counsel, Joseph Welch, captured much of the mood of the country when he defended a fellow lawyer from McCarthy's public smears, saying, "Let us not assassinate this lad further, Senator. You've done enough. Have you no sense of decency, sir? At long last, have you left no sense of decency?"

The strongly Republican political party dominated committee in the Army-McCarthy hearings absolved McCarthy of any direct wrongdoing, blaming Cohn alone. The exposure of McCarthy and his methods before a television audience, however, was widely considered to have heralded the beginning of the end of his career. Cohn resigned from McCarthy's staff shortly after the hearings. However, on December 2, 1954, his colleagues in the Senate—including a fair number of embarrassed Republicans–voted 67–22 to "condemn" his actions. Humiliated, McCarthy faded into irrelevance and alcoholism and died in May, 1957 at age 48.

Jacob Roth Whitesides was a nonentity who was never even called to testify. His name was stricken from the public records, and the "red scare" petered out into obscurity over the next decade. Jacob, however, found out that just to have been condemned by McCarthy was to have a profound negative influence on his future.

CHAPTER 7

Jacob Whitesides' early educational career, 1953-1960

WITH NO REAL OPTIMISM, JACOB applied again for a position of surgical resident at twenty well-known surgical programs. One by one they replied with a refusal of acceptance, without stating the reason why. But Jacob knew why: it was primarily due to his having been named as a communist or a "fellow traveler" and secondarily as a Jew. Antisemitism remained alive and well during the 1950s-1970s. Jacob had to swallow his pride, deny his deeply held Jewishness and Communist leanings, damp down his bitterness, and even his desire to be an academic surgeon, a status that would have greatly pleased his parents; but they also had no choice but to accept the reality that their country still harbored such antiquarian prejudices.

His father suggested that he could be accepted at the University of California Davis School of Medicine, in partnership with Kaiser Permanente Northern California, an eminently pragmatic surgical school. In fact, Jacob received an acceptance letter for the surgical program; but sadly, that was rescinded shortly thereafter without so much as an explanation or an attempt to justify the obvious underlying reasons.

Senior Rabbi Guzik–a long time and genuine friend of the Whitesides family–suggested a solution for Jacob's educational dilemma. He had friends in Texas who informed him of the mental health care crisis developing in the state, and their difficulties of getting serious young students seeking a medical education to apply to a new school–Texas Tech University

Health Sciences Center. Jacob's father called the new dean directly to find out if his son could be accepted or not for the medicine and psychiatry program at Texas Tech. The news was more than positive. Depending on how impressive Jacob Jr.'s transcript of credits proved to be, Jacob would be received with open arms. None of that foolishness about antisemitism. Jacob Sr. wisely left out any mention of McCarthy's Senate Permanent Subcommittee on Investigations.

The additional piece of good news was that Jacob was eligible for the Accelerated Track of a three-year path to the degree of Doctor of Medicine as long as he committed formally to matriculate in the school's psychiatry residency postdoctoral program. That was not all the good news: Jacob was also awarded a two-year scholarship to the medical school, and a promise of being awarded the same type of scholarship for the psychiatric residency provided that his grades were solid Bs or better during medical school. Under the state's Health Professions Education Assistance Program for student scholarship programs, Texas increased the maximum loan amount from $2,500 maximum scholarship per student/year and $2,500 maximum annual loan per student, to creating loan forgiveness programs for graduates who agreed to practice psychiatry or family practice in rural Texas for five years.

Jacob Roth Whitesides could not get his acceptance letter off to Texas Tech fast enough. Two weeks later, he was accepted; and two months later, he was in Lubbock, Texas looking for an apartment. It was hardly his dream—nobody dreamed of moving from lush Los Angeles to Lubbock as their life's dream—but it was better than nothing which was what he had the week before.

It did not take Jacob long to realize that Lubbock was something short of a tropical paradise–about five minutes after stepping off the bus. Flat dusty plains as far as he could see in every direction. Lubbock is located in the northwestern part of Texas, in the Great Plains region, and is part of the southern end of the High Plains. The city is characterized by flat, open, plains and low-lying terrain, with no significant elevation changes within its borders. The Yellow House River runs through a portion of the city. Lubbock originally developed as a ranching center, but artesian well water brought mixed farming to the plains. The topography of Lubbock and its surrounding areas is characterized by flat, open plains, and low-lying terrain, typical of the High Plains region. To the east of Lubbock, the terrain gradually slopes downward towards the Rolling Plains region, where the land becomes more undulating and the vegetation transitions from grasslands to scrublands and woodlands. To the west of Lubbock, the terrain rises slightly towards the Caprock Escarpment, a prominent geological feature that marks the edge of the Llano Estacado, or Staked Plains.

He was hungry; so, he walked to Clovis Road to the Jim Dandy and had a "Texas" burger, fries, and a root beer (his first such drink), then made his way to the university hospital. The 3601 4th Street, Lubbock, address was becoming known as one of the premier treatment centers, research, and educational, medical schools, in the country. Texas Tech was earnestly striving to make its psychiatric treatment and production of notable psychiatrists equally well regarded.

Jacob found his way into the main building and proceeded to the appropriate floor–the 3rd floor administration office of the Department of Psychiatry. He turned in the direction pointed to by a sign that read, "Psychiatry Residency Program Office".

A friendly simply dressed dish water blond smiled at him and said, "How y'all doin' this fine mornin'"?

"I'm fine, thank you Ma'am. I am a new resident in the program."

"What's y'all's name?"

"Jacob Roth Whitesides?"

"Date a birth?"

He told her.

"Oh, perfeck. Y'all come at the perfect time. We been lookin' forward to you joinin' the staff."

That sounded like a good start.

"Mind if Ah call y'all Jacob?"

"Not at all."

"Ah'm the infamous Miss Perkins, Gladys to y'all."

She stood; so, they could shake hands.

"Glad to meet you, Gladys. Glad to be here in fact."

"This will seem pretty abrupt, but we need for you to start work soon's we can git the paperwork over with. Fill out this here form, if y'all don' mind, Jacob."

It took all of five minutes, and Dr. Jacob Whitesides was officially a member of the medical staff.

"Now, Hon., y'all need to git over to Sunrise Canyon Hospital pronto. The night call psychiatrist is pooped and is waitin' for y'all to relieve him. Ya know where Sunrise Canyon Hospital is?"

"I don't. This my first day in Lubbock... ever."

She gave him the address—and made a call down to the hospital front desk.

"Hi, April. Can y'all git holt of Ephriam, I got a new doctor he needs to carry over to Sunrise."

"Yeah, he looks like a keeper."

She gave Jacob a warm smile.

"A, huh. Right away. Poor little Doctah Creple is plumb tuckered out. He has been up the better parta two days, and he sounds a bit grouchy."

"Ah'll have Eph up ta yer office in two shakes of a dead lamb's tail. Say 'hey' the Doctah Michaels from alla us in the reception area."

"Ah'll do it. Have a blessed day, now, ya heah."

"Back at y'all, Hon."

"Rest yer bones, Jacob. Good old Ephriam'll be here right away and carry y'all to Sunrise. Doctah Creple'll give you the orientation speech, and then you will be the head shrink in charge over there until Friday."

Sunrise Canyon Hospital [aka Lubbock Regional Mhmr Center (Mental Health and Mental Retardation)] is a mental health facility which provides short-term psychiatric treatment in a 30-bed inpatient facility to both men and women 18 or older located at 1602 10th Street, Lubbock. It was an attractive little place and an easy prelude for a psychiatric training experience.

Ephraim was ever determined to be helpful; so, when the elevator arrived, he said, "Ya'll need tah mash two. That's the big shots' office."

He mashed elevator button number two for Jacob. Jacob was sure he would catch on to how elevators worked sometime in the future. He made every effort not to show that in his face.

Looking tired and a bit exasperated, they were met by Dr. Creple when the elevator door opened.

"Hi," he said, "I'm Wil. Wilber T. Creple, M.D. formally. The residents and interns are not formal with each other. However, Dr. Solomon Reichmann is the chief of the department, and nobody calls him Solomon, probably not even his wife. He's Jewish, by the way, but that doesn't make any never-mind; he's the best of the best psychiatrists and teachers. That's all that matters."

"Glad to hear that it doesn't matter. Thanks for the heads up."

"It was nothing."

Wil stood about five foot two in his stocking feet, weighed 120 pounds soaking wet, and had a mild Slavic face, somewhere in the grey tinges of color and with rigidly straight, stubborn smokey grey hair. He had on a lab coat with more than a few specks of what had to be vomitus, some suspicious yellow spots, and some areas that probably once had been food. His shoes were mottled but were probably once brown. One shoelace was untied. His plain grey-blue tie was loose at the collar and looked worse for the wear.

"I'm Jacob. Jacob Roth Whitesides, M.D.. I prefer Jacob to Jake."

"Good to know. I'll show you around, then I'm outta here."

They made the rounds, met the nurses, administrator, the six psych inpatients, a lady psychology PhD, and a medical doctor. It took all of twenty minutes, then Wil was outta there.

Jacob was shown politely to the resident's reading and sleeping room, told about how and where to get food, and then left to himself. He had just picked up a thumb worn copy of Freud's the *Ego and the Id*, written in 1923. He did not make it through the introduction when a call came in for him to go to admitting.

"Dr. Whitesides, please come to the admissions office. We have something of an emergency in progress here."

"On my way."

It took him four minutes to get to the main office area. The emergency was glaringly apparent.

A handsome adolescent boy with blond curly hair and a rather pretty face was standing in the middle of the open lobby of the administration building. He wandered about aimlessly shouting to people unseen in a gibberish tongue and gesticulating aimlessly. His eyes were wild; and he avoided approaching any person in the room, even his parents. He was as genuinely frightened as if he had seen a ghost, or maybe a roomful. He made faux punching motions at the psyche techs, and at Dr. Whitesides with no effect.

"What is going on with our son, Doctor?" the distraught middle-aged mother, Mary Margaret, pleaded.

The boy's father, Walter A. Preston III, remained quiet, looking anxious, and stood grim faced twisting his hat into a cloth pretzel.

"Let me examine him and have a chance to talk to him before I give you a diagnosis. What is his first name?"

"Reginald. We call him Reggie," she said.

He was already sure that he knew what was wrong, but he did not want to blurt it out without a good basis.

Two burly psyche techs holding a strait jacket were edging towards Reggie. Jacob stopped them.

"Let me have an opportunity to get the boy alone and calmed down before we do anything physical."

He took the shift nurse aside and quietly asked, "When I get him into the examination room, bring in a syringe of 50 mg of chlorpromazine and another of phenobarbital 50 mg for IM sticks."

"Yes, doctor, but pardon me, what is chloro... something?" the somewhat disquieted nurse asked.

"Chlorpromazine–generic for Thorazine."

"Oh, yes, I know Thorazine. I'll get right on it."

"Come with me," Jacob said to the trembling and terrified young Reggie.

Reggie looked at Dr. Jacob as his savior and followed him with grateful docility into the interview office.

"Have a seat, son," Jacob directed and pointed at the comfortable divan facing the soft cushion arm chair.

Reggie did as he was told and slumped exhausted onto the comfortable couch.

Jacob smiled at him. Reggie managed a wan return smile.

"So, Reggie, how about you tell me about your name, address, telephone number, and about your family… all right?"

Reggie was hesitant at first, talking in a staccato pace in what amounted to a syllable salad, making no sense.

Jacob listened quietly until the tired boy began to wind down.

"Slow down a bit, Reggie. I need to know about you; so, I can help you get to feeling better."

"Wha… What did you say your name was, Doctor ?" Reggie finally said in his first coherent sentence.

"I'm Doctor Whitesides, son. I'm here to help you. I want you to understand what is going on inside yourself and how we can calm it down. Would you like that?"

"Oh, would I!" the boy responded entreatingly.

"So, let's try again. Tell me about yourself, your family, your brothers and sisters, your dogs and cats. We'll get to know each other some. Okay ?"

"Yes, my prince," Reggie said without sarcasm. Then he looked at the wall and said, "and you don't get to interrupt me or call me names while I talk to the prince. Shut up Eric."

About that, he was emphatic and quite lucid sounding except the fact he was talking to a person who was not there.

"First," said Jacob, now fully the psychiatrist, even though it was his first day, "tell me what happened today at your high school."

Reggie floundered here and there in his communication, but Jacob was able to string together something of a history of the day from Reginald Preston's point of view.

The day had started out like most others. Reggie ate a solid breakfast, caught the bus, and arrived at school fairly early. Nothing unusual in any of that. When he went to put his things in his locker, a classmate walked by and made a comment about the beauty and girlishness of his blond locks. Reggie saw that as something clairvoyant; the boy could see into his very soul.

Some of the boys were roughhousing as he entered his first class of the day, an elective art class, which featured decorative colored flowers in a copper pot. One of the boys, a general class bully, snidely chided Reggie with,

"Hey, sissie boy, couldn't make the football squad; so, y'all went gay-boy on us?"

That was the last straw. Now everyone would know.

Reggie's face turned purple; he grimaced in agony and fury; and he dashed out of the classroom, out of the school house door, and into the open field leading to a mile wide perimeter of scrub oak and juniper trees. He found a trench between the grassy field and the wooded area, flung himself face first into it and placed the palms of his hands over his ears to drown out any external noise. He could not escape the voices coming into his head from the surrounding bushes, the drainage pipe, and the ravens perched on the telephone wires above. He began to scream.

Jacob had to get the rest of the story from witnesses of the events including Reggie's mother, his two jeering classmates, and the vice-principal of the school. In brief, Reggie's "crazy" behavior attracted considerable attention and drew a crowd out of the building and over to where the distraught boy lay screaming and obviously hallucinating.

He was described as shouting such things as "I am not!" "Don't tell no one!" "Don't say nothing to my dad; he'll have hyssy fit!", "No," "No, no, no," "Never!" "Don't you touch me!" "Of course I like girls. Who don't? I ain't any kinda sissy-boy. Shut up!" and most of the time "Shut up, shut up, shut up," over and over again, apparently directing that demand to the ravens on the phone wires above.

The vice-principal informed Reggie's parents and grand father, the police, and the Methodist parson. Everyone assisted in getting Reggie into the ambulance and over to the nearby mental hospital. There, they had the good fortune to encounter a fresh psychiatrist who had written his university graduation thesis on Dementia Praecox.

Jacob administered the intramuscular injections of chlorpromazine and phenobarbital and waited until the drugs took effect. Reggie became lucid, then calm, then sedated, and finally fell into deep sleep on the interview room couch. Jacob had the techs come in and place the boy on a gurney and take him to a padded room on the second floor where a suicide watch was put into place, and round-the-clock psychiatric nurse surveillance kept him from any potential harm to himself or other people.

Then Jacob returned to the lobby and introduced himself to the anxiously waiting Preston family.

"Hello," he said, "I am Dr. Jacob Roth Whitesides."

He shook hands all around.

"What's goin' on with my boy, Doctor? What gives in a case like this?"

"What is going on with Reginald is not particularly rare. His diagnosis is dementia praecox, and its becoming seriously evident today was triggered by a well-known phenomenon, known as "homosexual panic"."

"My boy ain't not sissy boy; don't go sayin' he is, ya heah?"

"I am not saying that, Mr. Preston. What I am saying is that he has been harboring a fear of becoming gay or of having people think he is secretly gay. That does not necessarily mean that he has ever had a homosexual experience or even has those kind of thoughts."

"Is he crazy?" asked Mrs. Preston.

"Good question, Ma'am. We don't say crazy nowadays. He is mentally ill, and this is just the first episode in a serious mental illness called schizophrenia. You will have to brace yourself for a long drawn-out process over years."

"Any cure?" asked Millie, who was Reggie's elder sister.

"No. Not yet, I'm afraid. But, there are treatments, including medications, and some other things we may have to suggest down the line as his mental problems demand."

Mr. Preston continued to be angry and belligerent.

"We don't wanna hear nuthin' about that German Frud stuff about how his mother was bad to him, that kinna claptrap."

"And you won't in all probability. This a genuine physical brain disease, not a psychological problem like a phobia, or a mood problem. A lot of study is going on to find the causes, the kinds of chemicals and other things that might help, even surgery."

"No one's cuttin' open my boy's head. Ya'll listen heah ta me. Nevah."

"Walter, we ah goin' tah do what we must fa our boy, ya heah me. Now hush up about what we will and we will not do. Doctah knows best. Y'all know that. Let's see what is gonna come; and the doctah heah will guide us along."

Mary Margaret Preston had a determined look on her face that Walter had long ago learned to heed. He clammed up and listened.

"Yes, so, I gave him a sedative and an anti-psychotic medication which we will continue to use during his stay here. He is resting quietly and is at peace. I'll keep checking on him and make decisions as to what to do for this early period starting tomorrow morning. You need to get some rest yourselves. It has been a long and stressful day for you. Get on home, now; and let us take care of your boy."

"Okay, thanks," said Walter, still a bit grudgingly.

CHAPTER 8

Jacob Whitesides' psychiatric educational career, 1955-1960
Artist's wife who saw visions.

THE TEXAS TECH PSYCHIATRIC RESIDENCY was not a particularly difficult one as residencies went. It did not include psychoanalysis, a personally wrenching experience for aspiring clinical psychiatrists, for example. The patient load was busy but not exhausting, a purposeful decision based on a firm belief in healthy rest periods for trainees and patients. The group of hospitals involved in the residency included didactic learning in psychology, psychopathology, behaviorism, modern pharmacologic and psychotherapeutic approaches, neuropharmaceuticals, physical treatment such as lobotomy, electroconvulsive shock, isolation therapy, restraints, and psychotherapy [talk therapy].

Texas Tech faculty and residents had realized a need for a formal classification system of mental diseases shortly before Jacob arrived, and he was involved in the formulation of its principles in several scholarly papers. This led to more efficient and targeted mental health services and the creation of the first edition of the DSM [*Diagnostic and Statistical Manual of Mental Disorders*] of which Jacob was proud to make a small contribution.

The prevailing views of early recorded history held that mental illness was the product of supernatural forces and demonic possession, and this led to primitive treatment practices such as trepanning [creating surgical burr holes in the skull] in an effort to release the offending spirit. Relatively little in the way of improvements were achieved throughout the European Middle Ages, and later in America; and the oppressive sociopolitical climate saw many sufferers of mental illness being submitted to physical restraint and solitary confinement in the asylums of the time. It was not until the late 19th and early 20th centuries that modern theories of psychopathology began to emerge. Texas Tech was in the forefront of modern thinking and treatment policies. However, such enlightenment was slow in coming to less modern facilities of the country.

Around this time, two main theoretical approaches began to inform an understanding of mental illness: the psychodynamic theory of Austrian neurologist Sigmund Freud and the theory of behaviorism advanced by American psychologist John B. Watson. Freud's theory of psychodynamics centered on the concept that mental illness was the product of the interplay of unresolved unconscious [subconscious] motives and should be treated through various methods of open dialogue with the patient—a very prolonged process, and one only peripherally based on scientific study.

Behaviorism–on the other hand–suggested that psychopathology was more closely related to the effects of behavioral—operant–conditioning, and that treatment should focus on methods of adaptive reconditioning, using the same principles of classical conditioning elucidated by the Russian physiologist Ivan Pavlov. The studies of Pavlov were reproduced at Texas Tech, and Jacob authored several learned papers during his residency on Pavlovian conditioning in humans.

Texas Tech hospitals offered outpatient and hospital inpatient treatment including provision of psychotropic medication, newly introduced activity and group therapy, opportunity for patients to be outside and to exercise regularly, to have physical therapy and medical treatment by professions. The system's hospitals provided patient care and supervision for patients referred from the court/judicial system. Psychiatric services provided by the hospital included enlightened case management, court-ordered outpatient treatment, and integrated primary care services. The system served all comers, including people who are poor and vulnerable.

During his residency, Jacob became proficient in differentiating psychopathology from malingering or subconscious manifestation of illness such as Munchausen and Munchausen by proxy illness, performance of electroconvulsive therapy for depression, treatment of people who had been tortured or otherwise traumatized, and how to deal with violent psychotics who were a danger to themselves, their families, and society at large. He learned how to do neurological procedures such as lumbar punctures, pneumoencephalography, and even myelography to rule out physical as opposed to mental illness.

From a pharmacological perspective, the catecholamine hypothesis, published in the 1950s, was an influential milestone embraced by the Texas Tech system and resulted in the residents becoming serious scientists rather than "feeling" or just "talking" doctors. This led to research into the actions of drugs like reserpine and monoamine oxidase inhibitors. The catecholamine hypothesis proposed that depression and other affective disorders were likely caused by decreased levels of catecholamines such as norepinephrine. With that knowledge and attitude, the residents were ahead of their time, and that would lead to clashes with older, more experienced, and more hide-bound-to-traditional-care providers.

Jacob Whitesides' psychiatry training was innovative and conducted with several new concepts not generally part of training elsewhere or in earlier teaching centers. The residents, faculty, and patients, were a diverse group—diverse in background and well as diverse in their clinical interests and specializations. The clinicians cared for veterans, the community, college students, health professions students, children, elders and even diverse races, religions, and ethnicities without discrimination. The residents became proficient in the of addiction as a disease, dementias like Alzheimer's disease, bipolar disorders, autism, schizophrenia, and minimal chronic brain trauma. They cared for the incarcerated, for the homeless, the dependent, for every patient in our region who survived a serious suicide attempt, whether by burns, falls, ingestions, gun shots, or attempts by use of sharp object.

As in most training facilities and programs, the residency was two years long with some residents granted a third year to become especially proficient in a specialized area such as child psychiatry or forensics. Jacob was content to get through two years and enjoyed the learning and hands-on environment with progressively increasing responsibility.

Texas tech approached the training mission systematically by combining closely-supervised intensive clinical experiences in multiple settings with a comprehensive didactic program. Experiences were aligned with the health care reform demands of the contemporary era in giving residents clinical responsibilities within an integrated continuum of progressive complexity on the wards and in the clinics. Mentorship and elective experiences beginning in the PGY1 year and continuing throughout training provide residents with the opportunity to explore specific areas for professional development and master a topic area more deeply. One area of training particularly pleased Jacob. He was able to follow the patients he was given for his entire residency.

One example was particularly important to him. During the last quarter of his first year of training, he was assigned to see a very prominent, rich, well-educated, woman who was the wife of a famous Texas portrait painter who had a rather benign form of schizophrenia. Mrs. Farber became Evelyn, and Doctor Whitesides became Jacob during their association. Initially, Jacob tried psychotropics, then ECT [ElectroConvulsiveTherapy], ice baths, seclusion, and sleep deprivation—all to no avail. He and Evelyn finally settled into a peaceful, even pleasant, relationship which provided the socially prominent woman with what she needed most—someone to talk to about her auditory and visual hallucinations without feeling the need to communicate about them to a wider and probably unsympathetic audience of her peers. He saw her three times a week for most of his two-year residency and was able to release her from care by the time he graduated from the university psychiatry training program. A typical session would be like this:

"Good morning, Evelyn. Thank you for coming right on time. How are you feeling today?"

"I believe punctuality is an important part of the social contract, Jacob. Besides, I enjoy our sessions. I believe you are an insightful and caring mental health professional."

"Do you trust me, Evelyn?"

"Do you mean, am I certain that you will never betray me or what we share in our 55 minute sessions ?"

"Exactly."

"I do, or else I would never have continued to see you."

"Do you talk to other people about what you tell me."

"I don't. Not even to my husband. Nobody else could understand. You convinced me of that, and you are my sole outlet. My secret is safe, and I can unburden myself of the things going on with me without being humiliated by fools."

"Good. So, it has been almost five days since we last got together. Can you bring me up to date."

"It has been eventful, I must say. I met with the Mormon missionaries—two sweet girls from Utah. I have become quite converted to their religion, and that has put new life into my audio and visual… happenings."

"Tell me about them, Evelyn."

"Since last Friday night and every night since, I have been visited by fascinating and important beings. Joseph Smith, the Prophet, came to me twice to show me his golden plates; Peter, James, and John, came to teach me the gospel, and Brigham Young has begun teaching me how to achieve celestial life. They all were so kind, honest, and genuine. Last night was the greatest experience of all. Jesus Christ, the Savior, came to me in a burst of light. I was so overwhelmed and thrilled that I could not speak, and I cried. He comforted me and assured me that everything was going to be all right. It was wonderful."

"Were they real people, Evelyn?"

"They were real to me."

"You are going to remember only to tell me about them, right? Other people might not understand."

"I know that, Jacob, and it kind of makes me sad."

"I can understand, Evelyn, but it is important that you keep such things between us, okay?"

"Oh, I know, Jacob. I'm not stupid. I might even be crazy, but I am not stupid!"

Jacob smiled with the indulgent smile he had mastered, which helped to calm Evelyn and the others.

"Of course not, my friend. Oh, the time has flown by. Our hour is up. I'll see you on Thursday, as scheduled. Is that your understanding ?"

"It is, and I have to tell you, I have a premonition that I am going to be able to chat with Moses and Elijah, and maybe even Mohammed this week. I will tell you all about it."

The training domains took place within case conferences, supervision, and individual courses, in addition to the close and personal clinical experience. The neurobiology, psychopathology and phenomenology, sequences began in the PGY-1 year courses. Clinically, the residents focused on an introduction to emergency psychiatry, and addictions. Reinforcement of these concepts occurred within Case Conferences on the Inpatient Units and the Consultation/Liaison-Emergency Room Case Conferences throughout the two years. PGY-2 year included Developmental Psychiatry, Child Psychopathology, Neuropsychiatry, and Geriatric Psychiatry. Forensic psychiatry course. Summer of PGY 2 required the main psychotherapy sequence.

A PGY 3 was a requirement to gain in depth learning about Forensic Psychiatry as were advanced psychopharmacology, and expertise in ECT, TMS [Transcranial Magnetic Stimulation Therapy, a developing therapeutic modality] and DBS [Deep Brain Stimulation, a pioneering treatment under the control of the brain surgeons]. A separate year was required for residents interested in an academic career which included research tracks. Other tracks included training in developing areas of advanced psychopharmacology and somatic treatments; case-based discussions of side effect management and complex pharmacologic approaches to refractory psychiatric disorders of all types, including discussions of major psychotropic medication groups beginning to appear, such as antidepressants, mood stabilizers, antipsychotics, anxiolytics, sedative-hypnotics, stimulants, and other agents, in adults and child patients, and some insight into established and emerging neuromodulation techniques.

By the time of completion of PGY 2, the residents were required to pass a strenuous examination to certify their competency in supportive psychotherapy, cognitive behavior therapy—including didactics, interactive classroom skills-building sessions and individual and group CBT supervision, group therapy, family therapy, and psychodynamic psychotherapy.

In oral examinations, his professors and Jacob himself became confident that—after two years—he could manage acute and subacute medical and neurological conditions in the inpatient setting; apply appropriate methods of patient assessment and formulation; understand broad categories of psychiatric illness and implications for treatment and prognosis for a variety of psychiatric patients; accept and appreciate the milieu concept of inpatient psychiatric services; understand the responsibilities and roles of other mental health practitioners integrated in team treatment of patients; understand at a basic level the multiple treatment modalities: psychological, pharmacological, physical, and rehabilitative—employed with psychiatric patients.

Newly hatched psychiatrist, Jacob Roth Whitesides, was full of himself and ready to get a job healing the mental problems of the world, at least in the Texas world.

PART II

DANNY MCGRAW

CHAPTER 1

Farmer's Branch, Texas, July 30, 1930

IT WAS GOING TO BE a scorcher of a day in Farmer's Branch, Texas; and that always portended a significant upsweep in major crime. Detective Second Class, Hector Lopez McGraw fretted about it because his sickly wife, Lucinda, was due to deliver their third that very day; and Hector was on call. Her bag was packed and in the truck; he sat by the phone in the DPD detectives' office ready to head for home if she called with her first pain. They always came quickly with Lucinda.

He was about 10, maybe 15, minutes from the DPD headquarters in the basement of the Municipal Building to home on 328 Danny Lane, with lights and siren, which he had every intention of using. It was one of the perks of the job. He tapped his fingers on the desk in front of him until his partner, Det. 3, Clay Perkins, could not stand it any longer. He wanted to get to his fifth of Gallager and Burtons White label whiskey in peace.

"Go home, Hector. If you don't go right now, the first homicide of the day is goin' ta be ya'll. Git outta heah!"

Hector shrugged. Clay was right, he was useless as a third leg. He sighed, put on his Sam Brown belt, and made for the door of the Beaux-Arts architectural style Municipal Building–a two-story building at Main and Akard streets. The city offices occupied the second floor. Stepping out of the door was like entering a blast furnace. Dallas was having one of its hot, dry, thirsty, spells.

He was slowed by a small parade of KKK marchers making some sort of protest or other in front of the Municipal Building. There was not a black face anywhere to be seen. Even the Whites avoided being near the frequent parades, since violence was not all that rare. During the heyday of the Ku Klux Klan in Dallas in the 1920s and 30s, a sizable number of DPD were KKK members, including police commissioners and police chiefs. One list of members included at least 106 Dallas police officers, which at the time was the majority of the police department. During this period, the DPD did not protect the non-white community in Dallas and did not pursue cases involving racial violence against Blacks. It was a serious health risk for any cop to do so.

The run of the mill cop in the city was not known for being particularly peaceable. Dallas—at the time–was notorious for police violence. For years, the third largest city in Texas had had a higher per-capita rate of police-involved shootings than Chicago, New York, or Los Angeles.

Finally, he spied a little break in the kluckers' ranks and took advantage of it to get on his way north. He was determined to get Lucinda to the hospital if it killed him. He decided to use one of his few perks and turned on the lights and siren. He barreled through the familiar streets at almost double legal speed. No traffic cop would ever stop Sgt. McGraw knowingly; and this time, it would be worth more than their life to make such a rash mistake.

He squealed to a sliding stop in front of 328 Danny Lane, threw open the car door, and ran into the house almost tearing the door off its hinges.

Lucinda was a dish-water blond and had her hair up in a practical bun ready for the time coming when she would not be able to tend to herself much. Her face was wan, and she looked uncomfortable, not really in great pain. She never showed pain or distress; it upset Hector too much. For all his leathery tough exterior, he was a softy inside when it came to her and the children. She was wearing a faded light blue gingham dress. It hung loosely on her spare frame, making her easy to get at by the doctors and nurses.

"Let's git y'all up, woman. Time's wastin'. How quick are yer pains acomin', Dear? I left the squad car a runnin', and we'll turn on the lights and sireens soon's I start carryin' y'all off ta the hospital. Don't give my no sass, Girl. Giddyup and let's git outta here, like pronto."

"My pains er not comin' quick-like yet, Hector. Settle down. We can drive over there like regular folks with good sense. No big hurry 'bout it, yit."

"Easy fer y'all tah say, Lucinda. Y'all ain't the one that hasta do the worryin'."

She gave him her patented "calm-down" look. She often laughed at his overly solicitous outbursts, but this was not the time nor place. He was downright serious. He paid her no mind, picked her up, and trotted out the truck. They made the twenty-minute drive in something short of ten minutes, and Lucinda breathed a heavy sigh of relief.

"My laws, Hector. It's by the grace of God that we made it. Now, y'all gotta be nice to the doctors and nurses. Y'all git more from folks with honey that vinegar. Y'all recomember that, ya heah?"

The baby arrived fourteen hours later, a big ruddy eight-pound-six-ounce boy already fitted out with a two-inch long head of black hair. He howled his way into the world, and his father thought that was a very good sign.

The moment he was born, the baby immediately became Hector L (for Lucinda), McGraw, Jr. as determined by his father who also determined that the boy was going to be a doctor, not a copper like his daddy. It did not much matter that Lucinda had wanted to name the baby, Ernest Giles McGraw to incorporate her good father's name into the mix, if the baby turned out to be a boy. Father Hector had not been willing to talk about Lucinda having another girl. Might hex things. Lucinda wanted her son to be a banker; Hector thought that was sissy and would not even think about it as a profession for his only son, nosiree, not when that boy got educated and became a man. The plan was fixed.

CHAPTER 2

Farmer's Branch, Texas, 1930s

BACK THEN, FARMER'S BRANCH WAS the quintessential one horse town. Fourth street was the edge of town; there were no street lights, no city parks, and no Black people or Hispanics. There were four Protestant churches, five saloons, two cafes and one school, K-12. There was not a single Roman Catholic, Jew, or Mormon, in the town, and the KKK was determined to see to it that the demographic would never change.

School years for boys in Farmer's Branch in the rudimentary school were Darwinian in character. School yard fights were a daily occurrence, often two or three a day, most days. There was no such word as bully, nor was there any concept of fair play or Marquis of Queensbury rules. It was the survival of the fittest, day to day. Young Danny McGraw came from a rough and tough nuclear and extended family, and he was expected to learn to fight from day one. That proved to be a steep learning curve for the detective's son, if he was going to succeed in the hierarchy of boyhood there. The first contests were settled by fists over who's taw hit the most marbles out of the rough circles in the sand. That advanced to the sandlot football being more or less a "no harm, no foul" set of rules, and "losers eat your own dead" understanding.

Danny McGraw had the great good fortune to have good genes. By sixth grade, he was as big as the biggest boy in the school, the best technical fighter owing to the seasoned experience of his father, whose career consisted of brawlers on both sides of the law, and by his personality flaw of being completely free of fear or compassion for his opponents. He had a broken arm or two, broken fingers, a few missing child's teeth, and scars through both eyebrows. He had a handsome 45° angle left facial scar from some beastly boy from the wrong side of the tracks who wielded a knife. That boy got the worst of it, Detective Second Class, Hector Lopez McGraw, was proud to announce when his son got stitches at the doctor's office.

In Texas at all levels, football makes the man; there were no tennis or chess players in Farmer's Branch. The football field—such as it existed—was a dirt and sand acre plot of land belonging to the mayor and KKK Grand Dragon. Boys got hurt, broke parts, and developed scars in a place which was summer all year long. No one ever sued or thought about doing so. No one reported grossly unfair practices, and the scoring was iffy at best. The two teams employed the double wing offense, and Danny was the running back for his team. Neither team had a name, and both were basically made up of boy gangs. Danny earned his stripes and some notoriety for his reckless play. All the boys would probably have done better if they had had pads or helmets. Concussions were commonplace and may have accounted for the rather significant degree of diminished mental function in the town. It was also possible that close intermarrying played a role, but that concept was strictly off limits for conversation.

Danny was intelligent, but school work was not his thing. He loved auto mechanics classes, wood shop, and phys ed. It became clear by grade ten that he was never going to be any kind of scholar, was not going to go on to be a doctor or lawyer or such, or probably even graduate from the town's school. His father had to admit that his only son was not going to become a prominent physician, or attorney, or politician; so, he arranged for him to begin police training in a junior police academy for boys like Danny—big, strong, bright, but not inclined towards book learning. He made the decision for Danny before the very active young man could get himself into serious trouble.

The training was rigorous, and the dropout rate was high. Danny excelled in the rough environment, which was perfect for him. He soon developed the reputation as the best at hand-to-hand combat, small weapons defense, and the most accurate marksman with several types of weapons. He was too young to enlist in the marines when the beginning of World War II was foisted on the United States, but he was fully prepared to enlist when the Korean War started on June 25, 1950.

CHAPTER 3

The Korean War Years, 1950-1954

AT THE END OF WORLD War II the Allies agreed to establish a four-power trusteeship for the peninsula nation of Korea, which, until that time, had been under the control of Japan. This decision, reached at the Yalta conference in 1945, resulted in the establishment of two different Korean governments: the Republic of Korea (ROK), the democratic nation of South Korea, and the Democratic People's Republic of Korea, Communist North Korea. The 38th parallel was defined as the boundary between the two nations. By 1949, North Korea had obtained a massive amount of weaponry from the Soviet Union and Communist China and was poised to invade the non-Communist south.

The Korean War took place between June, 1950 and July, 1953. It began when North Korea sent 75,000 Communist troops to invade South Korea. The war quickly escalated and is seen as the first major military action of the Cold War. The Truman Doctrine–also known as the policy of containment–laid out a key tenet of Truman's foreign policy, which stipulated that the US would provide political, military, and economic, aid to democratic countries under communist threat. US and United Nations forces intervened on the side of South Korea, and Chinese forces intervened on the side of North Korea. On June 30, US ground troops were deployed.

The war ultimately ended in a stalemate after three years of bloody fighting. The United States never formally declared war against North Korea, and called it by the euphemism, a "police action." While Korean

War dates show the war ending on July 27, 1953, the ceasefire maintained the prewar status quo of a divided Korea, a situation that continues to the present day. Danny McGraw was not given the choice of ending his tour of duty until a year after the other recruits, because of the critical need for his services in the uneasy aftermath of that war.

When North Korea invaded South Korea in June 1950, there were some MP units already stationed in Korea. One of those was the 55th Military Police Company, which had been assigned to Camp Ascom in December, 1948. Most of those military police units that arrived during the months of the war came from Japan, where they were serving as occupation forces following World War II. Danny arrived in South Korea with the first contingent of US troops–part of Task Force Smith, the 1st Battalion, 21st Infantry Regiment of the 24th Infantry Division. They landed in Busan airport on July 1, 1950, to begin the Korean War. The next morning, the troops were sent to Taejon, where they were put to the test on July 5 when North Korean tanks approached Osan. This battle is considered the first US ground combat in the war, and Private Danny McGraw was in the thick of it.

Because of his early exposure to police training, his impressive size and skills, and his quick mind and devotion to police and military discipline, Danny had been drafted into the USAMPC [United States Army Military Police Corps]–the uniformed law enforcement branch of the United States Army. His early performance resulted in an elevation through the enlisted ranks, a field promotion to officer status as a captain, and assignment to the Provost Marshal General's Office. He became a Special Agent of the CID [Department of the Army Criminal Investigation Division] coded as 95D.

Danny led from the front, never asked a man (or woman) to do anything he would not do, and regularly stood up for his people, who were no more popular with the rank-and-file of the enlisted and the officer corps than cops are anywhere. He was—by nature—a fair man, but rigid about enforcement of the UCMJ [Uniform Code of Military Justice]. He often took on individuals and even small groups of perpetrators of crimes against the UCMJ , the laws of warfare, the Korean people, and women and children. He earned a reputation as a first-class fighter to be respected and feared and was quickly invited into the hearts of his CID unit to the point that to a man or woman, his 12 subordinates would fight for him or die for him.

After being promoted to CO of the 90th MP Special Investigations Unit, he was given the rank of Army Major—the highest possible rank for a Mustang [slang for an enlisted person promoted to the officer corps]. He was proud to wear the insignias, patches, and badges, of the MP force and frequently took down detractors of his branch of service found in the physical strife world of war-torn Korea.

United States Army Military Police units have combat zone responsibilities in addition to their law enforcement duties. The Military Police tasks can be separated into three disciplines and one integrated function; that function was Maj. McGraw's principal responsibility: Security and mobility support operations; Police operations; Detention operations; and Police intelligence operations (integrated function across all disciplines).

These responsibilities include mounted and dismounted patrols, response force operations, area damage control, route reconnaissance, cordon and search operations, critical site security, and convoy and personnel escorts. Operationally, these duties fall under the "security and mobility support" discipline of the Military Police Corps. The United States Army's Military Police provide an important function in the full spectrum of Army operations as a member of the Maneuver, Fires, and Effects, division. The MPs provide expertise in policing, detainment, and stability, operations in order to enhance security and enable mobility. They were regularly tasked to direct military traffic on supply routes. During the Korean War, Military Police kept supply routes open. They guarded enemy POWs. Subsequently, Military Police monitored the exchange of prisoners and patrolled the demilitarized zone.

The rank-and-file have a running joke that MPs sit around waiting for someone to go one mph over the posted speed limit. In truth, the military (in the form of the MPs) in war needs to be a force that takes control and care of people who act in a criminal manner.

Maj. McGraw and his CID team did all that during the war. There is one other function they had. One that is not widely known and not widely talked about. If the order came down "hold at all costs" or "no retreat", it was the MPs who had to enforce that order. When a line broke–and the troops began to run for the rear–the men with pistols shooting the soldiers that run were the Military Police. And square jawed, tight lipped, Major Danny McGraw was one of their leaders, another reason for the MPs' lack of popularity and particularly for the large man in front. There is a reason their branch symbol is crossed pistols.

The standard personal semi-automatic side arm of the United States Army military police was the venerable 45 Caliber Colt 1911. Danny and his brigade also carried 5.56 M4 carbines, a 40mm Grenade Launcher Module, the M2 , a M249 Squad Automatic Weapon (SAW)/M240B, and the Mossberg 500 shotgun or M26 Modular Accessory Shotgun System, as need demanded. MP team leaders like Danny were assigned an M4 with an M320 grenade launcher. As brigade leader, Danny was assigned a 320 50 Cal. submachine gun.

Investigations are conducted by Military Police Investigators or Special Agents with the United States Army Criminal Investigation Division (USACID), commonly referred to as CID. The Military Police Investigations (MPI) office is responsible for the investigation of all misdemeanors and several felony crimes including aggravated assault, housebreaking, and larcenies under a thousand dollars committed within an area of military jurisdiction or violations of military law committed by military personnel anywhere (Title 10 Section 805, UCMJ Article 5). MPI Investigators (31B ASI V5) are MPs who attend the Military Police Investigations course at the Military Police School, located at Fort Leonard Wood, Missouri. Army CID is the Department of the Army's criminal investigative organization, reporting directly to the Under Secretary of the Army. CID Special Agents investigate felony crimes, regardless of the incident location, which has an Army nexus.

Special Unit Patches/pocket or sleeve insignia signify membership in a special unit like transportation corps, medical corps etc.. Danny was proud of his uniform and its insignia: an MP brassard bearing the shoulder sleeve insignia of the 90th MP Brigade, and another simply the letters MP. Korean war military police were distinguished by a brassard worn on the left arm when on duty in the Battle Dress Uniform. The brassard was black with white lettering for garrison law-enforcement duty and could include extra designations such as "Customs" MP or "K-9 MP" (for dog handlers). Tactical brassards–like Danny wore–were green with black lettering for temperate climates and sand with light brown lettering for desert duty, both extant in the Korean theater. He wore a shirt pocket shield with a gold color metal and enamel device emblazoned with brown axe and rods, a balance and in saltire overall, a key with bow in the left base and a sword with hilt in the right base. The shield was enclosed at bottom and sides by a gold scroll of three folds inscribed *ASSIST PROTECT DEFEND* in green letters and surmounted at the top by two crossed gold pistols. Military-police soldiers wearing the ACU [Army Combat Uniform], Class A or B uniform, were authorized to wear combat boots instead of regulation low-cut shoes.

The Korean War–also referred to as the Forgotten War–lasted from 1950-1953. It was a conflict between North Korea (supported by China and the Soviet Union) and South Korea (backed by the United States). The war resulted in more than 36,000 American soldiers losing their lives while fighting for democracy and freedom. When men went missing or died behind enemy lines without proper identification, they still carried their own unique patch which would later help identify their remains when found. Without these identifying marks it would be nearly impossible for loved ones back home to know what truly happened. Wearing a patch also conveyed pride in serving that particular unit–something tangible which could be seen even if it could not be spoken.

The United States Army is a strong proponent of the special reaction team mission for the Army Military Police [from regulation FM 19-10] which is how Danny came to be awarded the Medal. Major McGraw was seconded from his CID brigade to a SPR team organized as an emergency to save the freezing soldiers fighting around Chosin Reservoir, South Korea from Inchon up to near the Yalu River. He was accompanied by a teammate, Lieutenant Anne Rogers, a nurse. They were assigned to an all-Korean MASH unit which was one of the first to receive incoming wounded and frozen men. Danny and Anne were given vague orders, "to help".

The most acute shortage was with doctors, particularly specialists. A doctor draft was instituted in August 1950, and the first medical draftees arrived in Korea in January, 1951. Although Korea was liberated from Japanese colonial rule in August, 1945, it had no army or army medical services of its own. With the support of KMAG [Korean Military Advisory Group—officially United States Military Advisory Group to the Republic of Korea], the Korean Army was able to build a nationwide evacuation chain during the Korean War. However, the expansion of the medical evacuation chain resulted in instability.

The United States and its allies hastily invented the Mobile Army Surgical Hospital and the aeromedical evacuation system, based on the casualty/medical evacuation helicopter system. Rotary-wing evacuation had previously been considered a means of last resort. The primitive to nonexistent road network in Korea forced commanders on the peninsula to reassess that doctrine and seek a faster alternative solution.

By the following year, 90 percent of the doctors stationed in Korea were draftees. Combat medical care doctrine in Korea consisted of a relay system. The first line of care was organized around two groups: a battalion aid station and a separate forward collecting station. The latter contained eight men composed of a doctor, medics, and litter bearers. Wounded would be gathered at the collecting stations and an initial diagnosis, triage, and tagging was performed.

Danny and Anne were assigned to K181 MASH unit, an all-Korean medical team situated as near to the front line in Chosin as it was possible to get. Their regular police duties seemed moot; so, the two pitched in to help wherever they could. In the midst of the ferocious battle with its torrent of wounded, the doctors were forced to develop a system of setting priorities in their gory duties they called triage. Danny and Anne pitched in, got bloody and exhausted like everyone else. In addition, Danny became the chief of security and took his turn on sentry duty. That resulted in multiple incidents of firefights with invading Chinese regular army soldiers.

They were in constant danger of being attacked by the enemy, overrun by the enemy, being shelled by artillery, shelled by mortar, and grenades thrown into the station. Danny had to stand as the lone defense against marauders and was responsible for killing hundreds of enemy soldiers. He was superficially wounded twice but held his position both times.

In July, 1950, the Air Force deployed the 3rd ASR [Air-Sea Rescue] unit trained to rescue downed aircrews behind enemy lines or in the sea. It opened a way for Danny and the other litter bearers to get the second worst wounded to evacuation helicopters in time to be flown to help and survival in Japan. The battle ended on December 13, 1950, and no survivor ever forgot even a moment of the horror he or she endured. It cost many of them fingers and toes; many had even worse direct wounds. The snow came. The temperature dropped to 40 below zero. The potential evacuees arrived at the MASH units with faces covered with ice, feet and hands frozen, to find their food and water there frozen. The army and marines fought in sub-zero conditions and all too often in hand-to-hand combat. Survivors call themselves the "Chosin Frozen," and Marines who fought there are known even today as the "Chosin Few."

When the wounded arrived in need of surgery, they had to put on their stretchers supported by saw-horses for lack of operating room tables. Everyone worked for 16 or 18 hours] until they were ready to drop, then somebody else would take over and work until they were ready to drop. To Danny and Anne many of the casualties were just young kids, and the hallways were filled with the wounded and dying. The two MPs learned how to inject the local anesthetic procaine into the affected limbs to deaden the pain. Since 90% of the cases were to deal with frostbitten feet; in a large part, the mission became a campaign to save the black and gangrenous limbs.

Then came the fateful day, December 1st, 1950, for both MP soldiers who were at the time assigned to work as litter bearers. The task was complicated by the dire straits the wounded were in, the fact that they took sporadic enemy small arms fire, and because the helicopters could not wait to leave for Japan for such frivolous reasons as wounds suffered by the bearers, bleeding by the patients, or the impossibly difficult slick icy terrain that had to be covered in record time.

They were left to themselves to pick which patients to carry to the helicopter and which to leave until later. Danny and Anne selected two young Americans to carry on one stretcher who were badly but not emergently injured. Three Chinese communists burst into the tent opening and were able to wound six sentries and both Danny and Anne. Danny had a through and through GSW in his left deltoid which was not life threatening but it felt as if he had been axed and then scalded. His arm was weakened. Anne sustained a scalp graze and a bullet wound that passed through both her buttocks. Her pain was agonizing, but she was able to carry on. Danny flew at the Chi-Coms like a Greek Fury and killed all three of them with his bare hands.

They had to admit that they could not carry the two good-sized Americans; so, they gently set them aside and told them to wait, help was on the way. The helicopter was on the ground and had taken on two wounded passengers. The pilot was gesticulating that they had to run with their next patients or be left. The stretcher was destroyed in the fight; so, Danny found a very small man with a very big chest wound lying on the ground with a transfusion running. Beside him was another small Korean, writhing in pain from a bleeding stump of a leg. Danny made up his mind in a hurry.

He hoisted each little man onto his shoulders, told Anne to carry the IV bottles and paraphernalia, and they started out at a miserable trot towards the copter. Two-thirds of the way, a North Korean special forces squad opened fire on them. They unceremoniously lowered the wounded Koreans to the icy ground, and both Danny and Anne began firing their M-14s at the attackers. Danny was hit again, this time in his right thigh, a fairly superficial, but painful wound. Anne took a round to her right flank. They succeeded in killing all of the North Koreans.

"Can you go on, Anne?" Danny asked her, concerned because she look pretty grey.

"I can, boss, how about you?"

"I'll have to. Let's give it one more try. We owe it to these two poor buggers."

The helicopter pilot was screaming at them. He was dramatically counting down on his ten outstretched fingers. Much as Danny wanted to show him one finger of his own, he refrained. The two poor buggers were worth more than any adolescent display of having been disrespected. They slowly picked up the patients who groaned in pain and began inching along towards the copter. A corpsman had his arms out ready to lift them aboard.

Danny never heard the bullet that caused such damage to his left thigh; fractured, dislocated the femur, and a blew away a softball sized glob of his hamstrings. He collapsed into unconsciousness at the doorway of the helicopter.

The corpsman leaped from the plane and tried to lift Danny aboard, but he was too heavy. Anne helped to get the two small Korean soldiers aboard, and the copter lifted off with alacrity; but that was tempered by sympathy and empathy.

Anne started to drag the big man back to the MASH tent, but it was futile. Two litter bearers behind them set their stretchers down and ran to the aid of their fallen comrade. They put Danny on their stretcher and lifted him into position to be carried back to safety. An enemy machine gunner got Anne in the belly, and she was out of commission and bleeding severely. Both litter bearers were killed.

Danny became conscious enough to realize that to stay where he and Anne were would mean certain death, and he was dead set against that bit of future. He rolled himself off the stretcher, uttered a few choice Texas back country epithets, and slowly—very slowly—dragged his wounded partner and himself across what seemed like a dozen miles of frozen tundra to the warmth of the MASH tent and safety. He was thereafter unconscious for the next three days.

CHAPTER 4

To the end of the war and back to Dallas, 1954

THE SURGEONS SAID DANNY WAS too tough to die. The nurses and medics pushed him to the limit to get up and about after he was operated on, transfused, and alert enough to know what was going on. His first question was about how his partner Lt. Anne Rogers was doing. When he learned that she was alive and still fighting to get well, he was somewhat enlivened. He walked on the fourth day, and he and Anne were transferred by ship to the 343rd General Hospital at Camp Drew, north of Tokyo.

A Japanese surgeon told him he would be mustered out of the military and sent home, but when he was evaluated by the hardened veteran American surgeon, he received instructions and orders. He was formally declared to be a "mission-capable wounded soldier" and after a month-and-a-half of rest and recovery, Danny was sent back to his MP unit, where he served until a year after the armistice was signed.

On December 21, 1955, Danny McGraw of Dallas, Texas was awarded the Congressional Medal of Honor by the former supreme commander of WW II allied forces, and then 34th President of the United States Dwight D. Eisenhower, a fellow Texan. The ceremony took place in the East Room of the White House with his entire family in attendance. Although thrilled and deeply honored by the award, Danny was deeply disappointed that Anne Rogers received only the 2nd highest award, the DSC [Distinguished Service Cross]. His fellow MP veterans told him frankly that it was because she was just a woman and a nurse, and she was lucky to get any recognition. Furthermore, they reminded him, had either he or she been a Black person, they would not have been considered at all. It was just the way things were.

By that time, Danny was a member of the Dallas Police Department and was being considered for advancement to the rank and responsibility of detective. That came six months later after he passed the detective test and was approved by the Chief of Detectives and the police chief. His highly respected father, Assistant Chief of Detectives Hector Lopez McGraw, was quietly instrumental in the rapid advancement, calling in a number of markers.

The Chief of Ds, Gustav "Gus" Abrams, decided to give the new detective an important test as his first case. The mayor's mistress, Gerty Anne Sawyer, was arrested in a nighttime surprise raid on a gambling and brothel establishment located on the sixth floor of the Magnolia Oil Building at Commerce and Akard. She was arrested in a drunken state of dishabille in charge of a Texas Holdem table. Newsie photogs accompanying the raiding vice cops caught excellent photos of her pneumatic chest accoutrements. The photos were especially well done in terms of detail, and there was no mistaking the individual in the center of the gambling table with one hand on a tall pile of chips and the other on a scatter of currency.

The problem for the vice squad, for the Chief of Ds, and the Chief of Police, quickly became Detective 3rd Class Danny McGraw's problem. What could possibly go wrong here? he thought.

He was sternly warned against talking to the mayor or anyone in his inner circle or to the arresting officers. Better to let sleeping dogs lie and for the arrest and charges to go magically away. One problem was that Gerty was very vocal and very public about who her boyfriend was and how much clout he had.

She was "gonna be outta jail in two shakes of a dead lamb's tail because, her boyfriend, Hank, would say the word, and she would have a "get outta jail free" card.

The mayor's office was publicly silent; but in private, he was on the back of the police officials, including the detective in charge, continually threatening to "pitch a hissy fit, to git-r-done, or I'll be fixin' to come down on the buncha ya'll like a ton a bricks, Ah swear!"

Mayor Henry "Hank" Kendall was a portly man with jowly cheeks, a florid complexion, and had the "Dunlop syndrome" [his large belly done lop over his belt]. He was sweaty when he was worried or angry. At the moment, he was both. Everyone in the room nodded their heads or pointed a finger at new detective Danny McGraw. He decided not to speak unless spoken to and kept an expression on his face like a soda cracker. That made Mayor Hank even angrier.

Hank got up the gumption and the anger to walk right up to Danny and take hold of the lapels of the new man's new suit.

"Whatta ya'll got ta say fer yerself, Boy? You even shave yit?'

Danny said quietly but in sotto voce; so, everyone in the room could hear, "I don't like people puttin' their hands on me."

Danny was a foot-and-a-half taller, thirty years younger, and a known hero for whatever it was he did in the war. He may have had a bland expression, but his eyes were like sharks', unblinking and completely devoid of warmth. It was how he came across to snotty kids in the army who thought they were tough. They were wrong.

The mayor picked up on the expression from the young man and backed up two paces.

"You got a solution for this cock-up, Boy?"

"I'm working on it, and I'll let everybody know what I get it fixed. And, with all due respect, Mr. Mayor, nobody calls me 'boy' or 'son'.

"No offense meant, Detective McGraw. I'll look forward to hearin' frum you purty soon. Thanks fer yer time, now ya heah?"

"You can count on it," Danny said.

The other cops in the room were holding their collective breaths until the mayor sauntered slowly out of the room.

The Chief of D's looked at Danny with a minimal smile, "Ya'll braced the lion in his den, and he blinked… this time. Watch your back, Danny, he never forgets a slight or forgives an enemy."

"Yes, sir. Now, if it's okay with you, I need to get back to work on the case. I need your permission to interview the lady in question."

"You got it. Tread lightly and keep the questions away from His Honor."

"That, I intend to do."

Danny had Gerty Anne Sawyer brought up from the tombs and placed in one of the interview rooms. He left her to stew in her own juices for an hour before opening the door to the room.

"Sure took your sweet time, Boy. Whatta you want with me? Is this where you apologize and erase my record?"

"Nope. This is where I give you a bus ticket for someplace far away."

Gerty looked at the young detective as if he had slapped her.

"Whatta you mean?"

"Let me be clear, Miss Sawyer. You have had a good run, and it is now over. You have to make a choice about your future. You have to make it now. You can push your luck in the local justice system that is not inclined your way. You could easily get a hefty fine and jail time. Whatever choice you make, you are not going to have any contact his His Honor ever again. Or, you can hop on the next bus out of Dallas, out of Texas, and out of the South. If you are a nice girl about all of this, I can probably rustle up some traveling money."

"What about me getting a rap sheet?"

"Depends on how good a girl I think you are."

"Okay, Copper. You got me. I guess I always knew my romance and my lucrative career would eventually come to an end. Help me out, okay."

"Deal."

"If you don't mind me asking, what do you get out of this?"

"I don't get fired."

It was a good week, a good start for Danny. His second case during his first seven days was simpler, more direct, and decidedly more dangerous. That is why the Chief of D's assigned him to find and arrest one Timothy Gonzales O'Neill, the local Irish gang leader and chief thug in Dallas County who had been a thorn in the side of the police and sheriff's departments for a decade. He was a cop killer—a charge never having enough evidence to get anywhere—a gun runner, a flagrant pimp, and a trafficker of young Hispanic girls to points north of the state. O'Neill was known to talk very little, to communicate with bullets when confronted, and to lie with Gaelic ease.

First, Danny had to find the thug. That presented no great difficulty. Danny found a couple of young punks in the tombs who were regular visitors there for a variety of perpetrations. He offered them the chance to beat their current charges in exchange for accurate information about O'Neill's whereabouts on any given day.

They swore him to secrecy, and he agreed. That produced two results: two more thugs went back on the mean streets, and Detective Danny McGraw got the opportunity to meet Timothy Gonzales O'Neill in his primary place of business. The place had no address except it was on Meandering Way, half a block from Big Mike's Grocery Emporium.

Danny prepared himself for the encounter by donning a bulky, uncomfortable flak jacket made from ballistic nylon, arming himself with his .45, an ankle .38, and a 12 gauge scatter gun with a pistol grip under the crook of his arm. For dramatic purposes, he put on his none-too-clean, unpressed, duty-worn, olive drab uniform complete with MP insignias, and much scuffed combat boots. He was ready to hunt bear.

He walked into the bar without closing the door behind him. His presence in the room drew attention not because he was so heavily armed but because he was the only White man in the room. No one recalled with any certainty what the man was carrying; but it was notable that on the day in question, it was the first time a White person had ever been on the premises.

Danny walked slowly at first adjusting to the darkened room after being in the strong sunlight. He looked about the place to find Timothy. The windows were smoky from the dirt; the floor crackled from empty peanut shells; and there was a heavy smell of stale beer and marijuana smoke. Aside from a low murmur from gravel throated men, the place was rather quiet.

"Who ya'll lookin' foah, Whitey? We don' get all that many piggies in heah, don' ya know it?"

Detective McGraw touched the tip of his hat and said in a quiet voice, "I am here to see one Timothy Gonzales O'Neill."

"Senior or Junior?"

"Both, please. And, may I ask who it is I'm talking too?"

There was a pause, then came the answer, "Senior".

Raucous laughter filled the room.

The voice of a prepubertal boy was then heard, "and Junior is also heah, Suh."

Danny walked purposefully in the direction of the manly voice.

"How come y'all ah packin' so much heat, Po-po?"

"Heard some things about this part of South Dallas, Mr. O'Neill. I wanted to be part of the peacekeeping process, and I thought my being well armed would serve as a deterrent to violence."

"Heard wrong, Porky. Just makes us be on edge, don' ya'll know?"

"My purpose is peaceable."

"And what's ya'lls purpose?"

"To arrest Mr. O'Neill and take him uptown for booking on an assortment of criminal charges."

The room erupted into an uproar of hooting, hollering, and guffawing. It was a cacophony. Taking advantage of the diversion of attention taking place, Danny—having fully adjusted his vision to the murky room—moved briskly to where he could see a large black man in a flaming red broad brimmed hat, glowing yellow pearl snap button shirt, and orange pants, standing next to a boy who looked to be no more than eight-years-of-age.

"Timothy O'Neill, I presume," Danny said and tipped his hat.

O'Neill was quick, but Danny was quicker. The criminal raised a long barreled shiny steel pistol and was starting to squeeze the trigger. Danny's 12 gauge pivoted from the crook of his arm and fired two barrels of OO shot into the undefended chest of the infamous outlaw. O'Neill's gun fired one harmless slug into the ceiling knocking out a light fixture.

The little boy sat back on his bottom and began to sob.

Men and a few terrified women scattered for the doors and windows. The action was so sudden and definitive that apparently no one had the presence of mind to fire at the tall, muscular Dallas Police Officer.

He took two steps and stood over the inert body of the once most feared man in the south side of Dallas.

He said laconically, "You are under arrest, sir," and placed a single symbolic hand cuff on the man's shooting wrist.

Danny reached down and scooped up the traumatized child and cuddled him to his big chest until he stopped crying.

"Where's the phone, barkeep?" he asked the man whose eyes were just peaking over the side of the long, wet bar.

"Rat heah, suh, Ah gots it ready fa ya."

Danny called the Chief of D's office and asked to speak to Chief Gustav "Gus" Abrams, personally.

"That you, McGraw?"

"Yes, sir."

"Why'd you call me up?"

"I have arrested Timothy O'Neill in his bar. I need an ambū-lance and some forensics folks down here. There has been something of a ruckus."

"I'll just bet. Me and the crew are on our way as we speak."

CHAPTER 5

Making his name in the Dallas Detective Bureau, 1953-1954

DANNY BECAME ELIGIBLE TO TAKE the Detective 1st exam at the end of his second year with the Dallas PD. His exploits were well known and resulted in favorable recommendations from Chief of Ds Gus Abrams, and from Mayor Henry "Hank" Kendall. The test was thorough, but Danny was much better prepared than his competitors. There were ten total applicants, of which two were veterans, and only two who had been on the force for over three years.

The Background Investigation had to be completed before the day of the test. Applicants had to submit a complete, detailed, and accurate, Personal History Statement. A certified detective conducted an extensive background investigation to include all but not limited to, contacting all prior/present employers, references, co-workers, ex-spouses, family members, and schools. Also, the applicant's residential history, record of financial responsibility, military records, and driving history are investigated. Background investigations typically took two to four months to complete. Ten applicants appeared for testing.

The preliminaries dug deep into the applicants' personal lives and histories. All applicants had to complete a pre-polygraph questionnaire in preparation for a polygraph examination and to complete it without discovering attempts to deceive. That reduced the number of applicants by two.

The physical test was easy for Danny and the other vet. It consisted of candidates being required to succeed at minimum requirements of vertical jump (minimum 6.5 inches), bench press with free weights (to a minimum 56% of the persons' body weight, i.e. (Current Body Weight X 0.56 = Benchpress Weight), Illinois Shuttle Run (maximum time of 24.9 seconds), sit-ups (minimum of 14 repetitions in 1 minute), 300 meter run (maximum time of 110 seconds), push-ups (minimum of 4 repetitions), 1.5 miles run (maximum time of 19:09 minutes). The physical tests weeded out three applicants leaving only five, including the two vets.

All applicants underwent a long and thorough psychological examination. Applicants completed two psychological written tests and were interviewed by a staff psychologist. There was also a medical examination with the applicants' physical and medical conditions being evaluated to ensure that he/she can function safely as a police officer. All applicants passed without finding problems. However, all applicants underwent alcohol and drug screening. Applicants provided samples of urine and blood for analyze to detect the use of illegal drugs. Two failed. The third applicant was a woman, and she failed on general principles.

The written test was a new form of testing which made grading easier—a set of multiple choice (guess) questions. Examples:

> May be considered _____ when all logical leads have been exhausted and no outstanding leads can be followed, although the investigator has not resolved the case to a logical conclusion.
> (Detective policy) The Detective Bureau supervisor or assigned lead detective shall report to and assume command of the scene when relinquished by the _____ on scene.
> (Detective policy) How often will an audit of vehicles being held by the detectives for investigative and/or prosecution purposes be conducted by investigative services command?
> (Detective policy) An investigator may release a felony or gross misdemeanor prisoner from custody with no charges filed for just cause, i.e., victim refuses to prosecute,

insufficient evidence, etc. The investigator will notify the jail to release the prisoner by _____
(Detective policy) A closed case may be re-opened for investigation anytime the _____ or additional information is received that would warrant further investigatory activity.

Solvability factors
(Detective policy) On all officer involved shootings, homicides, attempt homicides, and violent deaths not related to traffic fatalities, _____ will respond to the scene.

Only two men passed the written test. That left Danny and Kent Thacker as the two new first class detectives for the year. In recognition, each man was given a SIG-Sauer P226 and a box of .357 SIG ammunition. For a couple of weeks, Danny McGraw had the same Dallas PD Detective rank as his well-known father, something that gave Hector real pleasure. Shortly, though, Hector became the third ranking officer in the Dallas Police Department when he was promoted to the rank of one-star deputy chief, and that gave Danny serious behind-the-scenes insights and protections which would soon prove to be critical for his growing career and reputation.

With his new designation, Danny could choose the cases he would pursue as lead detective most times. And most times, he selected out the more interesting and usually more dangerous cases, especially when the alternate choice would have been a detective with a wife and children facing the danger. For that reason, he gained respect from both his superiors and those lower on the ranking lists. That he was unflinchingly brave, assiduously honest, and intuitively smart, which produced a following of lower ranking detectives that thought he walked on water and was an Einstein level genius.

He had his detractors, even enemies, as one particular case brought to the fore. It was early August, and Dallas was unbearably hot and humid. Lieutenant Foster Chico Rodriguez caught a case involving a possible child trafficking ring. Nominally, Danny was his subordinate in the investigation. Danny began to notice that his investigative results and those of Lt. Rodriguez were different and early on diverged in direction. Danny's evidence–vetted by men in his unit whom he trusted completely, including undercover officers—pointed at a local Hispanic businessman, Don Rodrigo Valentino Degollado, who was also on the County Council, the board of Parkland Hospital, and the influential Dallas Citizens Council. Degollado was generous to the south side people, Black and Hispanic, and was held in near reverence by that community. He was considered to be an untouchable by the police department, and so were his close associates.

Lt. Rodriguez and his subordinates pursued leads suggesting that the national bicycle gang, the notorious HAMC [Hell's Angels Motorcycle Club], which was founded in 1948 and grew to alarming power and ruthless over the ensuing years. They threatened and frightened the humble working-class Blacks and Hispanics in South Dallas, strong-armed them by extortion, and were responsible for a number of especially gruesome murders throughout Texas. They were easy to hate by the citizens, easy to suspect by the cops, and had proved to be most difficult to dismantle or eliminate over the past decade and a half. The mayor, city council, Dallas Citizens Council, and most of the senior members of the DPD took a simple, valuable, and safe, viewpoint that the detectives should concentrate their attentions on the HAMC. Bringing them down would be a major feather in the department's and city's caps.

The Hells Angels Motorcycle Club (HAMC) is an international outlaw motorcycle club whose members typically ride Harley-Davidson motorcycles. In the United States and Canada, the Hells Angels are incorporated as the Hells Angels Motorcycle Corporation. Common nicknames for the club are the "H.A.", "Big Red Machine", "Red & White", "HAMC", and "81". With a membership of over 6,000, and 467 charters in 59 countries, the HAMC is the largest outlaw motorcycle club in the world. They earned every bit of fear and notoriety their presence generated, and the DPD decided to mount a war against them. Danny found himself on the outside looking in.

Danny recommended against the first foray in force against the HAMC on the grounds that their evidence was scanty, and their numbers and weaponry were inferior to the gang's numbers and arsenal. His voice was a lone call in the wilderness, and he was roundly ignored. While the task force formed up and readied for the surprise nighttime attack, Danny and his men and women continued to pile up actual evidence against the popular Don Rodrigo Valentino Degollado and his ongoing criminal conspiracy which included the completely reprehensible child trafficking.

The plans for the Hell's Angels roundup, arrests, and incarcerations, were set for a week later, on a nonholiday Saturday night. Danny and his team worked over boxes of printed data to establish their case against Degollado–unknown to the perp–while the rest of DPD, and the task force getting ready to brace the outlaw motorcycle gang in its lair, a biker bar called the Deer Lounge, on 108 N. Fitzhugh at Columbia in old East Dallas.

The place had the deserved reputation of being the meanest bar in Dallas. It was taken over by the Hell's Angels from the mean old farmers who used to come there on weekends to drink beer and fight. The habitués roughed up two Texas Alcoholic Beverage Commission agents who went in to investigate the conditions. Another time, they threatened to take prisoners away from four city cops.

The cops who had had cause to enter the joint reported unanimously, "The people in there are just plain mean. You can feel meanness in the air."

That was especially true when the lounge came under new biker approved management. The old manager fired a pistol at a couple of customers and lost the license, which—incidentally–belonged to a man who had died under mysterious circumstances. The old manager (pre-Hell's Angels) just kept operating under the dead man's name. The bar was located in the bastion of middle-class hard work where clean play and brawling saloons and clip joints still abounded.

Dallas began as a swashbuckling, gambling-and-whoring frontier town; and that legacy had never completely left the town's blood. The Deer Lounge had a special milieu: sleazy, flabby go-go girls and stale, rancid, beer smells. The décor in the place was early tacky, with deer antlers on the wall. The go-go girls were frumps with protruding bellies and flabby bosoms.

It specialized in being a hangout for thugs. The two security guards had been hired to patrol the premises and throw out the more obnoxious drunks. But–that proved to be an overly hazardous career choice–so, for the most part, those guards carried out the trash bags full of empty beer cans, bottles, and cigarette butts. Knowing that the Deer Lounge which employed them was a fight-my-way-in, drink-my beer, and fight-my-way-out kind of place, the bouncers usually kept to themselves in the back storeroom.

The task force consisted of select members of the police vice squad, Texas Alcoholic Beverage Commission, ATF, and SWAT. Police Chief Robert V. Murray remembered very well several of Detective Danny McGraw's more important cases and demanded that he be on the task force. He waved off the Chief of Ds and Danny's protests with a dismissive wave of his hand.

"He is part of this. We need a warrior. Get me three or four more Danny McGraws, and we don't need this army you got lined up."

Like it or not, Danny was in. He had to leave the investigation of the vicious human trafficker to his 2nd in command, Jesus L. Gomez, whom he had to admit was at least as good at the collection of evidence as he was.

At midnight, Saturday, August 9, 1952, a force of over 100 heavily armed task force members gathered in the gloomy streets around the Deer Lounge in East Dallas. Danny McGraw was there, once again loaded for a bear hunt.

CHAPTER 6

The infamous Deer Lounge War, Saturday, August 9, 1952

DANNY LOOKED AT THE UPCOMING war at the bar as being much like similar raids he had conducted as an army MP during the recent Korean War. So, he dressed accordingly in full combat gear, even his none-too-clean, unpressed, duty-worn, olive drab uniform MP battle ACU uniform, the same bulky, uncomfortable flak jacket made from ballistic nylon, and he had an augmented armamentarium to carry around for the likely battle. He had his trusty .45, ankle .38, a 12 gauge scatter gun with a pistol grip under the crook of his arm. He added cross chest bandoliers of extra OO shot, and an extra belt to carry grenades. Both for utilitarian purposes and luck, he put on his MP insignias, and much scuffed combat boots. He was ready to take on the outlaw gang and was trusting and confident in his fellow fighters.

The task force moved in to surround the infamous lounge undercover of the starless night shrouded in fog and smoke from the neighborhood's factories. The streets were potholed, and their signage had long since been vandalized and removed. There was no mistaking the biker bar; a string of 42 Harley-Davidson motorcycles were parked neatly on the street under a blinking neon sign which read "*D_er _oge, Welcome*". The streetlight just north of the lounge had been shot out.

Danny and his squad were assigned to break through the rear door of the lounge, and SWAT was designated to enter the reinforced front door on the task director's count. Danny's squad had to tread carefully around and among the scattered upturned trash cans and piles of cardboard boxes, strewn about paper cups, beer cans, and brown glass bottles—mostly broken. When he was ready, he gave his mic one click and received back two separate one click messages—one from the task leader and the other from SWAT. Everyone was ready.

"3, 2, 1," Crash!!, both doors caved in like balsa wood being hit by a pickup truck. The front and rear squads rushed in under cover of flash-bangs and began screaming, Dallas PD, ATF, and Texas Alcoholic Beverage Commission! at the top of their lungs. Two uniforms were tasked to tip over the stand of motorcycles and to shoot out the front and rear tires on all vehicles. That was a sight to see!

The fight began in an instant as if the bikers had been forewarned. Shotguns, handguns of all sorts, AK 47s and WWII M-14 Garands began to fire back at the invading cops. Danny threw grenade after grenade in the general direction of what sounded like biker voices, hoping all the while about not causing any collateral damage among the cops. Bikers surprised the cops by diving out of side windows of the lounge, and some from already placed second floor window ladders and the two fire escapes. The scene was utter chaos and had the beginnings of a fiasco—a euphemism not used by the members of the police force.

The task force had not planned for a general escape of resourceful bikers into the dark streets. The perimeter guards assigned to take control of such an eventuality saw no reason to stay outside and away from the action; so, they had all entered the lounge following the attackers. It was as the military vets called it, a complete "Charlie foxtrot".

When the smoke cleared, and police lights made visibility possible, the task force leaders did an assessment: four bikers and two policemen were KIA; six bikers and six policemen were WIA; only three bikers [all either stoned or in the late stages of drunkenness] were captured. The leaders of the Hell's Angels were nowhere to be seen; and a few kegs of illegal moonshine, several dozen boxes of illegal [no taxes paid] beer and cigarettes, were all the contraband found in the joint. No guns, bombs, hand-grenades, or other military materiel, were found after an exhaustive search. All law enforcement units involved were angry and disappointed. But no one dared speak the most likely reason how the failure had come about.

Danny McGraw was all but certain why the police task force had failed, but he kept it to himself.

CHAPTER 7

The first big case: August 9, 1954-1956

THE DALLAS POLICE DEPARTMENT WAS a scene entirely reminiscent of a funeral with both sides of the family at odds with each other. The mayor, police chief, and chief of detectives, were caught in the middle. No one actually said out loud what everyone was thinking because it was unthinkable. Detective 1st Danny McGraw was certain of the cause, but he could not decide to confide his suspicions for fear that he could be blundering into speaking confidentially to the actual traitor. Danny's unit–who had been investigating City Councilman Don Rodrigo Valentino Degollado—were angry at the DPD brass for being so pig-headed about insisting on going forward on the biker raid, but they were infuriated at the idea of a mole in their ranks who put their very lives at risk

Lt. Rodriguez and his subordinates who had been the leaders of the task force against the Hell's Angels, took it upon themselves to start a dragnet to bring in every member of the outlaw gang in the state, especially those arrested in the Lone Deer Lounge, and to grill them for days on end. The mayor's office investigators, the District Attorney's investigators, and the Chief of Detectives personally, brought in every law enforcement officer, civil servant, and secretary, who had even the slightest involvement in for a somewhat less brutal, but no less angry, interview with the sole purpose of obtaining a name. Police and ATF chieftains appointed a special branch to get to the bottom of the betrayal, and all finally gave up in frustration. They called in the FBI.

The decision was not lightly taken. Every chief down to each concrete pounding patrol officer had some basic dislike of the "fibbies". It had some basis in experience. When the FBI came in, the locals took the second fiddle seat and were lucky to get information back until the entire investigation was completed.

The FBI's Public Corruption unit moved in and took over almost every available office space, brought in their own secretaries, typists, accountants, and investigators. Upon arrival, the SAC of Dallas FBI, Denton Cartwright III, informed the DPD and ATF, where the bear slept. From that point forward, the investigation would follow the DOJ's Intelligence-Driven Strategy for Operations; and the FBI would call all the shots. No one was above suspicion; no one was going to escape scrutiny. The vast majority of the DPD personnel were perfectly innocent; the department turned into a psychotherapist's dream of a full load of patients all at once. The cops and staff had PTSD, anxiety, depression, and serious cases of paranoia all at once and en masse.

Besides ferreting out moles and revealing corruption among cops, the FBI's public corruption program also addressed environmental crime, election fraud, and matters concerning the integrity committee of the Council of Inspectors General for Integrity and Efficiency. It was that council that made the rules and gave the directions to the fibbies in the field. Because of the far- reaching criminal arm of organizations like Hell's Angels, the FBI created the ICU [International Corruption Unit] to oversee the increasing number of investigations involving global fraud against the US government and the corruption of federal public officials outside of the continental US involving US funds, persons, businesses, etc. The FBI's public corruption program had established and maintained liaison with the OIG [Office of Inspector General] for each government agency to facilitate a comprehensive and coordinated approach to known crime problems and to organize appropriate referrals between the OIGs and the FBI The FBI's public corruption program investigates violations of federal law by public officials at the federal, state, and local levels of government and oversees the nationwide investigation of allegations of fraud related to federal government procurement, contracts, and federally funded programs. That was the directed aim of the Dallas,

Texas, and federal law enforcement with regards the Hell's Angels and the possibility that there was a compromised law enforcement officer somewhere in the loop.

The FBI uses applicable federal laws–including the Hobbs Act–to investigate violations by public officials in federal, state, and local governments. Most violations occur when the official solicits, accepts, receives, or agrees to receive, something of value in return for influence in the performance of an official act. The categories of public corruption investigated by the FBI include legislative, judicial, regulatory, contractual, and law enforcement. A key tenet of protecting the nation from those who wish to do us harm is the NICS [National Instant Criminal Background Check System]. The goal of NICS is to ensure that guns do not fall into the wrong hands, and also to ensure the timely transfer of firearms to eligible gun buyers. FBI joint task forces—Violent Crime Safe Streets, Violent Gang Safe Streets, and Safe Trails—focus on identifying and targeting major groups operating as criminal enterprises. All of them converged on Dallas in the aftermath of the failed raid on the Hell's Angels.

The feds had learned something about both obtaining intelligence and successfully working with local law enforcement. Much of the FBI criminal intelligence is derived from state, local, and tribal, law enforcement partners, who know their communities inside and out. Joint task forces benefit from FBI surveillance assets, and FBI sources track these gangs to identify emerging trends. Through these multi-subject and multi-jurisdictional investigations, the FBI concentrates its efforts on high-level groups like Hell's Angels engaged in patterns of racketeering. That ongoing investigative model had enabled them to target senior gang leadership and to develop enterprise-based prosecutions.

Modern-day criminal enterprises are flat, fluid, networks with global reach. The process had been developed and honed by multiple experiences within and outside the country. The "traditional" organized crime activities of loan-sharking, extortion, and murder, were all in play in the Dallas crime kingpins of the biker gang.

In the meeting with the locals, SAC of Dallas FBI, Denton Cartwright III, told everyone of how serious the FBI and DOJ were to eliminate the Hell's Angel, "You have an impressive list of crimes charged to the Hell's Angels. I can include additional charges of drug trafficking, identity theft, human trafficking, money laundering, alien smuggling, public corruption, weapons trafficking, extortion, kidnapping, along with the other known illegal activities. We have a broad range of crimes to nail the gang, and an impressive force to pursue and to punish them. TOC [Transnational Organized Crime] networks exploit legitimate institutions for critical financial and business services that enable the storage or transfer of illicit proceeds. Preventing and combating transnational organized crime demands a concentrated effort by the FBI and federal, state, local, tribal, and international partners. We have put every one of those assets into play.

"I can tell you this about your primary concern—that of having a traitorous mole within your ranks. A recent federal investigation into the Albuquerque Police Department's DWI unit started with two people who knew something wasn't right and came forward. They took their stories about corrupt APD officers to long-time Albuquerque defense attorney who was alarmed by the possible involvement of a sworn defense attorney and took the information to the FBI.

"As a result APD has placed six officers on leave and two resigned. Our special agents also raided the office of a prominent defense attorney. Because of that ongoing investigation, the Bernalillo County District Attorney was forced to dismiss more than 200 DWI cases tied to the officers since their credibility was called into question. No one doubts the seriousness of our investigations into public corruption. You are to be congratulated for starting the process promptly.

"I want you to know that this is not our first rodeo, and we have learned from our successes and mistakes. Over the past few decades, great strides have occurred in the law enforcement profession. To begin with, many police agencies have avoided hiring candidates who have low ethical standards and have identified those onboard employees early in their careers who might compromise the department's integrity. We need to start with that in the Dallas PD. In addition, research has discovered new methods of testing candidates for their psychological propensity to act ethically. It is my strong suggestion that you now include such testing into your tests of recruits before they are allowed to join the force. However, we are not naïve; unethical conduct by the nation's police officers continues to occur in departments large and small. We are here to reduce that number.

"The profession of policing has a subculture unto itself. The morbid sense of humor perhaps illustrates one of the most widely known characteristics. That police subculture either can prevent the existence of corruption or be a vehicle to spread it throughout a department. It is always a most difficult aspect to address, but we all have to face it head-on and make the changes necessary, however painful.

"The subculture often becomes stronger than the officer's family ties. Additionally, work schedules outside the normal realm can lead to feelings of isolation that further strengthen the bond of the subculture and its willingness to overlook the crimes of its officers. It will be our purpose to test the officers, interview their families, and to document financial information, to find members who are living beyond the means provided by the city or county. Further—and moving forward—senior officers should test new members of the law enforcement profession regularly. For example, see how amiable recruits are to accepting gratuities, a gateway to more serious corruption as it provides the opportunity for corrupt intent which may be discoverable before the damage is done. Accepting the free cup of coffee is the example most often used.

"Accepting small gratuities is a test of loyalty. In the corrupt subculture, fidelity to the long blue line becomes more important than integrity, and officers learn that their peers frown upon morality and independence. There is an undercurrent of "go along to get along" which has significant motivational power to start and perpetuate corruption.

"When this loyalty to the subculture becomes too strong, the solidarity that follows can adversely affect the ethical values of almost all the officers. The typical "us versus them" mentality creates an allegiance to the members stronger than that to the mission of the department or even the profession. Officers begin to feel a disconnect and animosity between themselves and administrative policies and senior officers. Conflicts can and will arise when personnel face a choice between what may be ethically right and their devotion to the other members. This is going to be one of those times, and you can anticipate that multiple officers will leave the force, either by choice or after being convicted. None of us can afford to allow such a strong fidelity toward their fellow officers *over commitment* to do what is right causes members to trade their integrity for that loyalty. It is to your benefit, and it is your sworn duty to stamp out such attitudes and the men and women who hold them and especially those who reap benefit from them.

"Instead of a stubborn blue line of defense to protect wrong doers, the department must create a distinct line that provides constructive dedication that results in team cohesiveness and does away with misguided allegiance that pits a group or an individual against the overall law enforcement mission. Develop a means of gauging the atmosphere of your agency. Take pride in doing difficult and dangerous tasks and developing real esprit d' corps through action taken as a team. Encourage your people to share job experiences, a quality of known elite units. When issues of corruption arise, the shared pride leads the team to say, "we don't do that sort of thing."

"However, be mindful not to foster general feelings of superiority among team members. That can and does lead to separation from the rest of the agency. Such units may develop their own code of conduct, which may not align with departmental policy and procedure. If left unchecked, it can lead to a feeling of being untouchable and a misdirection of loyalty. Be strong leaders, strong enough to get rid of disloyal and/or corrupt individuals. It is past the time when you can say, 'We don't have corruption here', because you do. You have a mole, and maybe a corrupt unit backing that mole up."

Danny clenched his jaw as he listened to the SAC list off the facts he knew were happening in his police department. However, he was convinced beyond doubt that his personal investigative unit not only had no mole or corruption, but none of them had had an opportunity to connect secretly with the Hell's Angels, at least since he took over.

He mulled over the SAC's speech and put it into the back of his mind. He was determined to bring down the corrupt Don Rodrigo Valentino Degollado. To that end, he ordered his team members to a meeting in his office that same afternoon. He planned to hit them with invective if anyone of them was the mole, and to praise them for the quality of their work on the case, and how proud of them he was.

All of that proved to be moot. Before he could get to the meeting, Chief of Ds Abrams ordered him to come to his office. That proved to be career changing for Danny.

CHAPTER 8

Changing the first big case: August 9, 1954-1956

THE CHIEF OF DS OFFICE was spic and span clean, more spruced up than Danny had ever seen it before. In addition to that, there was a new thick wall-to-wall frost green carpet, spoonflower peel and stick floral large scale neutral grey wallpaper, and shiny new efficient steel filing cabinets, table, desk, and several uncomfortable steel chairs—all similar in color to the carpet. It was very much the new style and fully up-to-date. Danny was directed to sit on one of the chairs with arms and was immediately uncomfortable, which might have been the intention for all he knew. He thought the entire makeover looked more like late WW II military or fifty-year-old jail office style. He was not asked his opinion, and he kept his lip zipped. He was learning the social ropes.

He was immediately aware that this was to be an important get-together. In addition to the Chief and Ds Gustav "Gus" Abrams, and his right-hand-man, Lt. Klint R. Peppercorn, Police Chief Robert V. Murray, Mayor Henry "Hank" Kendall, and State Senator Walter Wilcowski, a Democrat representing Dallas came in fashionably late to attend the meeting that had been declared a top-secret committee affair. That was altogether true; no one knew that the meeting was taking place, where, or why, not even the attendees other than the two police chiefs. Another indicator that it was to be a serious and business-like affair was the absence of any refreshments, snacks, or real food, other than plain water. Also revealing was the fact that each participant was warned in advance that there would not be any alcohol or tobacco in any form allowed. That was almost unheard of in Texas. There was a low rumble of discontent in the room until the two police chiefs entered and asked for attention and silence.

"Thanks for coming, everyone," Chief Murray began, "firstly, why all the secrecy and why so few of us are to be in the know?"

Everyone else shrugged.

"Because we cannot have any cops other than us or outsiders be in the know. It's touchy. We are going to talk about what the FBI's investigation has turned up and what we are gonna do about it. Chief "Gus" Abrams will explain the details."

Abrams stood up and looked at each attendee with a scrutinizing eye, getting their measure.

"Gentlemen, we've never had a problem like this in our history; and we are here to setup a dragnet to find the mole, the traitor, who ratted us out to the Hell's Angels before we made our humiliating raid. I personally don't like to be humiliated or to considered a fool. I am pretty sure none of y'all feel any differently. So, this is what we're gonna do.

"The fibbies have just about turned over every stone in the department, the ATV, and the Alcoholic Beverage commission, as well as an intense canvass of the city and the suburbs. It comes as no surprise that the Hell's Angels were not forthcoming, or that the rank-and-file coppers were not much better. The FBI has drawn up a list of corrupt cops and another of list of the criminals they work with for filthy lucre, it pains me to say. Their evidence is rock solid.

"We have more than one cop who has been overly cozy with the Angels, as evidenced by their telephone and restaurant meetings. Several were obviously caught with their dirty hands in the department cookie jar and confessed with full allocution in return for partial immunity and no jail time. We have done the math with the fibbies and have narrowed the number of suspects down to five, none of whom are part of the obvious perps in the department.

"We are going to have to tread as softly asd butterflies making love on a thin leaf. The last thing we want to do is to spook them. On the basis of his past record—especially for honesty and freedom from accusations of corruption—we have invited Det. 1st Danny McGraw to head up the team. He has not heard about this, and we have not informed his father, Chief McGraw, Sr. None of his current investigative team is in the know either, and we intend to keep it that way. He will be given the chance to turn down the offer of heading all this up, of course. Presuming that he will accept, this meeting is to be a discussion of how this lone wolf should operate and to offer helpful suggestions."

Danny was totally surprised, but he was not altogether unsuspecting. In the last week, talk of the mole had died down to a rare whisper; and he took that to mean that something was up.

He looked around the room. Everyone was looking straight at him.

"I accept. Scares the crap outta me, but somebody has to do it; and I guess I am as okay a pick as anybody. I have to tell y'all, I am gonna have to have lots of help, no secrets, no blue line protection. More than that; anything good coming out of this will require a full reorganization of the department and a complete change in how our police society works. No one is going to like the idea; everyone will resist divulging what they know; and it will be like pulling teeth to get anyone to point the finger at any one cop. Nevertheless, that is exactly what must be done. I will accept the job if I know that everyone in this room agrees to those terms."

Gus Abrams checked out the room. Each man nodded, and the deal was made. They had a new mole "Tsar". Danny gave everyone a quiet "good night" and headed to his office to get to work. It was nearly ten o'clock, but he had an idea that could not wait.

He put pencil to paper and wrote and rewrote a brief note until it was perfect: untraceable to the writer, succinct, and just ungrammarly enough to have come from a poorly educated man, and enticing enough to draw some corrupt sucker in. The end result, on yellow lined legal paper in all-caps said, "GET THE WORD TO PRES. COPS & ATF ON THE MOVE TO THE BACK 9 BAR ONE OF THE NIGHTS THIS COMING WEEK. CAN'T FIND OUT WHICH YET. GET TO SAFEHOUSE RIGHT ASAP!!! MORE INFO WHEN I GET IT."

He had his regular unit distribute the photocopied note to every suspected mole in the department and ATF including the brass. Each note had an imbedded mark to make it unique and traceable to the recipient. He knew that a message that important would have to be delivered in person.

Danny put a three-man rotating 24/7 watch on the Back 9 Bar and changed the men on the watch every other day. They drove motorcycles, hotrods, convertibles, pickups, and old vans which were mixed, mingled, and moved haphazardly to prevent accidental recognition. Two men were in the bar as regulars but changed after no longer than two hours at a time. He enlisted some of the ATF agents who were both scraggly and trustworthy to be included.

Results came on the third day. Det. 2 Lincoln "Linc" Schribner stepped into the phone booth half a block from the Back 9 at 460 Belt Line Road and put a call in to Danny.

"One", Danny said.

"Five," Linc replied. "Have something; I think it is a breakthrough."

"Good work. I'll be there in less than five minutes. Go and stand behind the news stand on Spectrum Drive where it intersects Belt Line. Buy a paper and look interested. I will pull in behind you on Spectrum, and you can fill me in."

"Clear."

Danny put the pedal to the metal and moved as fast as he could in the late morning traffic. He was looking at Linc after four and a half minutes. He blinked his lights twice, and Linc sauntered over to where Danny was parked, still reading the exciting local news.

Linc tapped on Danny's car window, then slipped into the front passenger seat.

"Let's hear it, Linc."

"Okay, Boss. This is what I seen. I was sitting up to the long glass bar eating Southwest egg rolls, blackened tilapia sandwich, and sippin' a beer. A kid—maybe ten-years–old hurried into the bar and evaded the bouncers who are pretty fussy about underagers getting in. He was carryin' a small size manila envelope which he carried held against his chest all around the joint until he spied Big Mike Donovan, who I recognize from my last couple of times staking out the bar. Donovan saw the boy and waggled his finger at him to come forward. The kid trotted over and held out the envelope for Mike. Mike handed him a fin and said, "thanks."

"The boy turned around and fast trotted out, turned left up Belt Line, and then left again into the first small alley along the way. I had to move down a few feet to get a decent view, and you won't be able to guess what I seen."

"Astonish me, Linc. Get on with it."

Linc continued, "So, a big guy come outta the alley about six inches and handed the boy a wad of cash. The untrusting kid took his own sweet time counting the cash—long enough for me to get a decent approximation. About sixty bucks."

"Good pay for a few minutes effort," Danny said, "must have been important."

"You better believe it, Boss. First, I seen the guy's shoes, somethin' outta the magazines, beautiful black shinies—probable set him back than a C note. Then, I seen his suit. Better'n Brooks Brothers, probably custom made. Fit the guy like a glove. Silk white shirt, fresh boutonniere, and a wide cowboy belt with a rodeo buckle that had to have been genuine."

"Recognize the guy?"

"Not right off, but after scratchin' my head a little I remembered standin' by him as we watched the recent rotten Hell's Angel's raid. He seemed to smilin' and thought at the time that was kind of funny; I mean funny odd, not funny ha ha. Oh, and now I recomember his hair. Real different. He had nearly coal black hair except for white temple and sideburns hair. His whole do was slicked down with Brilliantine or axel grease or somethin' way old fashioned like that."

"Got a name for me, Linc?"

"I called into the unit and gave the desk sergeant a description. He come up with name real quick. It was none other than Deputy Chief of Vice, Cody Samuelson, hisself. You coulda knocked me over with a feather. I spent nearly five years working for him, and I would never have imagined that the chief was dirty. Ya never know, do ya?"

"No, you don't. Look, Linc, I want you to go back to the station, straight to vice, and find out anything and everything about Samuelson you can including even opinions and guesses—all on the low down, you hear me?"

"I will stay mum until I get to talk to you next. Thanks for the trust, Boss."

"Well earned. Now get over there and convince that you are detective first material."

Danny rushed back to his office and got two secretaries working double time to find the whole story on Samuelson, including the department's sealed files. While they worked for two days, the stake-out on the Back 9 produced only one result. The cops filmed the place clearing out of every last Hell's Angel. Following them proved to be fruitless since they scattered in all directions, and all of them out of Texas.

IA proved to be a minor gold mine of information. Police Chief Robert V. Murray, himself paid Chief Raymond R. Colgate, head of Internal Affairs, a personal visit.

After pleasantries, the two friends got down to business.

"Look Ray, I have a huge problem, and I need you to do something for me to fix it… on the strict down-low, okay?"

"Sure Robert, anything legal."

"To make it legal, here's a written order on office paper and signed by my hand."

"Good enough for me. What do you need?"

"Everything you have on Deputy Chief of Vice, Cody Samuelson; and I mean everything… personal, financial, marital, complaints, suspicious activity, love life… everything!"

"Sounds serious, Boss. Samuelson is hot stuff among the guys. He is as much a part of the tradition around here as J.C. Arnold from 1881 on."

"Even more, even worse. Look, I hate to impose on you, but I really need it ASAP."

"You got it. I think I can round it all up by tomorrow noon. I'll put my best people on it. "Frankly, Ray, I would prefer that you do it yourself."

"In that case, look for it at the end of the day watch tomorrow, that's the best I can hope for."

"Just do your best, as always, Ray."

Ray interrupted the chief's lunch the next day with a phone call to the head waiter at Mister Charles restaurant at 3219 Knox Street Suite 170. He left a brief cryptic message: CALL ME. As soon as Chief Murray received the note, he excused himself and abruptly got his driver to get him back to his office.

"What's up, Ray?"

"Big stuff… not for the phone, Boss. Head over. Your eyes only."

Chief Murray trotted all the way to the IA office and told the secretary that her boss wanted to see him pronto.

"Go right in, Chief Murray, he's waiting for you."

"Show me," he said, and walked around to look over Ray's s shoulder at the open dossier on the IA chief's scratched up steel top desk.

Murray picked up the dossier for a closer look. He read the ten pages four separate times to take it all in and to charge his memory.

"How did all of this escape the disciplinary board, or the Police Commission for that matter, Ray?"

"Robert, all I can say is the blue wall of silence, the blue code, and blue shield. Take your pick. This is probably the worst example that I have seen in my entire career. Here is Deputy Chief of Vice, Cody Samuelson, with no clothes on."

The summarized dossier contained a treasure trove of raw evidence incriminating Samuelson and at least a dozen other police officers associated with him for the past nearly forty years. The roster of dirty cops including members of vice, homicide, robbery, burglary, and fraud divisions, nearly two hundred past and present bad cops. Fifty-six of them were still on the job. Danny set in motion a major secret factory to record and codify the crimes, the perpetrators, and the crooks, in the city who profited along with them from the sweat off the backs of the decent citizens. It became a work of love, a dedication to the complete change in the social structure of the large police force.

Eventually, several hundred judicial convictions were overturned, eight hundred new trials commenced and lasted nearly ten years. 400 police officers lost their jobs and pensions, and another 125 went to prison along with 186 of their co-defendants in police aided crime. The newspapers and radio shows never ceased delighting in the debacle and its attendant shame for over 15 years, almost the time when Danny McGraw retired from service.

Danny himself saved Deputy Vice Chief Cody Samuelson for his personal interrogation after the many crooked cops under his control had caved in, ratted on him, and revealed the mountains of irrefutable evidence linking him to the ongoing criminal conspiracy.

Danny was unshakably polite in his questioning. Samuelson was dressed in black and white striped jail clothes and not at all the smug dapper egoist who had roamed the city streets a few months before.

Q. Good morning, Deputy Chief. You look well. Are you ready for my questions?

A. I guess I will have to be. I thought at least I would be grilled by one of the other chiefs and not some two-bit flunky.
Danny ignored the insult.

Q. Mr. Samuelson, state your name, date of birth, present age, rank and department, for the record.

Samuelson growled, hemmed and hawed but finally settled in and answered the questions posed. It was tiring to put up a personal barricade of defensive insult question after question asked by the taciturn, all-business young detective who had an intimidating military persona despite his unflagging courtesy.

Q. Now, we will get too it. First, how much did you bribe your former chief of vice, Eric Conrad to be made deputy chief 22 years ago?

A. Uh… Uh… how did you know about that?

Q. I know everything, Mr. Samuelson. I have an entire room full of evidence for reference. Don't even bother to lie to me.

A. Aright, aright, I think it was five Cs, which was good money back then.

Q. What was the name and address of the first brothel madam you started to extort; so, she could keep in business with a minimum of vice squad interference?

A. Mary O'Donnel, I don't remember the exact address. She had a couple a three story walk-ups in Frogtown, maybe you know it as the Reservation. She controlled more'n 200 of the 400 girls who rented out small two-room cribs, and the guys that used to stand out front to get customers. Maybe you already know, but I got to be partners with Dr. W.W. Samuel who owned the buildings. He was a big shot down there. A park, a road, and a high school, were named after the guy. They was goin' to name somethin' after me, but I ixnade that—bad for business.

Q. Tell me about the gambling dens, prohibition booze running from Canada, and most recently the guns and drug business.

Samuelson took a deep gulp, squeezed his eyes shut, then—realizing that the jig was entirely up for him—he poured out a detailed description of the money involved, the locations of the still functioning crime locations, and the distribution routes. He held back on naming names or giving out secret bank account numbers, especially those in the Caymans.

Q. Mr. Samuelson, I get that info, or you go down for the long stretch in Huntsville making bricks—like an "all day" sentence. Maybe you have some idea how much the other cons like coppers in stir.

A. And maybe I know some stuff that'll get me immunity, whatta ya think about that, young McGraw?

Q. Not a whole lot. Immunity is something you can dream about while you're in the sweat shop there. Get real.

A. What if I can give you a list of names and a secret record I kept for the whole forty years I operated? I got madams, big-time gamblers, hit men, gun runners, drug smugglers, lawyers, judges, politicians—including a coupla governors–the whole lot. That's gotta be worth cutting my sentence down to maybe two-to-five and followed up by WitSec?

Q. It would have to be very good, very detailed, and very usable, Cody. You'll get at least ten years, even if it's the best allocution ever tendered. You are a murderer, a thief, a corrupter of young cops, and the vulnerable public, including politicos, and a thoroughly dirty cop. Everyone in the country is going to know your name, man. I said, get real, and I meant it. I am a man of my word, as you well know. I can make that happen, but I am no magician.

A. … Okay. I'll cave. You better not cheat me on this young McGraw. I still got pals in high places who would love to get the hit contract on you if you do.

Q. Bribes won't work. We're way past that point. Threats don't scare me. Better men than you have threatened me; most of them are pushing up daises. Start writing, and I promise I will see what I can do.

The end result was that Cody Samuelson spent two weeks feverishly writing names, dates, locations, crimes committed, and profits gained. He never went to trial; his allocution was enough to get his sentence down to 12-20 years in protective custody at Huntsville and a written guarantee of WitSec protection for his entire post incarceration life. Unfortunately for him, he was shivved and died after spending five years in the strict protective area of the prison. That crime was never solved.

There was no limit to the humiliations, prison sentences, reputations destroyed, and changes made in the governments of the state, counties, and cities of Texas. The court system was jammed with related cases for more than a decade. No one thanked Danny, except for the Chief of Police who gave him the Meritorious Conduct Award, given for a heroic deed involving exemplary courage, risk, and danger to personal safety; or for meritorious service in a duty of great responsibility where the officer performed in a distinguished manner. He also received a special rank promotion to lieutenant of detectives in the newly created Major Crimes Division.

That promotion was about to lead him to the most celebrated case of his long career.

PART III

JACOB ROTH WHITESIDES

CHAPTER 1

Burkheart Asylum, Sanatorium, and Destitute Orphans Home, Coppera's Cove, North Central Texas, 1960-1965

JACOB COMPLETED HIS PSYCHIATRIC TRAINING residency and was honored in a small graduation ceremony to which even his parents came. He was given that year's "Most Likely To Succeed" award in recognition of his stellar performance as a resident, a teacher, a scholar, and a trusted mental health professional. His mother went about the small crowd dragging her embarrassed son and introducing him to everyone as "This is my son, Jacob, the doctor." It took some effort to try and get away from the laughing eyes that replied to the obvious motherly hubris she radiated. His fellow residents, instructors, and psychiatric nurses liked him and told him that they would remember him with fondness.

The hospital administrator gave a small congratulatory speech in which he wished all the graduating senior residents "success, since there is no such thing as luck". He admonished them to serve the public and their patients, to keep the promises of the Hippocratic Oath, and to be scientists who would further the improvement of mental health care in Texas. He then handed out hand embroidered white lab coats with the newly hatched psychiatrist's name, followed by M.D. and below that, "Psychiatrist". Rebecca shed unashamed tears of pride for her successful boy.

Jacob had not told his glowing parents of the difficulty he had in getting a job, despite the crying need for trained psychiatrists throughout the United States, and even Texas, from which he was a well lauded alumnus from one of its best training programs. It was the old recurring problem raising its ugly head again. In doing their due diligence every psychiatric hospital to which applied—including those in California, New York, Chicago, and New Orleans—somehow discovered his having been subpoenaed to testify before the House Unamerican Activities and to suffer interrogation by the famous red baiters, US Senator Joseph McCarthy and Attorney Roy Cohn. He was forever branded as a Communist, it appeared.

Shortly afterwards, an article appeared on the *Los Angeles Times* reporting that–among others–known Communist, Jacob Whitesides, a Jew from Brooklyn Heights had been turned down as a doctor because of his "continuing" association with the Communist Party. That he was a Jew was mentioned three times in the article, and the article was reproduced in all the big city papers around the country. Not only was he a Communist, the hospital admissions committees observed, but he would turn out to be the first Jew on their staff, and none of the hospital staffs were willing to go that far in their desire to be modern and even to make steps toward diversity.

Finally, his favorite professor came to his aid, and got him a position in a little known Northcentral Texas hospital in a place called Coppera's Cove, a town neither of them had ever heard of. The hospital—the Burkheart Asylum, Sanatorium, and Destitute Orphans Home–was desperate to hire a new and modern psychiatrist. So much so, that they did not care a bit if he was a Communist Jew or had green skin and horns. They were glad to have him; and he was glad that at least one place was willing to hire a Jew, a Communist, and a persona non grata almost everywhere else.

Copperas Cove is located at the southern corner of Coryell County with smaller portions in Lampasas and Bell counties in the Limestone Cut Plains of central Texas. The town is situated within an group of hills situated between the Lampasas River and Cowhouse Creek valleys, known as the "Five Hills" area. It was founded in 1879 as a small ranching and farming community and had not changed much socially in the decades since. Locals usually referred to the town as just "Cove".

Inspired by the taste of nearby rather strange poor smelling, poor tasting spring water, residents amended the name to "Copperas Cove" [Copperas is a green hydrated ferrous sulfate $FeSO_4 \cdot 7H_2O$ used especially in making inks and pigments]. It is usually used in commercial grades not to be used internally]. The train depot at Copperas Cove served as the shipping point for farmers and ranchers in the area between Cowhouse Creek and the Lampasas River. By 1940, only 356 people remained in the town which was failing to thrive.

In 1942, Copperas Cove received new life when the US government located Camp Hood next to the struggling community. By the time the cantonment was upgraded to Fort Hood in 1950, the town had over a thousand residents. The population continued to increase rapidly, reaching almost 5,000 in 1960 at the time of Jacob's arrival. The city's economy became closely linked to nearby Fort Cavazos [formerly known as Fort Hood which was changed because that name came from a famous Confederate General, John Bell Hood of the Texas Brigade].

The hospital was founded in 1899; and for nearly fifty years, had served as a self-sustaining institution and community for many hundreds of mentally ill patients. The facility was intentionally placed twelve miles outside the city limits owing to the persistent fear of "crazy" people being "possessed by the devil". Someone had to deal with such people, and they had to be housed somewhere. Burkheart Asylum, Sanatorium, and Destitute Orphans Home, was that place. Originally, it had been a rather handsome campus with four Victorian light terracotta colored brick structures. The red color came from iron oxide/rust–a prominent mineral] in the clay soil of the region. When burned in the presence of excess oxygen, the iron oxide gives bricks a red color. The Victorian style, there in Texas, included elaborate ornamentation.

The Burkheart Asylum, Sanatorium, and Destitute Orphans Home's flourishes of Victorian architecture included steeply pitched roofs, towers, turrets, bay windows with ornate wood trim and gingerbread cutouts, bright exterior paint, and wrap-around porches. Key design principles in Victorian architecture include asymmetry, verticality, textural contrasts, polychromy, and a blend of historicism and maximal ornamentation. These principles are marked by combining traditional craftsmanship and mass production methods. Most of that was attempted in the construction of the new asylum, but cost consciousness and overcharges limited the ultimate success. Some critics called it hodge-podge.

The introduction of modern plate glass enabled more intricate designs. Victorian architecture's defining characteristics were incorporated into the new mental asylum with a carefree flair including eclectic and ornate brick, slate, glass, cast iron, timber, and ceramic tiles. The exteriors showcased eclectic styles, steep roofs, towers, bay windows, and vibrant colors, while interiors are adorned with dark woods, heavy fabrics, and decorative elements like carved newel posts, inlaid wood floors, heavy fabrics, intricate fireplace mantels, and decorative elements such as ceiling medallions, carved newel posts on staircases, inlaid wood floors, and gilded picture frames. This room differentiation was highlighted through architectural detailing like raised decorative wall panels, ceiling medallions, and elaborate crown molding.

The asylum was loosely patterned after Italianate Hamilton's Dundurn Castle in Canada with its adapted patterns for institutional purposes of the characteristic Italianate style. Formal areas like parlors, libraries, and dining rooms, contrasted with more intimate spaces like bedrooms and nurseries in the original design but had to be opened up for the purposes of accommodating the guests of the asylum. The rooms were then filled with heavy wooden furniture, patterned rugs, draperies, and cluttered decorative objects, most more than a bit dusty, the furniture looking as if it had undergone a less than average job of purposeful antiquing. The overall effect was that of a seedy appearance like an old man's favorite but ill-fitting and none-too-clean three-piece suit showing its age.

Funding for the buildings and campus originated from federal money and was maintained—such as it was—by Texas State and Coryell County budgets. Neither the state nor the county had any great enthusiasm for the place, and the local citizenry generally liked to think of it as a necessary evil, if ever they had to think about it at all. When first built, the four buildings on the grounds were fairly handsome examples of the popular institutional style Victorian architecture of the time—later in Victoria's reign, roughly from 1850 and on in both England and the United States, especially in the old Confederate South. As a result of new technology in that period, construction incorporated metal materials as building components. Structures were erected with cast iron and wrought iron frames, which—unfortunately—were rather weak in tension and did not bear up well over the decades.

There were two gates into the property; the second gate had rusted shut and was no longer functioning. The front gate was an arch with ornate wrought iron fencing. There were uprights that had rusted through, and the bottom of its three hinges had broken. The neglected curved sign on the top of the archway now read, B^{u}rkheart _syl^{u}m, Sana^{t}or$_i$um, and D$_e$sti^{u}te Orph_ns $_H$ome. The expansive lawns were in need of mowing, and there were large brown spots in obvious places in the grass. Hedges were not pruned; dead trees stood as skeletal specters; and a broken-down tractor sat forlornly by one of the desiccated old elms.

It was late spring, and already the heat was oppressive–96° F., a possible new record for the time of year. Jacob was frustrated that his shirt had sweated through and was plastered to his chest. The sign hand-written by an indelible marker on the front door read, "Enter here for office."

He found the office easily. It was the only room in the spacious hall with a person in it. The secretary was a late middle-aged suicide blond with probable surgical enhancement of her chest and reshaping of her very white face into a long, misshapen horsey look. Her eyes were too wide open; her ears set too low for her new face; and her blouse and skirt were too tight and too short for her age and girth. She was chewing gum.

He knocked politely, and she did not look up from her comic book. He knocked again, a little louder, then again once more without success. He pushed the door open and walked and stood in from of the secretary's desk.

"Ma'am, I am Doctor Whitesides. I am reporting in to begin working here as the new psychiatrist."

She looked up somewhat startled. She pulled out a cotton ball from each ear—improvised ear plugs—and said, "Couldn't hear you. Please say it again."

He did.

She bothered to put down her reading material, rearranged the clutter on the stained desk top, and looked at him with interest.

"Oh, good, we been expectin' you. I have a packet for you. Has your master key, ID lanyard, and some papers to fill out to make it all official. We're glad to have you, Doctor…"

"Whitesides. Jacob Whitesides."

"Okay, then. Take your stuff up to the third floor. You are going to be in charge of the main schizophrenic ward for now. We have two others; they're for the kids and for the oldies. You have the middle group. Find Mrs. Cantrell on the ward; she'll get you oriented. Tell her Marianne sent you up. Good luck."

He found Nurse Cantrell easily. She and two burly psych techs were in the process of wrestling a grey-haired, wild-eyed, screaming, man to the floor and putting him into a strait-jacket. They were very efficient at it; practice, he presumed.

He waited until they locked the inmate in a dark isolation room before he interrupted.

"Nurse Cantrell, I presume," he said and extended his hand.

She wiped her brow on the back of her hand and shook hands with him.

"Glad you're here. Tell me your name. Mine's Dina. Dina Cantrell. I'm the head nurse on three. You're the new shrink, that right?"

"I am."

"Look, I have a couple of more tasks to attend to, then I can have a walkie-talkie to get you oriented. Your office is next to mime. It still says Doctor Muñoz, Chief Psychiatrist, but will get that repainted with your moniker tomorrow… God willin' and the crick don't rise."

She smiled for the first time. He took her up on her offer and sauntered down the hallway towards the office spaces. Nurse Cantrell kept her eyes straight ahead or occasionally looked down at a stack of papers she was carrying. Despite the noise, catcalls, solicitations, and pleading, the nurse did not look side to side or down anywhere dregs of humanity were sitting, lying, or leaning. She refused to be sullied by the sights, sounds, and smells, emanating from the vacant eyed, semi-stuporous, wraiths passing their lives on the floor. Some were catatonic and silent; others were silent out of anger and rebellion; some stared blankly at the ceiling, or floor, or the wall, depending on the position their eyes had come to when they assumed their usual inert position for the day.

The dingy walls had a fairly even patina of grease, garden dirt, grass stains, and furrows caused by belt buckles and pocket brass fasteners as inmates intentionally scrapped lines or simply etched them as they slid to the grubby floor. The hallway floors were once polished inlaid hardwood tiles, but now there was a grease smudged and spotted background—some suspicious for bodily fluids–for walls that were originally gloss white and regularly scrubbed by inmates.

Jacob and Nurse Cantrell passed the pad-locked pharmacy office which was surrounded by windows to make sure no improper transactions took place, and for the security of the pharmacy nurse or tech. The windows were so grey with smut that much passed the notice of passersby. Mrs. Cantrell nodded at her office as they passed it. The door had a clean, clear glass window which revealed an OCD creation of neatness personified—a place for everything; everything in its place; and apparent cleanliness of walls, floors, carpets, desktops, shelves, lamps, writing materials, and a fresh new ink blotter, so strikingly different from the rest of the building and its offices that Jacob was sure a surgeon would have been satisfied to perform surgery in Cantrell's office.

The office to be of Jacob Whitesides, Psychiatrist, was not only as dirty as the halls and walls that led to it, but there was a degree of clutter worthy of a diligent hoarder. He had to kick aside the clothing, curtains, mounds of papers, and boxes that hid the existence of a few pieces dilapidated metal passing for furniture done in Early Depression Style. The utilitarian olive drab chair, table, couch, and desk, had been purchased from surplus when the old county building was renovated seventy-five years ago. There was a narrow vertical cleft in the wall that served as a laughable closet. In it hung three very old, ragged, and very dirty, lab coats embroidered with the name of Doctor Muñoz, Chief Psychiatrist, and Burkheart Asylum, Sanatorium, and Destitute Orphans Home. Jacob's first goal was to get those coats burned and to obtain from somewhere, somehow, sometime, some clean white heavy cotton doctor coats which actually identified *him*.

There were both mouse and rat droppings in the closet and on what probably had once been an eating table. Living and dead cockroaches competed for space on the repugnant and cluttered table top. There did not seem to be any closet space, book shelves, or anywhere to keep food. The last item—an unused mop and bucket–was the only one that met with approval by the new psychiatrist who was not a serious germophobe or eccentric minor obsessive compulsive disordered young man. He had his limits, and the room he had been assigned was well beneath any minimum standard of living he was willing to endure.

Jacob cleared a place on the odious couch and began to plot his course for the next several days. This place had been a cesspool long enough, and it became his solemn pledge to make it less averse to change, cleaner, more secure, less brutal and repressive, more humane, more modern and efficient, and less foot-dragging. He was a fighter by virtue of where he was brought up. He was sure that a real fight was waiting him in this backwater forsaken and forgotten quarter.

CHAPTER 2

The Coppera's Cove Asylum, War of Resistance to change, 1960-1965

JACOB HAD CHOSEN A PARTICULARLY difficult time of the year to get his proposed changes for the long neglected quarter of rural Texas: neglected in the sense of failing to modernize institutions, to alter fixed habits, despite evidence to the contrary, and to get men and women in positions of power and influence whose careers depended on maintenance of the status quo ante to acquiesce. Change would mean doubt about their accomplishments, a threat to their security and longevity in office, and perhaps even a requirement to admit they were wrong. Lawmakers at every level and at every historical time, have resisted all such, and this was not going to be any kind of expected upheaval from such unfortunate new ideas and attitudes.

It was hot and muggy; the boiler had broken down again; half of the grounds crew had quit over a pay dispute; and the nurses were working at tearing off the old scab of uniting in a union of nurses, techs, and other hospital workers. The chief administrator, Quentin Carver Driggs, PhD already had a migraine, to boot.

His secretary (who now had to be labelled as his "executive assistant") Ms. Gywneth P. Rogers, opened the door to his office, entered quietly, and said, "Sir, the new psychiatrist, Dr. White is here to speak with you."

Dr. Driggs looked a bit puzzled. White?, did they have a doctor named White?

"Is it perhaps Whitesides, Gywneth?"

She paused to look at Jacob's name on his lab coat.

"Oh, yes, Dr. Driggs. You are right as usual. I think I was a bit flummoxed."

"Show him in."

Jacob recognized that he was not off to a good start.

"Sir, I know you are very busy; so, if it is all right with you, I would like to get right down to business."

"By all means, yes. That would be refreshing indeed."

"Sir, I have just started on Ward 3, the adult schizophrenics. I have made observations there and have toured most of the clinical portions of the hospital and the grounds. I believe some changes should be made and soon."

"Such as?"

"Well, pardon me, but the areas I visited are unclean; patients are listless and most are sitting or lying on the floor. The pharmacy rooms are inadequate in both staffing and stocking, and I saw numerous examples of unacceptable rough treatment of our patients. Where I trained, none of that would be acceptable... Sir."

Dr. Driggs' eyes turned hard, and his lips tightened noticeably.

"I presume you trained at one of the very well funded centers which has time for coddling both the residents and the clients. It may come as somewhat of a surprise to you, but we have no time or money here for anything but the old tried and true methods."

Jacob was not to be dissuaded.

"I did observe many psych techs, nurses, other staff and even groundsmen taking prolonged smoking breaks, extended coffee breaks and lunch times. I also observed most of them coming in late and going home early. Finally, I gleaned from my observations that most of the clinical staff had little knowledge of modern changes in psychiatric care—a more humane and civilizing program for the mentally ill."

"And, I take it that you possess those missing but beneficial talents and knowledge."

"Frankly, yes. What I have learned in my training is no more than common knowledge and function in the world of psychiatric care. I believe I can help, if you will support my efforts."

"Ah, to be young. Dr. Whitesides, let me tell you about a good friend of mine who happens to be the governor of Utah at the present time. J. Bracken, Lee–a fine Republican and a true conservative–is the ninth governor of Utah. Lee's family came from a Mormon background; I'm not sure you've heard of them, coming from a Jewish background as you have. First of all, let me assure you that there is nothing to the so-called the Judeo-Masonic conspiracy–an antisemitic and anti-Masonic conspiracy theory involving an alleged secret coalition of Jews and Freemasons. He is in fact active in the Masonic Order, though, obtaining the thirty-second degree. I have it on good authority that he is not much of a Jew lover... suspects them of secret criminality.

"Lee did not graduate because he chose to enlist in the army in April, 1917, two months before graduation, to serve in World War I. A real American patriot. After discharge, he served in the Army Reserve as a second lieutenant until 1935. He gained popularity and some fame as mayor of a little town called Price. His accomplishments as mayor included putting the city hospital in the black, paving streets, and installing a new water system—all without breaking the bank. He was a true conservative, you see.

"He was an unsuccessful candidate for Congress in 1942 and for governor in 1944, but he was a persistent son-of-a-gun. In 1948, his determination paid off; and he was elected governor. As governor, Lee almost immediately gained national attention because of his battle against the federal income tax and his ideas on economy and reform in state government. Although Utah had no bonded debt when he took office and indeed had a surplus of some nine million dollars, Lee nevertheless called for additional reserve funds and deep cuts in many state agency budgets.

"Although corporation franchise and motor fuel taxes were increased, Lee convinced the Legislature to *lower* individual income taxes. He also influenced the simplification of the state's fiscal structure and maintained Utah's debt-free status. He vetoed many bills and deleted numerous appropriations in agency budgets during his eight years in office.

"That pitted him against educators. Lee's often-stated low opinion of teachers and administrators made him a foe of increases for school financing, as he was towards mental health facility renovations and new structures—considered them to be an extravagance.

"My friend, Governor Lee's battle with the Internal Revenue Service continued for many years, and he became a hero to tax rebels throughout the country, especially here in the true conservative South. After his stint as governor is completed, he tells me he wants to be mayor of Salt Lake City. He considers the place to have a wasteful and corrupt city government. I am sure that he'll get that house in order as well.

"That was rather long-winded, but here's the point. I hear with affection his usual response to the wastrels who want something new, expensive, and of questionable value to the body politic. He answers the beseechers with a famous question, 'Where're we gonna get the money?'"

"I am sure that you as a Jew know that money does not grow on trees. So, I put J. Bracken Lee's question to you for this foolishness: where're we gonna get the money?. I tell you right now, young Whitesides, I am to this institution what J. Bracken Lee is to the State of Utah. I am the protector of the taxpayers of Texas's money here in my little fiefdom. I tell you now, there will be now frivolous wasting of that sacred funding here in the Burkheart Asylum, Sanatorium, and Destitute Orphans Home. Don't come asking again. I am likely to get annoyed, and you won't like it when I get annoyed. Go back and tell your Jew and Commie friends that they will not be getting any kind of strong hold in this place!"

He seemed to be clearly overheated and gave Jacob a dismissive back hand gesture. Jacob took the broad hint and left. He knew that he had probably made the administrator into something of an enemy. He also learned that the man was a clear-cut antisemite, and professing anti-communist. He had clearly learned of Jacob's background. Jacob presumed that knowledge would not bode well for him.

CHAPTER 3

Jacob Whitesides sets out to change the world, one asylum at a time. 1960-1965

JACOB DISCOVERED A SIDE OF himself that he had not been aware of before. He was stubborn, almost self-destructively so. It was apparent to him, if not to anyone else that his hospital, his Burkheart Asylum, Sanatorium, and Destitute Orphans Home was a mess; and it was up to him to fix it. He started by going to the Coppera's Cove public library at 501 South Main Street and began an exhaustive study of psychiatric facilities in the United States. Irmgard Johannsen, the head librarian had never had a patron with such an intense educational interest, and she enthusiastically set about to help him to learn everything there was to learn about the subject. It became a mutual and serious project for the two of them, and they became fast friends.

At age 82, Irmgard was a dynamo with all the vigor and zeal of a 35-year-old woman in her prime. Moreover, she knew everyone in the town, had a finger in every organization that mattered, and was a bulldog when there was something for her to be passionate about. Jacob's work as a psychiatrist was not particularly taxing or time consuming at that point, because the system at the hospital was clearly designed to keep the attendants' workload to a minimum no matter how many patients were held there at any particular time. He had no interest in sports, girls, bar hopping, clubbing, or hiking. He quickly took on the project of beautifying the grounds and the buildings with his new partner and friend Irmgard.

They met three times a week at the Lil Tex Restaurant across the street from the library and plotted their long term and that day's projects. The administration and staff of the hospital were surprised and amused when concerned citizens' groups began showing up with volunteer construction crews, truck loads of lumbar, paint, and tools, and the men, women, and youth groups to get changes moving. Jacob dressed in his workman's outfit and assisted during a portion of his everyday duties. No one asked for a dime in pay; all materials were donated; and townspeople lined up at the library to sign on to help.

The chief administrator, Quentin Carver Driggs, PhD and his executive assistant Ms. Gywneth P. Rogers, watched with bemusement as the construction crews and flocks of volunteers began showing up at the usually completely neglected institution. They began to fret a little as the buildings and grounds began to transform into something approaching what the campus had looked like in its early days. Their concern was that change was bad, and it might even interfere with what a good thing they– the administrative council–and the staff had going for themselves. Their concern turned to be genuinely unsettling when the project appeared to be well-organized and not likely to go away anytime soon.

The regional Boy Scouts began sending boys there to get their Eagle Scout projects done; the Girl Scouts sold thousands of cookies to tourists and townspeople and began sending them out by mail to aid in funding; the Association of Junior Leagues International's local Coppera's Cove, chapter became so determined to see the project to a successful conclusion that it was able to get the national headquarters involved. The AJLI was guided by its mission to advance women's leadership for meaningful community impact through volunteer action, collaboration, and training, and committed to breaking down barriers that hinder women from achieving success. The Coppera's Cove, Asylum project became one of its leading and best publicized projects. As a result, Jacob and Irmgard never lacked for volunteer help.

Dr. Driggs could see that this thing was getting out of hand; he was losing his grip on the system; and it worried him. He could not see what he could accomplish by making a fuss with the local government about the project "interfering with the hospital's sacred duty to help the poor indigent mental patients" of the area. When the Lions Club, Kiwanis Club, and Rotarians came into the hospital buildings themselves, he knew he had to act, or the cushy job he had created for himself and his cronies would be lost to the Jew-boy/Com-symp do-gooder. He had to do something, and he had to do it soon.

Dr. Driggs made an emergency trip to see Governor Daniel Price and Lt. Governor Clinton Q. Boggs [who presided over the Senate, which held the real power to get things done, in Drigg's opinion] in Austin to enlist his help to stop this incursion by the upstart psychiatrist, Dr. Whitesides.

The meeting with Gov. Price was the height of brevity.

"Good morning, Dr. Driggs, what can I do for you this fine day?"

"I'll get right to the point, Governor. We have a problem in our psychiatric institution, and we need your executive help."

"Glad to be of help, if I can. Tell me about the problem. I have to say, mental hospitals are always in some sort of trouble, and the people of Texas are not much interested in dealing with crazy people. They see the hospitals as "out of sight, out of mind" places and don't want to even know that much about their goings on."

"Our problem is that we have some northern do-gooders comin' in and interfering with our operations."

"In what way, may I ask?"

Driggs explained about the hordes of workers who were renovating the grounds and the façades of the buildings, reinforcing crumbling portions, and now were cleaning, repainting, and refurnishing the interiors at an alarming rate.

"Tell me again how that is a problem, Dr. Driggs. Every governor I know would give his left hand to have such a problem."

He looked genuinely bemused.

"Well, sir, it boils down to who's running the place, me and my people who are paid by the state or some Com-Symp Jew and his cronies who want to take over."

"Who on God's green earth would like to take over an insane asylum. I cannot imagine anyway there could be a profit in that, can you?"

Driggs could, but he was not about to divulge that knowledge to the governor of the state. The meeting turned out to be a total failure for

Dr. Driggs; and more than that, it was something of a humiliation. Dr. Quentin Carver Driggs, PhD did not care for that in the least, not even a little bit. He went directly over to the senate building to work around the governor by dealing with his old pal, Lt. Gov. Clinton Q. Boggs.

If such a thing were possible, the meeting with Boggs went even worse. Once Dr. Driggs explained his problem, Boggs laughed. Uproariously.

"Sounds like you and your cash cow hospital are about to be seen in the light of a Texas day, Quent. I suggest you keep yourself out of the limelight and hope that his "problem" quietly goes away. The worst thing I can think of for you is that your little mission here to the capital might excite some organization to launch an investigation of your "problem". How do y'all think that would go down?"

Even Driggs' friends had turned him down. He was truly and thoroughly humiliated and forced to tuck his tail between his legs and drive back to Coppera's Cove and his tidy little empire, the Burkheart Asylum, Sanatorium, and Destitute Orphans Home. It took the man several weeks to get over being humiliated and to come up with a suitable way to deal with young doctor Jacob Whitesides. He wouldn't say to himself the word "revenge", but he had difficulty coming up with a better synonym that was more palatable and still amounted to the same thing. He was—by nature—a patient man. His view of revenge was that of the Frenchman Eugène Sue who said "Revenge is like vischoisse; both are better served up cold."

While Dr. Driggs, his staff, and his business cronies stewed over the changes being made, Jacob Whitesides began to figure out how to give modern psychiatric care throughout the improving physical plant of the hospital. He decided to rectify the most egregious measures he witnessed, starting on his own schizophrenic ward on the third floor. During one of their pleasant breakfasts at the Lil Texas Restaurant, he enlisted Irmgard Johannsen's advice and help.

"My friend," she said. "The asylum is a disgrace, even after we cleaned and fixed it up, and it looks better. But—as you know—looks can be deceiving. You are the doctor, and you need to make sure those unfortunate people get better care. We should first get the pharmacy room into shape; so, you can get the meds to the people without mistakes.

And so you can find them. I must say, I think you need a real pharmacist. Do you agree ?"

"Completely. Irmgard, do you have anyone in mind? Anybody who is a relative of friends, somebody just out of school."

"I just might know somebody. Would she get paid? Note that I said she."

"I like "shes" just fine, but this is still Texas; and the patriarchy rules. It will take some arm twisting and a little trickery, but I think I can get someone into the spot and paid, even if it is just a woman."

To ensure that they had the backing of the community, Jacob and Irmgard rounded up a group of effective women activists to come on a little tour he had planned. Besides Irmgard, there was Cecily Turner from the AJLI who was something of a young firebrand. Her mother had been a suffragette, and she passed that fire on to her daughter from a tender age. Karen Kinsey headed up the Girl Scouts and was determined to make it more than viable, she wanted the organization for girls to be important. When she heard how women were treated in the asylum, she volunteered herself, her three sisters, an aunt, and two cousins, all of whom were considered to be movers and shakers in North Central Texas as well as in Coppera's Cove. There was a lady doctor in town—Catherine O'Malley Connelly–and she had harbored grim suspicions about the asylum for years. She was fully ready and willing to enlist the American Medical Association, the Texas State Pharmacists Society, and every leader of a woman's group in the entire state.

Jacob and Irmgard decided a little surprise for the hospital would be the best way to hold the tour, deciding that it was easier to get forgiveness than permission. After a fruitful series of get-togethers, the members of the tour group were an impressive representation of women and of power bases in Texas. Jacob, Irmgard, Cecily Turner, Karen Kinsey, Dr. Connelly, Nurse Viola Dastrup—a mover and shaker in the Black community who nobody pushed around, midwife Janice Haskins, popular in the rural parts of a dozen and a half of North Central Texas Counties: Collin, Dallas, Denton, Ellis, Erath, Hood, Hunt, Johnson, Kaufman, Navarro, Palo Pinto, Parker, Rockwall, Somervell, Tarrant, and Wise. She was young and vigorous, and as influential as any woman in the state.

Minnie D. Cunningham, Pharm. D. was one of a very few woman pharmacists in Texas and jumped at the chance to get her message out. She did not care if Doctors or men, or the KKK did not like it. There were four out-and-out political activists showed up: Janet Forester of the Women's Health Protective Association, Maggie Harrison of the League of Women Voters, Travis county commissioner Annabelle R. Prentiss who became first woman in fifty years to win statewide office when she was elected to the first of two terms as state treasurer, Mary Margaret O'Hoolihan the Texas representative to the National Farmers' Alliance Congress of Mothers (who was also a prominent lady in the Catholic community), Dr. Ruth Taylor Goodington from the American Association of University Women, and Maria Innocenta Perez, vice chair of the Raza Unida party, to raise the visibility of Hispanics in Texas.

When they gathered–on time, and prepared with note pads and pens—it was likely the finest collection of brains and brawn centered in one place in the State of Texas in that half century.

Jacob and Irmgard laughed with each other as they welcomed their small but important army. They had to maintain placid facies as they passed the none-too-pleased administrators, senior nurses, long term psych techs, and the hospital attorney, who happened to be visiting for lunch that day.

The tour went as if scripted to show Burkheart Asylum, Sanatorium, and Destitute Orphans Home at its worst, and as if this were an altogether regular and most unfortunate day for the inpatients. The first bad impression came as the tour group entered the poorly ventilated, narrow and congested hallways where some patients slept on the floors, propped against the walls or simply sat staring vacantly into space. No one had anticipated such a tour; so, no attempt had been made to clean up the denizens of the hallway.

Irmgard spoke up and shared with the group that "this is an insane asylum, a home for the county's poorest people, and later on we will go and see the two cemeteries where the poor are buried. I have done the research and learned that there are over 18,000 bodies lying underneath the old grounds, their burial places unmarked."

These were tough women, but they cringed at what Irmgard shared.

The pharmacy room was a disaster; it was unmanned and unlocked. The main medicines on the shelves were aspirin, Lydia E. Pinkham's

Vegetable Compound, Leidy's Female Pills, Milk of Magnesia, Castor Oil, and Pepto Bismol. One lady found a bottle of haloperidol, and another found two containers of Codeine with Acetaminophen, and three each of phenobarbital and choral hydrate. There were antacids, Licorice Root: the entire root to be chewed raw or made into a tea; Ginger for nausea; Willow Bark (which had some aspirin in it) used as a first line for pain relief; Apple Cider Vinegar for various health issues; Echinacea Root to boost the immune system; and six cans containing prunes for constipation. The remaining shelves were filled with patent medicines claiming to cure ailments from cancer to coughs. All were clearly labeled as such on the containers.

The first time on the schizophrenic ward proper was a cultural shock of the first order. The halls, cots, doorways, and window wells, were inhabited by dejected-looking people with matted hair and tattered clothing. The ward was too small by half for the number of occupants; They were crowded and herded together like sheep in the shambles, or hogs in the slaughtering-pens", one of the women, a former farmer's wife said. Mary Margaret O'Hoolihan could not take the smell in the room.

She exclaimed, "For heaven's sake let us out; this stench is unbearable," and fled from the room with no destination in mind other than to be elsewhere.

On the adolescent ward, Jacob took them to a none-too-clean store room that was doubling as a makeshift operating suite. In it were six burly attendants, two young boys and three girls. They were all semi-sedated and waiting their turn to be sterilized (involuntarily), at least they were not aware of what was about to take place.

Maggie Harrison of the League of Women Voters said that, "What I have just witnessed was nothing short of an atrocity."

Everywhere the tour group went, they encountered dilapidated, overcrowded conditions that most rural state mental hospitals, like the Coppera's Cove Asylum were exposing their patients to.

At the end of Jacob's tour, Dr. Ruth Taylor Goodington observed, "There is little distinction between lunatic asylums, as the primitive mental-health facilities elsewhere are known, old English poorhouses, and Texas county jails. What an eye opener! How discouraging!"

The women talked to the house staff, doctors, and nurses and came away with a feeling of pure disdain for the popular pseudoscientific ideas, like eugenics and phrenology, that had become unusually popular ideas among psychiatrists. That kind of thinking led to atrocities like forced sterilization being imposed on patients.

Annabelle R. Prentiss went fully public and was quoted in the *Dallas Morning News*, the *Dallas Morning News Al Día*, and the *Dallas Examiner*, "Coppera's Cove patients were neglected and abused. There wasn't much treatment. People weren't fed well. The food was terrible, and I mean terrible–weevil-filled. The rooms swarm with vermin. An attendant told me that [and I quote], 'The cots and bed-clothing are literally alive with them. We cannot keep the men clean, and we cannot drive the parasites away unless they are clean.'"

Jacob and Irmgard uncovered reams of evidence to support a formal statement that political corruption was part of the problem that certain Dallas County officials involved with Coppera's Cove facility that it was being treated it as a patronage haven, hiring pals and cronies who had no expertise in handling mental patients. Employees got drunk on duty, partying and dancing late at night in the asylum. Some of the asylum's top authorities used taxpayer money to decorate their offices and hold lavish parties while patients were suffering in squalor. Everybody was a political hiree; so, consequently, they have nobody to report to other than the political boss. Jacob decided not to publish that evidence or to circulate it privately, if Dr. Driggs would clean up his act and that of the ongoing criminal conspiracy.

Driggs agreed reluctantly, but he was a man who held a grudge, as did many others involved. He vowed to "set things right", in a hypocritical way of defining the "right". For the time being, however, Jacob and his friends won. The place began to change for the better.

CHAPTER 4

Changes that come with a price, 1960-1965

THE CHANGES CAME SLOWLY, BUT they came. What did not change was Dr. Driggs', Nurse Cantrell's, and certain Dallas political, legal, and business figures' attitudes towards Jacob Whitesides, the whistleblower. They worked quietly and behind the scenes to interfere and thwart Jacob's changes, and to sully his reputation. It was a slow, but effective vendetta.

During the first week after his famous [or infamous, depending on the point of view held by the listener or reader] tour of the Burkheart Asylum, Sanatorium, and Destitute Orphans Home, Jacob met with Dr. Driggs three times. Each time, the hospital attorney, Phillip Delano Cranston III was in attendance, but remained silent.

The first meeting was not quite acrimonious, but there was considerable frost in the room. Jacob chuckled a little inwardly because his first item [demand] was probably the most expensive of all.

"It is time posthumous to get the facilities air conditioned."

"Not gonna happen."

"How about a compromise and just do the clinical areas?"

"And leave our offices still as hot as hades??!!"

"One of the choices. But the powers-that-be in Washington, have explained where the bear sleeps to empower the Texas Civil Rights Project which passed the good news on to the Texas State You know, Dr. Driggs, Texas locks up more people in more prisons than any other state, often in more inhumane conditions. Black Texans are imprisoned four times more than whites. 75% of people behind bars in Texas are not convicted of any crime but unable to pay bail for their release pending trial. That is the big issue with the feds. Airconditioning for a predominately Black hospital in a little Texas backwater is minor and is expected to happen quickly. All that is needed to avoid a major suit is the administrator of said institution to make the request. Take your pick."

Driggs ground his teeth and all but broke his face trying to manage some sort of smile.

"So, Dr. Whitesides, what about our offices in your grand scheme of things."

"Not a problem. Sign here."

He handed the administrator a completed document, lacking only a signature. Driggs signed with a scrawl that almost scratched through the paper.

"There... satisfied?"

"No. Let's go to item number two."

Driggs could not suppress a groan.

"Good, now that is agreed, here is the request. We have twice weekly group therapy sessions in all units throughout the year. That will require care givers who are unfamiliar with the new kinds of less brutal treatment to be trained and certified."

"And that will cost us considerable out-of-pocket for the universities to provide such training."

"Right. But I happen to know that you have set aside a fund for just such purposes, Dr. Driggs. If that seems to be overly difficult, we can always have the Texas State Auditor, Clement Packer check the books to see what is actually available. Would you like that?"

Driggs was livid.

"Shut your mouth about that, you little blackmailer. So, the gloves come off. Well, here is all you get. One: I'll sign every stupid document to get you what you want from the government which is at no cost to us. Two: I will authorize the training, and at our expense. Three: We have a rational talk about any future such expenses. Get my meaning ? Don't press your luck, young man. I have about reached the end of my patience."

"Now, item three."

It was as if Driggs had never spoken.

"Give it a try."

"Sure, and this is another freebie. You have the state infectious diseases unit come out here and fumigate the whole place, burn all the patients' uniforms and bed linens, and get new high quality, attractive, and long lasting materials to make the wards over."

"And you say it will be a freebie from Uncle Sugar, or our liberal friends in the State legislature."

"Already approved. I knew you would like it; so, I barged ahead. And… you're welcome," Jacob said working to keep the distinct note of sarcasm out of his voice.

Driggs knew he had been had, and he hated it. He stared daggers at Jacob, who looked him in the eye with pure innocence which made Driggs even angrier. But, he wanted to wait to vent his full anger for a more egregious proposal from the pipsqueak.

"Item five: in the next month, you hire a trained pharmacist, a trained x-ray tech, a surgical tech fresh out of the army or navy medic service to sew up wounds and to take care of the minor nonsurgical, run-of-the-mill GP complaints."

Driggs gave Jacob the evil-eye.

Jacob said, "The answer to your kind question, this is another freebie. Uncle Sugar is happy to oblige."

Driggs nodded his head.

"Item six: This is one to insure the institutions good reputation for the future. It will serve as a gauge for society's conscience and faith. We have many Black women, and they get taken advantage of. Too many get pregnant, and they receive abysmal care. So, you are going to get the credit for changing all of that. You need to hire three Black women to provide nursing care and midwifery services. There are plenty of women in the Black community near by who are excellent in the work and anxious to work. This is a good opportunity for you to shine, Dr. Driggs."

Driggs searched Jacob's face for signs that he was being disingenuous. He decided that Jacob was sincere, and therefore unshakable and unbribable.

He reverted to kind and blurted out his standard question before actually thinking, "Where we gonna get the money?"

He knew it was foolish, and he knew that Dr. Whitesides knew the same thing. Jacob had the good grace and the good sense to let it go.

"I have faith in you, Administrator. I am sure you can find the funding for such a good cause."

Jacob had a few more items to spring on the administrator and his lawyer, but he decided to leave them for the next meetings through the month. He politely bid the two men goodbye and left a parting message.

"See you next Thursday after rounds. Incidentally, the entire staff has requested to join me on rounds through the entire facility. Won't that be a welcome addition?"

He smiled and exited the overheated room.

When the attorney, Phillip D. Cranston III, was sure that Jacob was well out of earshot, he spoke to Dr. Driggs for the first time.

"Quent', that was an expensive little meeting. Tell me if I'm wrong, but I think we have inherited a real enemy in that one. If we don't rein him in, we are gonna lose this nice little cash cow. You got any ideas to get him to stop crusading or, better, to leave Texas altogether."

"We can't just shoot the man. The cops would be on us in a second. You know they have a pretty new and very highly respected incorruptible in the DPD now. Name's Danny McGraw. I don't want him poking around up here."

"I just had a brainstorm, it might be possible to make his life so miserable around here that he wants to go someplace as his own decision. We might could help him along by finding the man a new location, a promotion he would not be able to turn down. Whatta you think? Worth a try?"

"Bettern anything else I can think of. Let's get our thinking caps on overnight. You phone me up tomorrow afternoon, and we'll palaver. We have to come up with something right quick like."

CHAPTER 5

Gloves off, 1960-1965

DRIGGS AND CRANSTON DREW UP a plan of attack in some detail and included Nurse Dina Cantrell into their confidence. She, in turn, suggested that they include the oldest of the hospital's psychiatrists into their cabal.

"He's a right winger, somewhere to the right of Genghis Khan. I believe the rumors that he is either the local Grand Dragon of the KKK, or he is right close to the top. I mentioned a tidbit about Jacob being a closet Jew, and a true red Commie, and he went ballistic. He screamed at me that we had to rid the place of 'such human trash... Jew and Commie combined. We need to have a good old fashion lynching.' I swear, he said it just that way."

Both Driggs and Cranston agreed enthusiastically that Christiansen was just the kind of guy they needed on their new clean-up crew.

Three days later, Jacob arrived early to begin his rounds and was surprised and very much pleased to see almost the entire clinical staff waiting to accompany him on what they referred to as "teaching rounds", something many of them had enjoyed in training and were looking forward to resurrecting there at the asylum.

"Good morning all," he said cheerily.

"Good morning, Professor," the chorused back and everyone laughed.

The day was off to a great start. They entered the elderly "schizophrenic" section and were greeted by a babel of grey heads all talking at once. Some were talking to the home planet, others conversing to each other in word salad, and some were just yelling and berating each other in what seemed to be nonsense.

Jacob recognized that his request that the sedating medications be decreased throughout the schizophrenic ward had been carried out, and this was the result. At least they were clean—some of the men even shaved, and wearing clean clothes. He was very pleased to see some of the older women being coquettish, revealing something of normal personality. There were three fights between some of the patients with Alzheimer's Disease. He decided that was as good a place to begin as any.

"Please note," he said, "this is fairly common behavior in some with advanced Alzheimer's. They may become agitated or aggressive as the disease gets worse. Agitation starts with the patient becoming restless and worried, and they are not able to settle down. Agitated people tend to pace a lot, not be able to sleep, and sometimes to act aggressively toward others. They may verbally lash out or try to hit or hurt someone—including family and caretakers. It is behavior utterly foreign to the older person from his or her earlier years. Often these problems start to happen or worsen in the late afternoon or early evening, referred to as "sundowning". Anyone have suggestions about treatment?"

A nurse Jacob had not met before spoke up, "I'm pretty new here, but where I trained, we had a lot of these kind of patients."

"How did you handle them?"

"We found that it was important to find out what sets them off, and to correct that if possible. They can become agitated by pain, depression, or stress; too little rest or sleep, constipation, sudden change in a well-known place, routine, or person, a feeling of loss; for example, the person may miss the freedom to drive, too much noise or confusion, or too many people in the room, being pushed by others to do something; for example, to bathe or to remember events or people. Their disease has made the activity very hard or impossible; so, they become frustrated, feel defeated, and want to act out. And, maybe the most important reason is feeling lonely and not having enough genuine or warm contact with other people. "

"So, what is the answer to dealing with them successfully?"

"First of all, it is not helpful to sedate them significantly most of the time. It only contributes to the confusion and the problem. So does having a urinary tract infection, especially in women. It works better for some calm, easy going, person to talk soothingly to the patients and to draw them away from the place where agitation is building up. Get them something to eat or drink that they like. Give them a hug, praise their clothes or hairdo, talk about their family or interests without requiring them to contribute memories. Do urinalyses every couple of weeks; and no one is going to like this, but get a KUB [lower abdominal x-ray] once a week to see if they are badly constipated. Get the nursing staff to check closely to see if they are having regular bowel movements, diarrhea, or constipation.

"It is important to try and calm patient and try not to show frustration. Speak calmly. Listen to the person's concerns and avoid arguing. Reassure the person that they are safe, and that you are there to help. Use other communication methods besides speaking, such as gentle touching, to help them calm down. Little hugs go a long way in people who will permit it. Take deep breaths and count to 10 if you get upset.

"Create a comforting home setting. Try to keep to a routine, such as bathing, dressing, and eating at the same times each day. Reduce noise and clutter. Play soothing music and keep well-loved objects and photos around the home. Let in natural light during the day. Slow down and try to relax if you think your own worries may be causing concern.

"Try focusing on an object or activity. Distract the person with a snack, beverage, or activity. You could watch a favorite TV show, listen to music, go for a walk, read a book, or do a household chore, such as folding laundry, together.

"You may have to protect yourself and others if needed. Hide or lock up car keys and items that could be used in a harmful way, such as guns and kitchen knives. If the patient becomes frankly aggressive, stay at a safe distance until the behavior stops. Call the psychiatrist for the ward or the on call doctor. Be sure, he or she gets all the information, especially about medications. That may be the time to consider medication changes that may help."

"That was excellent, Ms. Carter. We're glad you are here," Jacob said with a wide smile.

He had won a friend there.

"Dr. Fitzpatrick, could you give a summary of the medications useful in this kind of situation?"

"Glad to," he said.

No one had ever asked his clinical opinion before, and he was flattered.

"I memorized this list while I was in training and have had experience with all of them. A note of caution, try not to overdose, oversedate, overprescribe, or use the drugs for an excessive period of time. Sometimes, it is worth while to change the kind of drugs around.

"These are most of what I have found useful: SSRIs [Selective serotonin reuptake inhibitors]; Risperidone (generic name)/Risperdal (Brand name); Olanzapine/Zyprexa; Aripiprazole/Abilify; Haloperidol/Haldol; Quetiapine/Seroquel; Ziprasidone/Geodon; and Brexpiprazole/Rexulti—a new one. Benzodiazepines such as lorazepam and oxazepam—relatively short acting members of that drug family–may also be prescribed off-label. We prefer to avoid diazepam/Valium because its half life is too long, and the blood levels tend to increase at varying rates and with different results."

Dr. Fitzpatrick went on to explain about the effects, adverse effects, dosing, recognizing problems with each of the drugs. When Jacob praised him, he blushed. Once again, Jacob had won a friend by giving the rather shy doctor a chance to shine.

Everything was going well until they came to the adolescent personal disorder unit. As soon as the group entered the ward, one of the more troubled Borderline Personality patients, a 16-year-old plump girl called out to Jacob by name.

"Hey, Doc. Jacob, you wanna take me into the exam room and check out my sore chest area again?"

She giggled and then laughed uproariously. Soon, three other girls—also Borderlines—were hooting, laughing, and shouting, inappropriate and accusative charges, suggesting or frankly stating sexual abuse by Jacob. He fought to remain calm, to keep a passive stoical face. It was difficult. If he protested his innocence, he would only stoke the flames of doubt; if he remained silent or hurried away, he would convince the intended audience that he had something to hide. He countered the conundrum by ignoring it. The four girls, Abigail Constella, Mary Anne Patterson, Petra

Sloweski, and Ingrid Pettersdotter, continued their harangue throughout the tour's visit.

Jacob elected to have the lecture on personality disorders in the classroom on the second floor where the interfering girls could not attend.

"Sorry about all that, ladies and gentlemen; but it is a genuine prelude to the discussion of serious personality disorders to be given here by Dr. Gladys Y. Jefferson, of our faculty and treatment services," Jacob said, relieved to be out of the line of fire, and into what he hoped would be a presentation of information that would show how difficult his–and the other caregivers for adolescents—tasks were.

"Dr. Jefferson."

"Thank you Dr. Whitesides. The talk has already been introduced during our tour time on the adolescent ward—specifically here, the girls' behavior issues. I will begin with a brief definition of the types of personality disorders and an idea of what we have to deal with. I regret that our own Dr. Whitesides had to be the victim of those girls in such a public display.

"First, a general description: personality disorders are mental health conditions characterized by lifelong patterns of thinking, perceiving, reacting, and relating; significant distress or functional impairment; inflexible and atypical behaviors; and problems with relationships, work, and social activities. They may manage stress by drinking or misusing drugs; so, our patients have to be monitored to be sure they are not getting illicit drugs from the outside. They have a hard time managing their anger and find it hard to trust and connect with others; we saw a prime example of that on the ward. If those girls acted alone, they were demonstrating signs of Borderline Personality to a clear degree.

"Next, let us consider Group A personality disorders. They have a consistently dysfunctional pattern of thinking and behavior that reflects suspicion or lack of interest in others. They include:
Paranoid personality disorder

1. Lack trust and is suspicious of others and the reasons for their actions.

2. Believe that others are trying to do harm with no reason to feel this way.
3. Doubt the loyalty of others.
4. Not willing to trust others.
5. Hesitant to confide in others for fear that others will use that information against them.
6. Take innocent remarks or situations that are not threatening as personal insults or attacks.
7. Become angry or hostile to what are believed to be slights or insults.
8. Have a habit of holding grudges.
9. Often suspect that a spouse or sexual partner is unfaithful with no reason to feel this way.

Dr. Jefferson counted off the numbers on her outstretched fingers.

Schizoid personality disorder

1. Appear to be cold to or not interested in others.
2. Almost always choose to be alone.
3. Limited in how emotions are expressed.
4. Cannot take pleasure in most activities.
5. Cannot pick up typical social cues.
6. Have little to no interest in having sex with another person.

Schizotypal personality disorder

1. Has unusual thinking, beliefs, speech or behavior.
2. Feel or think strange things, such as hearing a voice whisper their name.
3. Have flat emotions or emotional responses that are socially unusual.
4. Have social anxiety, including not being comfortable making close connections with others or not having close relationships.
5. Respond to others in ways that are not proper or shows suspicion or lack of interest.
6. Have magical thinking–the belief that their thoughts can affect other people and events or vice versa.

7. Believe that some casual incidents or events have hidden messages.

Group B personality disorders have a consistently dysfunctional pattern of dramatic, overly emotional thinking or unpredictable behavior. They include:

Borderline personality disorder
1. Have a strong fear of being alone or abandoned.
2. Have ongoing feelings of emptiness.
3. See themselves as being unstable or weak.
4. Have deep relationships that are not stable.
5. Have up and down moods, often due to stress when interacting with others.
6. Threaten self-harm and actually carry it out as in cutting themselves or swallowing foreign and harmful objects, or behave in ways that could lead to suicide.
7. Are often very angry.
8. Show impulsive and risky behavior, such as having unsafe sex, gambling, binge eating, and self-injury
9. Have stress-related paranoia that comes and goes.

"I would note that most of the girls on the adolescent ward are there because they are Borderlines.

Histrionic personality disorder
1. Always seek attention.
2. Are overly emotional or dramatic or stirs up sexual feelings to get attention.
3. Speak dramatically with strong opinions but has few facts or details to back them up.
4. Are easily led by others.
5. Have shallow emotions that change quickly.
6. Are overly concerned with physical appearance.

7. Think relationships with others are closer than they are.

Narcissistic personality disorder
1. Have beliefs about being special and more important than others.
2. Have fantasies about power, success, and being attractive to others.
3. Do not understand the needs and feelings of others.
4. Stretch the truth about achievements or talents.
5. Expect constant praise and wants to be admired.
6. Feel superior to others and brag about it.
7. Expect favors and advantages without a good reason.
8. Often take advantage of others.
9. Are jealous of others or believe that others are jealous of them.

"This is common among elected officials, and I predict that someday, a presidential candidate with this disorder will seek to be an American dictator. Beware.

Antisocial personality disorder
1. Have little, if any, concern for the needs or feelings of others.
2. Often lie, steal, use false names and con others.
3. Have repeated run-ins with the law.
4. Often violate the rights of others.
5. Are aggressive and often violent.
6. Have little–if any–concern for personal safety or the safety of others.
7. Behave impulsively.
8. Are often reckless.
9. Have little, if any, regret for how their behavior negatively affects others.

"Remember that I foretold the coming of a populist dictator for America? This set of behaviors will be indelibly etched into his or her personality. Again, beware."

"Group C personality disorders are quite different from and have little crossover with Groups A and B. C's have a consistently dysfunctional pattern of anxious thinking or behavior which include:

Avoidant personality disorder
1. Are very sensitive to criticism or rejection.
2. Do not feel good enough, important or attractive.
3. Do not take part in work activities that include contact with others.
4. Are isolated.
5. Do not try new activities and does not like meeting new people.
6. Are extremely shy in social settings and in dealing with others.
7. Fear disapproval, embarrassment or being made fun of.

Dependent personality disorder
1. Rely on others too much and feels the need to be taken care of.
2. Are submissive or clingy toward others.
3. Fear having to take care of self if left alone.
4. Lack confidence in abilities.
5. Need a lot of advice and comforting from others to make even small decisions.
6. Find it hard to start or do projects due to lack of self-confidence.
7. Find it hard to disagree with others, fearing they will not approve.
8. Endure poor treatment or abuse with apparent stoicism, even when other options are available.
9. Have an urgent need to start a new relationship when a close one ends.

Obsessive-compulsive personality disorder
1. Focus too much on details, orderliness and rules.
2. Think everything needs to be perfect and gets upset when perfection is not achieved.
3. Cannot finish a project because reaching perfection is not possible.

4. Needs to be in control of people, tasks and situations.
5. Cannot assign tasks to others.
6. Ignores friends and enjoyable activities because of too much focus on work or a project.
7. Cannot throw away broken or worthless objects.
8. Is rigid and stubborn.
9. Is not flexible about morality, ethics or values.
10. Holds very tight control over budgeting and spending money.

"Finally, know that OCH [obsessive-compulsive personality disorder] is not the same as obsessive-compulsive *disorder*, that is part of the general anxiety disorder spectrum which regularly includes several disorders at the same time, such as: anxiety, depression, OCD, and phobias. Many people with one type of personality disorder also have symptoms of at least one other type. The number of symptoms a person has may vary overall and at different times."

When the tour was over, the group met outside; and finally, Jacob felt compelled to deny the accusations of the Borderline Personality Disorder girls. He was vehement and explicit, and every person in the group believed him and sympathized. Still, he was severely disquieted and knew he had to do something to protect himself, no matter what. He did not like that feeling within his psyche; but, after a life of fending off antisemites and anticommunists, he concluded that it was time posthumous to take care of himself proactively.

CHAPTER 6

The start of Jacob Whitesides personal campaign, 1962-1965

DURING THE FOLLOWING SEVERAL WEEKS, Dr. Driggs, Nurse Cantrell, and Dr. Lyman Christiansen, the lead psychiatrist for the adolescent ward, and a satisfied financial member of the hospital's profitable cabal, worked steadily and cautiously to gain favor among the four Borderlines who seemed willing enough to go along with the plan to return to the status quo ante. A girl named Alice Ashton—who probably should never have been admitted to the asylum—was bright and curious enough to catch on to what was happening among her co-inmates. She believed they were basically criminals—the same as Driggs, Cantrell, and Christiansen. She was also smart enough to keep that to herself and saw the situation as a possible way for her to be discharged.

Jacob made night rounds after lights out on the adolescent ward. Every girl was sedated and asleep except one. Anticipating Dr. Whitesides arrival, she cheeked her nightly sedative and waited until the doctor made his rounds.

"Psst, psst, Doctor Whitesides," she whispered out of the darkness.

He shined his flashlight in her direction and whispered back, "Alice... is that you? What are you doing up after lights out? You don't want any trouble, do you?"

"I don't, but I have to talk to you... to tell you something important, Doctor."

"What is it that is so important, Alice?"

"You have to promise never to tell anyone what I tell you, all right?"

"Sure, I promise."

"We have to go to the classroom; so, we can talk without being overheard. I'll follow you and your flashlight."

Jacob made a point of standing at least six feet apart from the attractive young woman to establish protection if this turned out to be another dirty trick by Driggs and his cabal.

"Tell me your problem, Alice," he said.

"I'll get to that in a minute. First, I have to tell you about your problem, Dr. Whitesides."

"Yes."

"Please listen. I don't have much time."

"Okay."

She hurriedly blurted out everything she knew about the plot to blacken his name and get him fired and even put in prison. She was precise, concise, and detailed, naming names, dates, places, and quotes, she had written down.

When she finished, Jacob had to pause for a minute to take it all in. Finally, he responded.

"Alice, thank you. I have suspected as much for quite a while. I don't know what to do. I'm afraid for myself, for you, for the rest of the girls, and for the hospital. I feel like I'm hogtied."

"What if I agreed to testify in a court of law if it came to that?"

Jacob became suspicious.

"Why would you do that?"

"You know I don't belong in here. Get me out; and I will give you everything you need to get hold of me on the outside; so, you and the court can find me and get my testimony. Is that too much to ask?"

"No, it's not. We have to trust one another. I will work on your release starting tomorrow. I can't thank you enough, my dear girl."

CHAPTER 7

Gloves off, 1960-1965

JACOB SPENT AN ENTIRE WEEKEND pondering how to preserve himself in view of the obstacles and threats in his path. He was innocent of any crime or any other wrongdoing, but it did not matter since the administration of the hospital and their coconspirators were dead set on finding a way to make him look like a criminal and they would never stop. He knew that. He decided that the only thing he could manage was to eliminate the threats. That would buy him time, and probably allow him to leave Copperas Cove and Texas and to start over. Maybe, there was someplace in the union where they were not antisemitic or communist haters with whom he could reason. After all, he had rejected Communism and the party after he had the fear of his life in the House Unamerican Activities Committee. He had not so much as glanced at a *Daily Worker*, or walked on a street where communists congregated or where there was a Communist Party office.

He was cornered like a rat. But even a cornered rat will fight back. At the end of that fateful weekend, he had come to a plan—a complicated, expensive, and time consuming, but plausible, plan. He reckoned his advantages: he had time on his side; no one would have any idea of his plan; and he had thought about it seriously and carefully enough that he knew that it was flawless. Jacob knew that a secret was what only one person knew. He vowed to himself to keep that secret to the grave. He took a week of his vacation time the next week to set his plan in motion.

First, he sought out information about real estate. He knew exactly what he wanted, but he had no idea where such a place was located at first. He looked into real estate maps, advertisements, and talked to people at random to see if he could find someone with something to sell on the down low that Jacob wanted to buy without a lot of legal entanglements and bureaucracy. He spent the latter part of the week doing some traveling and finally ended up in Texas Hill Country.

The Texas Hill Country is arguably the most beautiful region of Texas. Its green hills and rolling rivers are a stark contrast to most of the state's flat and arid landscapes. The Hill Country is filled with jaw-dropping natural wonders. He motored around in his nondescript 1950 Ford 150 pickup which looked much like any other farm vehicle in the sparsely populated area.

Jacob was beginning to get the lay of the land. He turned onto highway 16 to Farm Road 1323 and head toward Willow City–the Willow City Loop off the beaten path between Fredericksburg, Johnson City, and Llano. It was a gorgeous 20-mile stretch of road that wound through green hills of Gillespie County. The route was perfect for motorcyclists and scenic drivers for its fun, winding drive, and beautiful scenery. But it had not yet been discovered by the tourist crowd and was sparsely populated by locals.

The timing of Jacob's trip was perfect. The area had had more than usual rainfall, and there was an awe-inspiring display of bluebonnets. Later, in the fall, he returned to see the gorgeous foliage of Lost Maples State Park. The park's Uvalde bigtooth maples were bursting with colors. With his binoculars he was able to glimpse some of the park's rare birds. Jacob thought to himself that perhaps he could just settle there permanently—no antisemites, no anti-communists, no cops. The park is north of the town of Vanderpool, roughly an hour's drive southwest of Kerrville. The towns would have all the staples he would need to live comfortably and to execute his plan.

The problem of finding some private land which would suit his peculiar needs still loomed as he neared his second visit to the area. The administration of the hospital's project to drive him out was incessant and increasing in its intensity. The young Borderline girls were becoming more and more brazen. He had to get his plan underway before it was too late. It was becoming an obsession for him.

Then, as he was beginning the return trip to Copperas Cove, he ran into a stroke of luck. At a sharp curve in the gravel road which passed through empty pastureland, several dozen neglected long ago plowed sections, and a single nice, well-kept farm. In front of the farm entrance an old man was laboring over his antique (1939 prewar) Ford 1-1/2 ton truck. He was obviously not getting anywhere because Jacob could hear him swearing a blue streak from 100 yards away.

Jacob parked onto the side of the road and walked to where the farmer was just then burning his fingers on the red hot radiator which was belching steam.

"Hey there," Jacob said, "anything I could do to help?"

"Nice of y'all ta axe me, but this old heap is due for a trip to the junk yard. I'm sick of it. I gotta say that it has served me since '39, and they don't make 'em like they usta."

"Maybe it's time to get a new one."

"Past time, but I just can't keep a doin' this anymore. Me and the truck and the tractor are all done in. I can't fix up the house or the barn. It's time fur me ta call it quits. I hate the thoughts a movin' ta the city, but I guess my boy's right, it ain't worth it no more."

Jacob's heart quickened a little.

"Any chance you've been thinking about selling your place, Mr....?

"Jimmy West. What's yours?"

Jacob quickly thought about the answer, "Michael Straight," he lied.

He had to keep his name out of any documents or anyone's mind who lived around the area.

Jimmy extended his hand, and they shook. It was warm and friendly, as if they had been neighbors for years. Jimmy evidently did not know about Jews, communists, or psychiatrists, and Jacob was determined to keep it that way.

"Y'all know what, Michael, I have been thinkin' a lot about that, and this here contraption is about the last straw fer me. Y'all thinkin' about takin' up farmin'?"

"Maybe, if the price was right. I'm not made of money like a lot of the city slickers I know."

"You know, we could make the right deal here and now, and I could just walk away. I don't think you are much of a cheater and neither am I. Are you serious about this?"

"Yeah, I am. Can we take a look around?"

"Sure 'nuff. Let's get us a beer, and we can saddle up my horses and ride around the whole place in under a hour."

Having never been on a horse in his life, Jacob took a little gulp.

"Great. Let's get on with it. I'm getting excited."

"I'm happy to hear that. Let's agree not to take unfair advantage of each other."

He spat on his right palm and extended his hand for another shake. Jacob followed suit and kept his face serious to avoid giving offense.

He watched intently as Jimmy put the blanket, then the saddle and cinched up the rear billet and front cinch strap. That was not too difficult, and he did a reasonable job on the horse provided him. Like Jimmy, he fiddled with the saddle and straps to ensure that they were neither too loose, nor too tight. He paid enough attention to recognize that the time to tighten up the cinch was when the horse exhaled. Some horses are tricky and they hold their breath; so, they can dump their unsuspecting rider when they got the chance. Putting on the bridle was a little more difficult. First, he had to determine what went in the horse's mouth, and what went behind its ears. He fumbled a couple of times, but the old horse was patient, and finally he had the bit in the mouth and the head piece and brow band in place; so, it was not mashing the horse's ear. He watched Jimmy casually place the reins over the saddle horn. Jimmy used a wood block to get up into the saddle, and Jacob did the same. It was unfamiliar but did not appear to be particularly difficult. He followed Jimmy out of the horse barn and around the farm, listening to the friendly old man chat on about the features.

After an hour, Jacob was determined to buy this place. It was perfect for his purposes, and he could see himself actually living there after some fixing up projects. Jimmy did not sugar coat the needs of the place.

"I 'spect y'all will want onna them indoor facilities. Never seen the need myself. The plumbin' is old and suspect, and the electric wirin' is definitely undependable. I don't have the money, the strength, or the time, to do all the fixin'. I know it needs a lot; so, whatta you think about somthin' on the order of… let's say around 28,000 dollars for the whole thing as is, lock, stock, and barrel. That'll include the livestock and equipment, such as it is. I'll be glad ta see the end of them. More trouble than they're worth."

Jacob had done his homework before ever leaving Copperas Cove. He knew it was a bargain among bargains, and he would never get another such chance. He had considerably more than that in his life savings bank account. He did not want to appear to be too anxious to say "yes".

He paused, rubbed his brow, then spoke slowly, "Jimmy, that's more than fair. I do want to ask a favor of you for the transaction."

"Name it," Jimmy said, his entire face lit up in a smile.

Jacob described his desire to pay in cash money, to put the property in his mother's maiden name as a surprise for her, and to do the legal work with only him, Jimmy, and Jimmy's son, knowing the details."

"Fine with me, Michael. I don't wanna seem ridiculous, but should we get the paper work done this very day?"

He was afraid he would not live long enough to get that much cash money and be rid of the burden and chores of the old farm.

"We can do it all, right away today, but I don't carry around that much cash in my back pocket. I can get to my bank first thing tomorrow morning and get the cash for you. Do you trust me enough to do that?"

"Look, my friend, we both spat on our hands and had a strong handshake. That's good enough for me."

They traveled to Vanderpool and met Grant West, Jimmy's eldest son. Together, they went to the land office and filled out a pile of forms, and shortly, Rachel Roth (Rebecca's mother, Jacob's grandmother) became the proud owner of a farm in northwest Texas, a fact she was never to know. Michael's dear friend, Jacob R. Whitesides, had the power of attorney to sign for anything and everything needed for the farm. It went as smoothly as anything could be in rural Texas, and far less complicated than if it had been in a city with all the security nonsense.

Jacob raced back to Copperas Cove and went straight to his bank, the local branch of the Mercantile National Bank, where he withdrew $30,000 in cash. The tellers had to rush around to several other banks to get the full amount. It was the largest withdrawal of cash any of them had ever seen. Jacob intended to pay the good old man extra to keep him on his side. He hoped it would pay off if anyone ever came snooping around.

Jimmy and Grant were tickled that they had gotten a kind of Baker's Dozen. In addition, Jacob told Grant he could take anything from the farm he wanted. It became a case of "one man's junk is another man's antique". Jimmy and Grant only wanted a few items of nostalgic value and nothing Jacob did not intend to keep or try to sell. It was a happy deal all around.

Jimmy settled into a nice little cottage in Vanderhoof complete with indoor plumbing which he grew quite fond of. Unfortunately for the family and the town, the fine old man died of a stroke less than two years after the sale. That left only one other person who knew about the transaction and could trace it back to Jacob Whitesides, if he was inclined to do any digging. He was not so inclined, and Jacob and Grant never crossed paths again.

CHAPTER 8

Getting down to do Jacob's "life saving" work, 1963-1967

JACOB WAS THE PROUD NEW owner of a property which had several attributes that suited his needs to a "T" [The etymology is interesting; it has a somewhat mysterious origin. It probably originated in the 1600s, and there are a couple of theories. From tailoring and clothing: In that context, "T" refers to the shape of a T-square, which is a common tool used by tailors and carpenters to make precise measurements and cuts to achieve precise fits. In early golf, players marked their scorecards with a "T" for "perfect"—a hole completed was a hole without any additional strokes. In the case of his new property, the place was distant from Copperas Cove, but not so far that it took much time for him to get to it. It was located in a rural and little traveled area, one unlikely to change much over the coming years. The farmstead herbage was overgrown enough to shield the areas beyond the roadway from public view. Jacob was going to be able to make additions and revisions to the property away from prying eyes, and that ranked highly in his planning.

A special feature was present, and known only to the late Jimmy West, not even by his son, Grant. Behind a low hillock which was well forested, there was an oval pond or sinkhole which was approximately 100 feet across and 150 feet long. The water was clean; and on a sunny day, Jacob could see nearly to the bottom, about 200 feet deep. The new owner made it one of his first priorities to find out what, if anything was down there.

The real world intruded upon him, and he had to get back to his work as a psychiatrist in a very needy small hospital. For three days, there were no incidents. On the fourth day, however, he was summoned to the administrator's office for a meeting with Dr. Driggs and Dina Cantrell.

"Good morning, Dr. Whitesides, Dr. Driggs will see you now. Walk right in."

"Thank you."

"I'll get right to it, Doctor, I know you are busy. You see, there has been... how shall I say it... an accusation against you."

"What sort of 'accusation'?" Jacob asked with something of an edge in his voice.

"Well, to put it delicately, one of the adolescent girls reported to the nurse that you... well... she said, you... how shall I put it?"

Nurse Cantrell interrupted, "Oh for heaven's sake. She accused you of groping her."

"Did she now? Who is 'she'? Precisely what did she say I did? Oh, and were there any witnesses of that so-called groping act?"

"No need to get testy now, Dr. Whitesides," Driggs said authoritatively.

"Sounds to me like 'testy' might be an understatement," Jacob responded.

Dina Cantrell put it bluntly, "You squeezed her bare breast even after she told you 'no'. How's that for precise, Dr. Whitesides?"

"Precise, but a lie. Again, any witnesses? Any corroboration?"

"Nurse Lily Fortunata talked to the girl immediately after you left the ward after touching her inappropriately. And the girl confided in one of the other patients. The evidence is damning, DOCTOR!"

The emphasis and tone of voice was unmistakable. Nurse Cantrell was out for his blood.

He spoke slowly, calmly, and deliberately, "What was actually witnessed and will be testified under oath? And I ask again, was there any corroboration?"

"They reported to Dr. Lyman Christiansen, the lead psychiatrist for the adolescent ward, how is that for corroboration, DOCTOR!?"

She was almost shrieking.

"This is not the time or the place for further discussion. I can see that this will require a more formal setting. I will personally arrange that, and all of you will be in attendance when I do. There will be other hospital officials present in all likelihood," Dr. Driggs said, and gave a dismissive wave of his hand.

The meeting was over.

Two more complaints came in over the next two weeks, and Jacob was informed of them; but there were no additional meetings in Dr. Driggs' office. He could not endure the acrimony. Jacob determined that to be forewarned needed to be forearmed. He left early every Friday and worked industriously through each weekend at his farm thereafter.

His first project was to find out about what was in the pond. He bought goggles and swim fins and made several deep dives. He realized that he needed to develop his breath holding skills if he was ever going to find anything useful about the pond. Any purchases he made were done with cash, in different stores and different towns every time. He used different names each time as well. In his mind, this was war.

At work in the asylum, it seemed as if every day held a new accusation and a new threat. By then, the deep underlying leitmotiv was becoming ever more evident. He began to hear, "Jew", Jewish People", "you Jews", and "Reds", "Commie", "Com symp", "Lefty", "Unamerican", and even "traitor" occasionally. He was under siege, and he acted accordingly. First, he never admitted to a thing; second, he took copious notes of everything that was said, including the ethnic slurs. Third, he took his remaining vacation time for the year and headed for a three week stay in the hill country at his out-of-the-way farm.

The work quickly became too much for him; so, he set out to find the perfect farmhand to help him get his myriad projects completed. He found that man in the person of Lemuel Pluxen. Lemuel was as big, strong as an ox, with an appetite to match. He was slow witted, forgetful, and had the attention span of a gnat. In Jacob's mind, the thirty-eight-year-old Lemuel was perfect. He was orphaned at an early age, graduated from the foster system at age eighteen without having completed grade school. He subsisted by doing odd jobs and the kindness of strangers.

Jacob fed him well, kept him clean, gave him a comfortable bed, and was nice to him. Lemuel quickly came to see him as the father he never had.

He worked long hours with a will and learned simple tasks with reasonable quickness to keep the work underway.

He could hold his breath for three minutes, a feat Jacob considered nothing short of miraculous, and he became an enthusiastic diving producer of information about the secretive deep pond. Lemuel reported that there was a side cave situated on the bottom of the pond which was invisible to anyone but an extraordinary swimmer/diver. Within the cave were piles of junk that had accumulated over decades, maybe hundreds of years—a perfect place to hide things.

Lemuel accompanied Jacob in the '39 Ford 1-1/2 ton truck and contributed the great physical strength required to acquire, transport, and unload the wide assortment of equipment and tools needed for Jacob's projects. A partial list included: a nondescript old bakery van, dozens of heavy ply opaque plastic bags and hard liquid glue to seal them. They had to be able to dissolve completely in water, both hot and cold, without leaving any traces, and to degrade when put in mud due to the reaction of microorganisms.

In Kerrville they bought large bolts of blue arts and crafts material called plastic canvas, which was usually used for needlepoint. These sheets of plastic mesh are perfectly safe for aquarium use, they come in all sorts of colors, and they were extremely cheap. The helpful store owner told Jacob about someone having come up with the creative idea to grow Java moss on sheets of mesh. Java moss is a slow-growing plant, and it takes its time; but once it clings and spreads, it makes an opaque, natural vegetative background for an aquarium or a deep pond. Fish appreciate the extra plant life as well; so, Jacob bought several tanksful of rapidly reproducing trout to confuse snoopers even further.

In the way of tools, he bought brick saws, a large industrial saws-all, heavy nylon rope, and an assortment of general carpenter and plumbing tools. Large purchases which required Lemuel's great strength to muckle included: a 754 Disc Industrial Wood Chipper–a portable unit that provides the pulp and paper industry with a highly productive machine. With repeated trips to different towns, different providers, using different fake names, the two men brought back to the farm a medium sized used backhoe for grading, surfacing, loading, lifting, material handling, excavating, trenching, and other jobs Jacob had in mind. Around since the 1950s, loader backhoes can usually be driven on public roads, thus enabling operators to drive them from job to job, saving them the time and expense of trailering the machines and towing them around with a truck.

The loader backhoe new to the farm could dig depths of nearly 17 feet. Their machine was able to haul up to several thousand pounds of material in the front loaders while maintaining the agility to navigate congested jobsites. Their new-to-them backhoe was a diesel Tier 4 compliant with an engine kicking out 100 horsepower.

He bought a STIHL MS 500i Professional 25" bar and chain chainsaw for $1,400. It seemed to be ghastly expensive but came with a 100% guarantee of good performance. Because he paid cash and did not ask for an insurance policy, the manager of the Ace Hardware store threw in a set of protective loggers' pants, high cuff reinforced security gloves, and NOS men's walker 1507 waterproof burgundy colored logger boots size 10½ D for $175 without charging him. They were a comfortable no blisters fit as long as he wore tall thick loggers' stockings.

At nights when Lemuel was asleep, Jacob investigated how to dissolve bodies, a legitimate regular need on a farm to rid carcasses to prevent odors and pollution; so, the librarians did not raise their eyebrows when Jacob requested such information. He learned that popular literature was wrong in saying that quick lime was the answer. What did work, he learned, was that you can dissolve organic material by chopping animal bodies into smaller pieces and suspending them in concentrated sodium hydroxide, then applying heat using a pressurized stainless steel autoclave or comparable professional kitchen equipment. He went to a Vanderhoof medical supply company and rush ordered two large NAUDH electric stainless steel autoclave pressure cookers.

He also learned that he needed large quantities of hydrochloric acid to dissolve bones and teeth. He learned that HCL was much safer [avoiding explosions] than other acids and base methods for high-boiling or temperature-resistant organic materials, including fats, oils, greases, and waxes. It was well established that destruction via hydrolysis of large biomolecules (such as proteins, lipids, carbohydrates and nucleic acids), with possible further demolition of smaller units was more easily and effectively accomplished with the acid methods. Acids at very low pH effectively destroy bone and teeth. However, he later learned by experience that destruction of bone in acidic conditions is no quick job; 1-3 hours at room temperature and atmospheric pressure, it can take nearly a day, or even longer, depending on the acid–for bone to dissolve when fully submerged.

Jacob Roth Whitesides was a strong believer in the belt and suspenders rule for living and avoiding trouble. For that reason, he visited Vanderhoof's largest and most complete DIY [Do It Yourself] hardware store and picked up three large mobile incinerators which he had been assured were the safest ways to handle the risks associated with carcass disposal, since it utterly destroys any trace of animal waste, whether it is infectious or not. He was informed by the store manager that the incinerators require a permit to be operated; he must also obey government guidelines to avoid air pollution and the expected very bad odors. He agreed readily and promptly forgot all about it. He had more important things to occupy his time. Besides, he had no intention of creating a paper trail.

Any conservative and cost-conscious farmer would have been content to have the cheapest, safest, and most effective, equipment for the job. Jacob's purpose was to eliminate all traces of the carcasses he intended to eliminate; so, he made his preparations to use all three methods: chopping into small pieces, dissolving in acid, and finally incineration.

Jacob was quite exhausted when his marathon three-week ordeal of "farm" work was over. His setup was complete, and looked ready to test, and final disposal in the pond was the culminating solution to any attempts by law enforcement forensics to find DNA, let along body parts of any kind leading to suspicion for Jacob or case solution for the cops. No habeas corpus [produce the body] was going to be possible ever.

He convinced Lemuel of the joys and fun in New Orleans. The gullible young man was thrilled to receive $300 cash and a one-way bus ticket to get there. Jacob was sick and tired of being discriminated against, falsely accused, and tormented. Once and for all, he was going to take care of Number One.

CHAPTER 9

Meeting the challenges, 1967

THE ADMINISTRATION OF BURKHEART ASYLUM, Sanatorium, and Destitute Orphans Home, decided that it had accumulated enough evidence and ammunition to get rid of the communist Jew, Jacob Roth Whitesides, once and for all, thereby returning to their previous quiet, peaceful, and highly lucrative, business ventures run through the institution. Nurse Cantrell kept a watchful eye on Dr. Whitesides while Drs. Driggs and Christiansen, along with the asylum's corporate attorney Phillip D. Cranston III, meticulously prepared their case against Jacob, including the types of questions to be asked of him and of the complaining witnesses. They were careful, and it took time. Accusing a doctor–especially getting rid of one because of crimes–was a touchy business, fraught with hazards for the accusers. Cranston was determined that they would have such a tight case, that Dr. Whitesides would likely not even put up a defense.

Jacob had friends in the institution who agreed with his disgust at the corruption flourishing there. One of them was Dr. Gladys Y. Jefferson, the expert on adolescent personality disorders. She pretended to be a good company stooge but supplied Jacob regularly with information from the administration office. She was well aware that the corrupt members of the clinical and administrative staff were making unconscionable use of four girls on the adolescent unit: Abigail Constella, Mary Anne Patterson, Petra Sloweski, and Ingrid Pettersdotter. She was not quite certain what that misuse was, but it was certainly anathema to the psychiatric well-being of the young and impressionable women.

Gladys telephoned Jacob.

"Hello."

"No names. I have news. The formal party starts one week from today at 0600. Capiche?"

"I do. I have to get to work."

He took a sick day the next day, a Friday. That gave him three full days to work. He set out immediately for his Hill Country home-away-from-home.

As soon as he arrived back at his hideaway, Jacob rushed to the trusty old tractor that Lemuel had restored to remarkably good working condition. He drove to the far northwest corner to work. The area had several distinct advantages: it was well away from any road; it was nestled into a deeply wooded area—tall pines, Ash, juniper, and live oak that were impenetrable to vision from even a few yards away and might only show a structure from an overhead plane. On a previous trip, he had created a rough serpentine gravel road that led to a corner section which measured roughly 100' X 150' but with intentionally ragged borders. He began a crude logging operation by pushing the trees over including their large roots.

He chain-sawed the downed trees into 14" six blocks and plowed them into a corner of the plot. He plowed the rough ground with the tractor and its plow attachment until it was reasonably clear enough of protruding roots, sage brush, and rocks, to hold buildings and equipment without them tipping too much. That took up his first day and most of his strength. It was an exhilarating feeling to do the physical work, so different from the day-to-day grind of his psychiatric practice.

The next day he moved all the accumulated brush to form a sight barrier along the approaches to his road. Then, he got his large truck out to move the equipment he had so carefully and secretly purchased. One-by-one he moved the heavy items to their semi-permanent places in the newly cleared area. The camo shed sat in the far northeast corner of the cleared area to hold all the tools, boxes of plastic bags and glue, plastic and metal containers, and the twenty polyethylene Anticor barrels of HCL. It was a cool, dry place as was essential for safe storage [according to applicable ASME, ASTM standards] of the corrosive acid; the three large mobile incinerators, the wood chipper, and the large lead acid pots, were hidden behind brush in the lower southeast corner with adequate room to move around as necessary. A side road provided access to that work area.

The next day, Sunday, he worked in and around the house making minor repairs, cleaning the floors, washing the windows, and testing out the stove, toilets, and faucets. He could not get everything done; so, he called in sick to the administration office of the asylum, the first time for him to do so since arriving for work. The third and fourth day at the site, he put together the water tower he had trucked in from Dallas the previous year and pulled it to a standing position using the truck and some heavy chain. He put together the tall ladder and fixed it in place. Jacob was satisfied that the large water barrel on top was not so tall that it could be seen from the road, or by chance fishermen from the river, or unless some interloper walked or drove out along his fresh gravel road all the way to the work site he had built.

Late that last afternoon, Jacob finished his work by pumping water from the river up into the tank via a heavy-duty hose and a sturdy IPT self-priming cast iron centrifugal water pump guaranteed for both industrial and commercial applications that require high-volume liquid transfer, waste-water drainage, and processing. The equipment lot owner showed Jacob how to set up and use the long-lived little pump and explained the safety and user-friendly features like buna-N seals, dual volute design, self-cleaning, clog-resistant impeller, and built-in check valve ensures consistent self-priming. The one phase 60 Hz+ ODP motor had a five-year manufacturer's guarantee. The equipment was untraceable because he found it in an equipment sales yard that was going bankrupt in south Dallas. The old Black gentleman was glad to sell the whole lot to Jacob for $800 cash and no records kept, a mutual convenience.

The water pumping exercise was particularly satisfying because all the equipment worked exactly as it was supposed to do—an unusual experience in the nonmechanical psychiatrist's experience, and it was fast and efficient. The large tank sitting 30 feet in the air was filled to capacity after thirty minutes of set-up and another forty-five minutes to do the pumping. Jacob removed the pump from the river and covered the hoses with camouflaging brush. He put the pump in the camo shed with the rest of the equipment and looked upon his newly refurbished domain with pride of ownership and accomplishment. So far as he could see, he was ready.

It was still light; so, Jacob decided to drive back to the asylum and to establish the "fact" that he had never left the campus. He made a point of making late rounds, talking to all the patients and staff, taking his supper in the village café, and chatting up all the locals. He even bought a conspicuous round of drinks for the customers and wait staff.

When he left the café, Jacob made a point of letting people know that he was heading home to get his necessary nine hours of sleep. He was sure that all the people he had encountered that evening would constitute a credible alibi should questions ever arise.

He waited until full darkness before setting out to do the work for which all his Hill Country labors and his elaborate subterfuges around the asylum had been intended. He put on all-black clothing, a face-hiding balaclava, black nitrile gloves, and the special soft soled black combat boots he had obtained from the surprisingly well-stocked army-navy store in Kerrville.

Before leaving his apartment, Jacob reviewed the equipment he packed into a black back pack: serrated hunting knife, .22 German Lugar pistol, sturdy nylon cord, plastic bags, a used 10" long leather wrapped Bean Flexible Police club with a woven handle and the original leather strap. He had purchased all of the gear at auction at the Kraft Auction Service in Valparaiso, Indiana. Everything was conducted verbally, and no written records were kept.

He double-checked everything and drove to the first of his destinations for the night—Number 12, Main Street in Medina, the home of attorney, Phillip D. Cranston III. The house was set off from the rest of the few residences on Main Street in a healthy apple orchard. Jacob and learned that Cranston was also the owner of Medina Love Creek Orchards Cider Mill and Country Store, a five-minute drive away on the Medina River. The house was what was known locally as "Cowboy Modern". Medina is a quiet little unincorporated village nestled in the Hill Country where everyone new everyone by name and by the back of their heads. No one locked their doors in Medina… no need.

Jacob was familiar enough with the lawyer whom he despised to know that the man was a bachelor, lived alone, seldom went out at night except to attend to his two little businesses. He had a 35% chance of being correct that the house on Main Street would be the correct choice. He parked his truck among the apple orchard trees; so, no one could see his activities, and crept up to the side of the house facing west. The lights were on in almost every room and obscured any view of a person lurking outside. He hit paydirt at the third window.

It looked into a comfortable office complete with white-tail deer, and coyote heads mounted on the walls, a large wood desk, and a comfortable cushioned swivel seat where his prey was seated intensely interested in a folder of papers. Phillip Cranston was balding small man with a neat pencil mustache. His eyes were too close together making him look beady eyed. He wore old fashion pence nez glasses perched precariously on the bridge of his nose. He was dressed in an undershirt, a pair of comfortable baggy khaki pants, and no shoes. His fingers were long and bony, and his face was pinched and mean looking—at least Jacob saw him that way. He was playing cowboy western music on a vintage zenith record player. Jacob could hear Cowboy songs of the Roaring West by the New Frontier Singers. They were belting out *The Big Rock Candy Mountain* at a level that could be heard two blocks away. Cranston was smiling and tapping his fingers to the music.

It was eleven p.m. when Jacob pushed the front door of Number 12 Main Street open, waited to see if any alarm would go off or if the owner would react. The music still blared, now shouting out a rendition of *The Last Roundup*, which Jacob thought was appropriate, perhaps even prophetic. He had time to reconnoiter around the first floor of the rustic home. That led him to a door in the room behind where Cranston was sitting at his desk. He tried the knob; it was unlocked. He very gently eased it open and found himself looking at the back of Cranston's head not six feet away. He slipped off his backpack and retrieved the plastic bag, glue, police club, the bottle of chloroform, and a clean handkerchief. Everything was ready at his fingertips.

Jacob wanted his victim to display no marks of trauma if possible to heighten the mystery if the body was ever discovered. He decided to try the chloroform for that reason. He soaked the handkerchief in the transparent liquid with an ether-like odor. The value of the choice–in addition to its quick effect–was that it was nonflammable, evaporated quickly, and acted too quickly for a victim to be able to fight his assailant off in time to achieve escape.

He held the wet cloth behind his back as he tiptoed up behind the intensely involved Cranston. With a sudden move, Jacob whipped his right hand with the handkerchief spread out in the palm around in front of Cranston's nose and clamped over the shocked man's nose and mouth. He held onto the back of Cranston's head with his left. Cranston made a feeble brief effort to evade his attacker but fell off his chair unconscious before he could accomplish anything of an effective defense.

Jacob waited a few moments to be sure Cranston was out cold, then knelt beside him, placed a plastic bag over his head and face, and glued it in place. He held a garrot ready just in case, but it was not necessary. He waited for a full five minutes, then checked Cranston's carotid pulse. It was absent. Jacob could not see any chest movements of respiration, and his ear on the lawyer's chest detected no beat. His pupils were fixed in the mid position, a sure sign of death his researches had taught him. He was dead. Jacob Roth Whitesides had just killed a man in cold blood with malice aforethought, and he did not feel the slightest pang of remorse. He stripped off all of Cranston's clothing, his glasses, his watch, and a diamond stud pinkie ring from his right hand, neatly folded the clothing, and placed all of that in a chest of drawers in the man's bedroom.

He went out the back door of the house and walked to the shed in the back yard where he found just what he needed—a wheel barrow. He returned to the killing room and hoisted the slight dead body into the barrow and left with all his belongings out the back and around to the orchard where his truck was parked. It had taken him forty minutes to drive to Medina and would take him that much to return to his house in rural county. The stealthy killing had cost him another half hour. Overall, he was satisfied with his preparations and accomplishment in a relatively short time but vowed to do better next time. He covered the corpse in a plastic sheet he had laid out on the floor of the cab. However, there was no blood or other fluids.

There was no trace of his footprints, tire tread marks, or anything to indicate what had happened in Phillip Cranston's house that night.

There was no one on the streets of Medina as he left town, and none of the houses had lights on their porches or inside the homes. Medina used county sheriffs to police their quiet and calm little burg, and there was no sign of a deputy or a sheriff's vehicle anywhere to be seen. It was as if a ghost had evaporated the man who lived in Number 12 Main Street and whisked him away into the ether-sphere without a trace.

He drove to his rental house and hid the dead body in a clump of bushes for the time being. His adrenaline was pumping ferociously, and his dormant killer instinct had come to the fore in full flower. He drove directly to the adolescent housing quarters of the asylum and parked his truck in the back among the night shift's vehicles, lost among them.

He knew were each girl slept, and he had his choice of victims to take out next. He did not want to attract too much attention to his crimes; so, he chose to kill only the girl who was on tap to present evidence on Monday morning against him. That was Abigail Constella, a loud and boisterous Borderline Personality Hispanic teenager who was small and wiry, probably weighed less than 90 pounds. He knew all the girls well enough to know that Abby was an insomniac, and she would almost certainly be the only person up and about on the unit. He pondered how to get close enough to her to use the chloroform again.

He decided to take a risk. He did not put on his balaclava and allowed his face to be seen clearly in the soft night lights in the hallway. He was going to act as if he were making midnight rounds if she saw him, and he planned to walk right up to her. His soft soled boots where soundless on the hallway floor as he neared the room she shared with two other girls. Abby was turning into the doorway of her room when Jacob slipped up behind her, silent as a snake. She was singing a vapid song popular with the country's teenage girls, *Maybe I Know*, the hit single of the Wrecking Crew.

Even in the dim light, he was sure it was Abby by her a Jackie Kennedy–style coiffure. Before she could close the door behind her, Jacob pounced and put her down with his chloroform cloth so quickly that she was almost unaware that she had been anesthetized and then be made dead. The same technique of the plastic bag over the girl's head and glued to her neck was quick and efficient for snuffing out the life of the teenage child painlessly and very quickly. No noise; no mess.

Jacob took every precaution to ensure that she was indeed gone, checked for any hint of evidence that he had ever been there, then stripped off her clothing and neatly folded the articles and put them neatly into her dresser drawer where they nestled inconspicuously with all her other neatly placed girlish clothing.

He placed his balaclava over his scalp and face as an abundance of caution. She was light; so, he put her naked body over his shoulder, looked all around, and trotted swiftly out of the building and to his truck where the plastic sheeting on the cab bed awaited the second victim of the night.

Jacob retrieved the first corpse and loaded into the truck with Abby's and took off as fast as he dared go—given the high need for local traffic cops to meet their quota of speeders for the day–to his house in the hill country. He hid the two bodies in the brushy area of the northwest corner where all the equipment had been set up, then made a return trip to the asylum as fast as he dared.

He had a small stroke of genius on the way back. It was only 3:30 in the morning; so, he could add another layer to his alibi. He hid his collection of antique watches inside their protective velvet lined mahogany decorative box under a loose floorboard under his bed where only a serious search could turn it up. He called the sheriff's office and reported that he had been robbed. A deputy in his cruiser was moving along the gravel road in front of the asylum at the time and responded immediately.

Q: What exactly was stolen, Dr. Whitesides?
A: Jacob listed succinctly and accurately the watches that he had been so lovingly collected for many years–Longines Tank 17 Jewels vintage 10K GF Watch 100% Authentic, Hamilton men's watch Boulton, Patek Philippe Nautilus 18K white gold watch, an Ernest Borel Kaleidoscope Selton gold filled rare vintage watch, and sixteen others. His recollections were remarkable for their precision and for revealing how valuable they were to him.
Q: What is the value of the entire collection, and can you list each item with its value?
A: Just short of $150,000. And I can give you the list you're are asking for. He could, and he did.

Q: Is the collection ensured, sir?"
A: Yes, indeed.
Q: Name of the insurance company?
A: Western Mutual, I'll call them first thing after they open their doors. They have a main office in Dallas.

"Thank you, sir. I think that will be all for today. Let's keep in touch as the investigation goes on."

Deputy Sheriff Andrew Keiting was thorough and pleased with the precision of the report. It made him look good. He made a note that he spent fifty-two minutes questioning the victim and doing a preliminary search of his living quarters. It was the largest heist he had ever heard of in or near Copperas Cove, and he could hardly wait to spread the news.

Jacob was happy to compound his alibi and called Western Mutual at 9:05 that morning to report the theft. His case was assigned an insurance investigator, Wendell Croft Edmonds NICB [National Insurance Crime Bureau]. Edmonds was in Jacob's house two hours later and was even more thorough than the sheriff's department. His search of the house went over almost every square inch (with the exception of attempting to lift up floorboards under Jacob's bed).

Q: Can you give me a list of people who are familiar with your collection or the inside of your apartment?
A: It was a short list. He told Inspector Edmonds that he had never told a single soul about the collection, its value, or its contents, let alone showing it to anyone.
Q: Have you any enemies who would want to harm you in any way?
A: Well… I guess I could list the administrators of the hospital, its attorney, and several young patients who are displeased with my forthright decisions related to their work or care in the hospital. He gave the short list which he knew would not be destined to improve his popularity at the institution. Nonetheless, he had a quiet inner satisfaction about doing so.

CHAPTER 10

An important meeting, 1967

IT WAS A BUSY WEEKEND for Jacob in anticipation of the fateful meeting in the administrator's office on Tuesday morning. Immediately after his interview with Dallas burglary detectives, he drove directly to his house in Hill Country. He was still on sick leave. He changed into his rubber morgue clothing and started up the engine of the sturdy old truck. It took about three minutes to get to the cleared area in the northeast corner of the property. He grabbed the handles of the wheelbarrow and wheeled it to where the bodies were hidden in a pile of brush. There was a minor telltale scent of early decay hanging in the air. He had waited long enough for rigor mortis to set in, and to allow the muscles to return to their soft, pliable original state.

He put them in the wheelbarrow and hauled them to the work area. He first scrubbed both corpses with a hard bristle brush, caustic lye soap and Clorox from scalp to soles of their feet. He then proceeded to follow the human dissection manual to dismember them joint by joint, all the work being done on one of the large clear plastic sheets he had purchased for that very purpose. When the body segments were small enough to fit, he turned on the large wood chipper and handed each segment one at a time into the chewing mechanism. The machine was doing its job thoroughly and sharply. Out of the other end of the chipper came pieces measuring less than 1' square. There was a fairly sizable pile of sludge from pulpified muscle, clotted blood, and unrecognizable bone fragments. To that point, Jacob had not even worked up a sweat. He secretly thanked God for getting the machinery for him.

Carl Douglass

The rest of the operation was slower and more tedious. Jacob gathered up the sodden chunky mass and transported it to the incinerators without allowing even a tooth sized fragment to hit the ground. The incinerators were effective and efficient, but their capacity was too small to make a serious dent in the pile in less than two hours of steady work. Jacob pitched scoop shovels full of the once human detritus into the incinerators—three of them—and set the heat register to its highest range. A pungent smoke came out of the small chimneys, and Jacob determined that the cremations were finished when that smoke ceased. He checked inside his incinerators and was pleased to see only ashes and fragments of bone and teeth remaining of what had been an accusatory lawyer and a girl.

When the incinerators and their contents cooled down, he shoveled out the grey contents and placed them in a sifter which kept the larger (½ inch bone fragments and most of the teeth) in the mesh and allowed a powdery pile of ashes to accumulate in a bucket. That amounted to two fifteen gallon buckets filled to the brim which he sealed temporarily and a third one filled about ¾s full. He then took a 12-pound sledge hammer and smashed the teeth and bone fragments into a coarse powder. He cleaned the sledgehammer and the metal plate he had pounded on in the river until there was no trace of what had been done with them. He scrubbed them with his mix of Chlorox, harsh soap, and his 11" hard bristle and Bi-Level Scrub Brush Extension Pole Attachment. The scrub brush was designed to scour ship decks, and brick house siding but it functioned quite nicely for the purpose at hand.

The last step in the erasure project was to dump the fine powder into his lead vat filled with hot hydrochloric acid and made sure that the material was fully submerged. It took all day Saturday for the mass of sludge to become a fairly smooth thick liquid with no resemblance to the original human source. He let the sludge cool, then shoveled it into the heavy ply opaque plastic bags and sealed them with the quick drying permanent liquid glue to seal them. He had studied a wide range of plastic bags and had finally purchased bags able to dissolve completely in water without leaving any traces, and to degrade when put in mud due to the reaction of microorganisms.

• 175 •

He placed the bags in the truck's bed and drove to the pond. He backed up and parked. Then he climbed into the back of the truck and heaved the innocuous looking bags into the deep clear water. He watched with satisfaction as they wafted to the bottom and off into the underwater cave and out of sight.

He checked the work area for any signs and congratulated himself on the remarkably clean and bucolic scene. Perfect.

As demanded of him, Jacob arrived at the asylum's administrative offices at six o'clock on Tuesday morning. He was carrying a portfolio of information with which he intended to make his defense. He stifled an insistent yawn; it had been a busy and rather tense weekend; and he was sleep deprived. As the other participants filtered in, he held his piece, since this was essentially the meeting called by and controlled by Quentin Carver Driggs, PhD and Dr. Lyman Christiansen, the lead psychiatrist for the adolescent ward, who nodded at Jacob as he walked by and took a seat at the far end of the conference table. Dr. Driggs' efficient secretary, Ms. Gywneth P. Rogers [more correctly, his "executive assistant"] and Nurse Dina Cantrell followed suit, until it appeared that they had a quorum. The potential witnesses were seated in the ante room to wait their turn. Driggs was careful to follow legal procedures as outlined by the institution's attorney, Mr. Cranston (as long as that technicality suited his purposes).

At first everyone in the room avoided eye contact with the other attendees. At six-thirty, everyone except Jacob began to fidget. He commanded himself to remain rigidly immobile and silent. At seven o'clock, some murmuring began among the others; and they were looking at each other. Dr. Driggs whispered to Ms. Rogers, who got up and left the room. She was gone for half an hour.

When she returned, she immediately resumed her seat and whispered in Dr. Driggs' ear. He stood up to make an announcement.

"Ladies and gentlemen, I am sure you have taken note of the absence of the chairman of our meeting, the institution's attorney, Mr. Cranston. In fact, we have not been able to find out why that is the case, or even where he is. So, unfortunately, we will be obliged to postpone the meeting to another, as yet unspecified day and time, when he can be here. I apologize for any inconvenience this may have caused you."

Without further explanation, everyone left the room somewhat bewildered. It was very much unlike the punctilious Mr. Cranston. What he did not bother to mention—since it was regarded as an incidental—the key witness for this particular meeting, patient Abigail Constella, was also not in attendance, but she was a Borderline Personality Disorder patient, and strict cooperation or punctuality were not really expected.

PART IV

Danny McGraw & Jacob Whitesides

CHAPTER 1

Missing persons, late August, 1967

THAT THE NEARLY PERFECTLY RELIABLE Phillip D. Cranston III, JD, Attorney at Law, did not show up for what the institution considered to be a crucial meeting at first created consternation. When Dr. Driggs and his staff were unable to find him in any of his known haunts (which were very few in number for the rather reclusive man), they began to be concerned. When the local and county peace officers made a thorough search, including digging up his past, and found nothing about him except a minimalist social media presence and a nearly nonexistent general social history—including attending no professional legal conventions, belonging to any church, never having married, had children, traveled, or vacationed, outside his small world between and the modest town of Medina, Texas and the Burkheart Asylum, Sanatorium, and Destitute Orphans Home, in Coppera's Cove, North Central Texas, the concern became worry. It was almost as if the man never left his house while in Medina, or the asylum when he was in Coppera's Cove.

It was a full month before the administration, clinicians, and caregiving staff of the hospital, began to entertain the idea that foul play might have occurred. Finally, a committee of the psychiatric staff met in a brief conference and determined to do something about the issue. None of them was particularly enamored of getting involved personally, most believing that it was a police matter, better left to the officers and not to have the institution get dragged into the news media coverage any more than it had to. Four separate individuals were nominated to head up a committee to approach Dr. Driggs, and—if necessary—to contact the state police or even the FBI. Two of them refused to accept the position if elected; one man, elderly Dr. Frances Kingman, was elected, accepted, then developed pneumonia and had to be hospitalized. The final electee, Dr. Jacob R. Whitesides, had never spoken up or offered an opinion. He had not declined election when it was offered to him, either. By default, he was elected; and Jacob did not seem to be either pleased or displeased by occupying the position. He did accept graciously.

Jacob reviewed the search progress—and lack of it–to date. He concluded that there was no other recourse than to go beyond the local police. He informed Dr. Driggs of the faculty's decision, and the administrator had no objection. He guessed that it was time to search more deeply, and reluctantly agreed that something had to be done, even if it brought unwonted attention to their beloved institution. As Jacob was leaving Dr. Driggs' office, he mentioned—as an afterthought—maybe they should include a search for the difficult patient Abigail Constella.

"If you think it is appropriate for the sake of completion, Dr. Whitesides."

"It might put us in a good light, sir. You know, we are not making a value comparison between a well-known and well-to-do male professional and a poor female asylum inmate."

"Put that way, I think you have a point. Be as thorough as possible; but, between you, me, and the fencepost, our real goal is to clear up any mystery about Mr. Cranston."

"Of course, sir. I am pretty sure we can slant the interest in that direction. After all, it is the right thing to do."

"Then, I'll leave it to your discretion. And thanks, Jacob. You are a real team player."

In his new capacity as the hospital's representative for the search committee (which consisted of only one person for the moment), Jacob made his first call to the Dallas Police Department.

" Hello, this is Dr. Jacob Whitesides from the Burkheart Asylum, Sanatorium, and Destitute Orphans Home, in Coppera's Cove, up in North Central Texas. We wish to report a possible missing person."

Q: Ike Nichols, Desk Sergeant, speakin'. How long has the person been missing?

A: A little over a month.

Q: What steps have been taken to find the individual? I presume he or she, as the case may be, is an adult.

A: Yes, he is attorney Phillip D. Cranston III, JD who lives in Medina and works in Coppera's Cove at the mental institution.

Q: It may seem like a somewhat awkward question, but is the attorney who is missing, someone of—shall we say—considerable importance?"

A: You might say so. At least he is to the hospital and its relationships with the local community and the organizations which deal with our institution.

Q: Likely to make the news, Dr. Whitesides?

A: Hmmh… I think so, but only locally.

Q: Okay, we'll look into it, but it will take a coupla days to get someone out there.

A: Fine. It's been a month; so, I don't think that two or three more days, one way or the other, will make much difference.

Q: Shall we list you as the "go-to" guy out there, Doctor?

A: I think that would be best. I seem to have been the one who drew the black bean.

The desk sergeant laughed. "So, expect a visit later in the week, sir. We will be as thorough as possible but as unobtrusive as we can under the circumstances.

"That will be most appreciated. On my end, I will help as much as possible; but I confess it won't be much. I hardly knew the man; he played things close to his vest, if you know what I mean."

After he cradled his receiver, it was Jacob's turn to enjoy a laugh.

The desk sergeant made a decision. The DPD was too busy; the Major Crimes Unit would not be interested in such a trivial missing case; and the Missing Persons' Unit had a fairly large number of guys who would be pleased to get out of the department for a while.

He called the unit and spoke to his old friend and drinking buddy, Sgt. Fred Simpson about the case. He explained the particulars, and added that the north Texas country was pretty nice this time of year. It would only take a few days—week at the most.

Sgt. Simpson said, "I'll get our newbie, Probie Karen Oppenheimer, on it. She is running for attorney general of the DOJ, if you get my meanin', Ike."

"I know the type. Maybe we can give her the big opportunity."

It was Ike's turn to laugh.

CHAPTER 2

The beginning of the search for the missing, late August, 1967

A WEEK LATER, THE OVERANXIOUS and overenthusiastic twenty-year-old probationary DPD police officer Karen Oppenheimer presented herself and her credentials at the front desk of the hospital and asked to see Dr. Jacob Roth Whitesides. She and her cred pack attested to the fact that she held the rank of officer and was assigned to the Missing Persons' Department. She was bucking for a promotion to corporal and was on her best behavior and most eager state of mind, facts she kept to herself.

Karen was well educated, especially in the growing new field of forensic internet. She had had modest successes in obtaining the better—not the best and latest—computational and transitional computers and software to be able to search out criminals, to follow their movements using their vehicle trackers and cell-phones for geolocation. She set up a tight and organized mini-bureau in the Missing Persons division, and worked almost constantly on her 1960 model which was marked by the conversion from vacuum tube to solid-state devices such as transistors and then integrated circuit (IC) chips. This led to primary computer memory moving away from magnetic-core memory devices to solid-state static and dynamic semiconductor memory, which greatly reduced the cost, size, and power consumption of computers. Even her accountants were pleased to give her what she wanted—an IBM 7090/7094.

The intrepid young blond blanketed the city, then the county, then all the counties in and around Dallas with not even suggestive results. She expanded the search to the entire United States by paring up with FBI, ATF, and nearby states' data bases, using her department's already harried co-workers to do the most in depth search for any missing person ever. Phillip D. Cranston III, JD, Attorney at Law, had dropped out of existence. Prior to the current search, his general news appearances were minimal and his social media presence was a cipher. Finally, Karen gave up and returned to Dallas to once again begin delving into the ever-growing stacks of Missing Persons.

During her search efforts, the radio, TV, and paper news outlets, were churning up a veritable wasp's nest-hit-by-a ball-bat storm of public interest. The demand was for real news and a stop to the omni-present conspiracy theories. Not only did Karen Oppenheimer's star cease to shine so brightly, but she was beginning to look like something of an albatross to the higher brass.

Missing Persons was eager to get rid of the Phillip D. Cranston III, case. By then, many cops presumed that the man had been murdered somewhere by someone, but did not have a viable clue to establish either hypothesis. Captain Ed Reach Strathmore of the Missing Persons finally decided to ignore the humiliation of asking for help, and contacted the Chief of Ds, Gustav "Gus" Abrams, for help. Gus could detect a lemon case when anyone tried to foist it on him. He kicked the matter up stairs to the Chief of DPD's office.

Gus said, "Look, Chief, the whole department has flopped trying to one finish up an MP case that is being oversold by the news."

"Let me guess," the Chief Murray, said in a tired voice, "maybe somebody from out in the sticks named Phillip D. Cranston III? How'm I doin'?"

"Right on Chief. Personally, it's lookin' like a permanent case we look at again every ten years, unless you have some kinda' good idea."

"I guess I'll go where I always go… to Danny McGraw. I feel sorry for the poor guy, when the stuff rolls down hill, it almost always hits Danny and sticks."

"Ya gotta admit that much of the time he comes through. He's got some kinda magic goin' for him."

"He's smart, like his old man. And he is tough and persistent. Where he's better than old Hector used to be is that he is very patient, almost irritatingly so. I'll take the path of least resistance and give him a call."

"He'll be thrilled," Chief Abrams said sardonically.

The chiefs had underestimated Danny. He had taken an interest in the perplexing mystery disappearance almost as soon as it hit the news. He was glad—if not overly enthusiastic—to get the case and to get away to the Hill Country he loved.

He came alone at first and checked in with the Copperas Cove's PD who were more than glad to get the albatross case off their shoulders. He was given free reign and roaming privileges along with free access to everyone who knew anything about Cranston's having become missing and seemingly with no hope of being found.

Danny did not bother with Karen Oppenheimer's findings–which he admired–but because she had been so thorough and comprehensive, there was no further use of beating that dead horse.

He decided to work for a different premise, a hypothesis, if you will, or one of his famous hunches. He determined to exhaust the knowledge contained in the brains of people who knew Cranston—including his fairly large number of enemies, his very few friends, and limited number of personal acquaintances.

He decided to work from the top down. His first interview was with Dr. Driggs, who was bored to tears from the constant interruptions to rehash the now hackneyed history of the missing attorney.

"I want you to tell me everything you know about Phillip Cranston, Dr. Driggs. Do not leave anything out; nothing is too trivial. I especially want to know about your personal experiences with him and how you feel about him deep down."

"Seems like a do this every day, but I'll give it another go. The man seemed to have come from nowhere if you are looking for details. There are 15 certified law schools in New York. He graduated in the middle of his class in Pace Law School, not one you are likely to have heard of, and for good reason. He was in the exact middle of his graduating class and had a GPA of 2.9. The man was lackluster in almost every way, and demonstrated that by failing to pass the New York bar exam three times and not being able to get any job as an attorney for three years. He apparently filled his time doing odd jobs—bus boy, waiter, bar keep, even a fish monger. He eventually got a job with a minor accounting task from which he was fired for reasons not made public, and that brought him to Texas.

"After a couple of lackluster tries, he got a boring position as the corporate position for a local Dallas Teamsters' Union charter; It was never apparent to Danny, the Teamster's president, or Karen Oppenheimer what he did there, but he made a potful of money. For some reason, he left that employment along with most of the other educated people and disappeared into the Hill Country. There, he got a job in a Copperas Cove ambulance chaser firm, where he again made serious money. He tired of that and came here to the hospital. That was five years before me."

"How's his work been?"

"There's not been much law work for any attorney to do… that is until quite recently when one of our psychiatrists began kicking up a fuss about how we do business. That guy, named Whitesides, believed—still does—that we're not modern enough. He rubbed nearly everyone the wrong way until we had to get Cranston on his case. He was disruptive, and he had to go. It fell to Cranston to find plausible cause.

"About the time Cranston started interviewing Dr. Whitesides, he up and disappears. Strangest thing you ever heard of, especially since Cranston was making good money here, had interests in several profitable businesses around the area."

"Besides this Dr. Whitesides, do you know of or suspect any other possible enemies, Dr. Driggs?"

"Not really. Some of the people he does business with some folks that look pretty shady to me, but what would I know about that sort of stuff?"

"I need a list of those 'shady' characters. Can you get right on that, Dr. Driggs?"

"Sure, anything I can do."

He left the room for ten minutes and came back with a list of five men and their companies with hardly any other information. Danny shrugged, thanked the man, and set out to eliminate the men on the list from suspicion. Their names seemed like a list of Italian mafiosos, but he knew it was neither fair nor profitable to jump to such a conclusion just because a guy had an Italian name.

He made a canvass of the local Italian business bosses. Their places of business were all quite rundown, but they were all turning more than healthy profits at typical unobtrusive businesses—garbage collection, upscale foreign cars which were all being sold to eastern European outlets, construction companies using almost entirely Black and Hispanic workers, and the local—and most profitable of all—fish wholesaler. Danny's suspicions were going up, and he could not shake his unease by visiting the establishments.

As was his usual practice, Danny started at the bottom rung in the companies and worked his way up the power and profit ladder. Mostly he hit a bland and uninformative dead end. In the Grenly Bros Fish Market, he met with a junior girl secretary who was cautiously irritated about the goings-on in the market. She hinted that there was something fishy going on there, and it was not the swimming around in the ocean kind.

"That's interesting, Ruth. I'm a detective with the Dallas PD, and there's almost nothing I haven't heard. If there's one thing I've learned it is to protect any informant who helps me. That's a gold bond promise on my part."

"I need to get something off my chest, even if I get labeled as a rat. I need to get a safer job anyway."

"Safe from what?"

"Like maybe a fall down the slippery stairs, getting accidently stabbed when you walk past a cutting table, or simply going missing after making a few complaints to somebody up the ladder, if you get my meanin'."

"I think I do, Ruth. How about you get me some sort of a list of those 'accidents' and what the beef was with the bosses with them. That would be a good start. We could meet somewhere away from the factory and the store some evening. Sound like a reasonable thing?"

"Sounds like a "maybe date" or the closest thing to it I've had for a while. You know any decent Italian places around here? Since I started at the fish factory, I've got a hankering for a good Italian fish dinner. That sound okay?"

"I know several in Dallas. Can I pick you up tonight after work at your apartment, say at eight?"

"Ummh, I guess so. Can I see your badge? A girl can't just trust anybody she only just met anymore, ya know."

"Here's my badge and credentials. Look, Ruth, I want to convince you that I'm legit, and you're safe. What if we brought along your mother or a sister, something like that."

"I know it sounds like a drag, but my sister is pretty cute and funny. She's also a good judgea character. She likes Italian, too."

"It's a date for three, then," Danny said.

CHAPTER 3

Jacob Whitesides investigation of the inner workings of the asylum, late August, 1967

JACOB WAS BEGINNING TO BE paranoid, even though nothing seemed to be happening around the asylum, at least anything involving him. Still–just because he was paranoid–it did not mean that he did not have valid suspicions. He decided that he had to develop a proactive plan. First, he needed a master key. To find that, he had to think logically, something he seemed not to be doing so well in lately. Where were keys kept? There must be more than one for the whole complex. The janitor's room was the most logical.

It was simple getting it. The door to the room was not locked, and all keys were hanging from hooks row on row. He examined them—all solid brass, the best grade of brass, Alloy 360/free cutting brass. From his work in a machine shop as a boy, Jacob knew that the alloy exhibited excellent machinability and formability, as well as suitability for soldering and brazing operations. It was great material; the only problem was that every key looked almost exactly the same as all the others. None of them were marked with a location identity. That erased the ease with which he had located the keys. Everything was going to be slow, the celerity of movement of a glacier; and he did not have that kind of time.

He tried to think, to be logical… but nothing seemed to come to him. He was trying not to have a panic attack. He had seen them, but he had never had any kind of feeling like that… before.

He had to start somewhere; so, he picked up the first key on the left of the top row. He held the next several up and saw that they were similar but did have some definite changes in the notches and size of the NATIKON KY-3 Hollow Barrel Brass Plated keys. He took a set of six keys in order to try each and to keep track. After all, he only needed to get one correct key into the one opening, that of the administrator's office.

It was very late and dark. Not a soul around. He turned his large flashlight and moved swiftly—a distance of nearly seventy-five yards between the janitor's room to the administrator's office. It took him three rushed trips and a lot of sweating before... at long last... a key slipped very easily into the lock, turned, and freed the doorknob. He walked in like he owned the place. His sense of panic was gone, taken over by an adrenaline rush of excitement.

Now, all he had to find was what he was looking for. There were nine metal drawer cabinets, each with four drawers. None of them had any signage on the outside. He started with the case nearest to Dr. Driggs desk. To his dismay, the cabinets all had separate keys, the keyhole much smaller than the master cabinet key. Surely Dr. Driggs was not so paranoid and security conscious that he was willing to walk all the way back to the janitor's room whenever he needed to open a drawer. Jacob checked closet doors and struck gold (more likely flimsy nickel and brass colored to look like gold). Although they can be plated in a variety of colors, most keys are typically silver or brown in color. These were older and flattered Dr. Driggs, Jacob reckoned.

There were 36 keys; Jacob squinted and found them all to be exactly the same; so far as he could see. He was right. It probably gave the eccentric asylum director some sort of pride to see so many keys, even though he knew they were all the same key. No one else knew that. Except now Jacob knew.

He opened the top drawer of his intended cabinet and found it to be empty. The second one down had file folders identified with a large alphabetically ordered letter printed with a calligraphic lettering done with black indelible marker. For the first time that evening, Jacob paused to think. He then quickly moved to the last cabinet where he assumed the Ws would be. He was rewarded by finding a large ornate W on a folder in the second to the lowest drawer where he had assumed it should be. He took out the folder, found his name and intended to draw out the pages one at a time until he found something useful. It was the very top paper, since it was the most recent one placed.

He found his name, a date two weeks away, and a list of people he knew. He figured out that the first names were of two girls from the adolescent ward–Mary Anne Patterson and Petra Sloweski. The next—and separate row—had nurses Nancy Wake Tompson, RN, Harriet Carson, RN, and Stanley Sutherland, Psych Tech. That would be too many to process in the time he had, and the disappearance of so many at one time would draw serious attention to the asylum and to him eventually, he thought. He had some serious decisions to make and to get his plans coming from that decision-making session.

Danny McGraw and his threesome date with pretty Ruth Pettigrew and somewhat less appealing Penny Pettigrew who seemed annoyed when he stated her full name. He flashed his badge to get a good table looking out at the expansive back lawn with trees lit up with ground lights. It was uptown and attractive looking. The girls were impressed with him, the view, and the restaurant's cultivated atmosphere.

The liveried waiter spoke with an Italian accent and asked what they would like to drink.

"Ask the girls first. I want them to have a good time," Jacob said with a smile radiating generosity.

Ruth ordered a Manhattan, and Penny asked a Remy Martin 1738 Accord Royal Cognac, although she was not at all sure what it was.

Danny had to keep his wits about him; so, he ordered Perrier water, begging off alcohol, "Got to be the sober driver," he said.

It turned out as he expected. Both girls were quickly mellowed by their hard liquor and became very loquacious and informative. Their initial dis-ease about the cop evaporated, and soon afterward, their determination not to reveal anything about the fish market's hidden goings on.

"I hate the place," said Ruth, her voice becoming slurred.

"I been there longer, and I hate it more," added Penny.

"What is it you dislike so much, if you don't mind me asking?" said Danny.

One more drink each, the girls unleashed a torrent of pent-up anger, frustration, and disgust, with the way the fish market operated.

"Look," said Ruth, "let's get real, the place is a mob front. The Italians are Mafia studs, brutes from Taormina, Sicily. They brag about being family, clan, or *cosca*. They talk about Mafia stuff like a clan is led by a boss a *capofamiglia* or *rappresentante* with an underboss a *capo bastone* or *sotto capo* and supervised by one or more *consigliere*. Under his command are groups *decina* of about ten soldiers called *picciotti*. Our big boss—who we haven't ever even met—brags about being a decina, and his vice-president of sales is his "*capodecina*" That kinda talk goes on all the time, like we don't know nothing. Everybody knows the Mafia is the biggest criminals in the whole world."

Danny did know a considerable amount about the Mafia from Dallas and even before that when he was in the army. He also knew a little about Taormina, which is a hilltop town on the east coast of Sicily. It sits near Mount Etna. He knew about *umirtà/omertà* or code of silence. The mafiosi Danny knew called the Mafia "*Cosa Nostra*"/Our Thing/men of honor/ or men of respect.

Heroin in Dallas was often distributed to street dealers from Mafia-owned pizzerias, and the revenues could be passed off as restaurant profits; the cops labelled it as the "Pizza Connection". For a time while he was on active involvement with Major Crimes the local wiseguys waged a campaign to dominate *Cosa Nostra*, and they also waged a campaign of murder against journalists, officials, and policemen, who dared to cross them. More and more informants emerged for Danny to interrogate. Many of those guys paid a high price for their cooperation, usually through the murder of relatives. He remembered a made man, Luigi Marino Loruca who turned state's evidence. His mother, aunt, and sister, were murdered. He had been so involved that he learned the incompany lingo and relationships. Mafiosi of equal status called each other "*compare*"/comrade; inferiors called their superiors "*padrino*"/godfather.

Danny remembered one case which might have relevance to what he was getting from Ruth and Penny. There was this butcher who wished to sell some meat to a supermarket without paying sales tax—just good capitalism. Since the transaction was a black-market deal, the guys involved cannot turn to the police or the courts if either of them cheats the other. The seller was supplying rotting meat, and the purchaser refused to pay. The mistrust and fear of being cheated with no recourse prevented these two marketers from making a profitable transaction.

To guarantee each other's honesty, the two parties had asked the local mafia clan to oversee the transaction from start to finish. In exchange for a commission, the mafioso promised both the buyer and seller that if either of them tried to cheat the other, the cheater can expect to be assaulted or have his property vandalized. The local Dallas mafioso capo's reputation for viciousness, impartiality, and reliability, was so compelling that neither the buyer nor the seller would consider cheating with him overseeing the deal. The transaction thus proceeded smoothly. That came out as a defense in a trial, and that led to Danny developing the butcher as a CI.

More to the present point regarding the thriving fish market, Danny was connecting the dots. Mafiosi provided protection and invested capital in smuggling gangs. Smuggling operations required large investments: goods, boats, crews, all of which were part of the fish market's operation. Danny was well aware that few people would trust their money to criminal gangs, like the actual smugglers. It is mafiosi who raise the necessary money from investors and ensure that all parties act in good faith. They also ensure that the smugglers operate in safety. He was pretty sure that this was what was going on.

He was also pretty sure that the Mafia and the fish market needed a fence or a money launderer, and that was where the elusive Phillip Delano Cranston III came in. Danny would have bet a month's pay that the attorney was crooked, connected, and had tried to hold back money from the local mob. His bet included the idea that the man probably slept with the fishes now. The idea that it was that putz, Jacob Whitesides, who wanted to avoid some embarrassment was laughable, and he put the man's name in the far back of his mind.

Mafiosi rarely directly involve themselves in smuggling operations. When they do, it is usually when the operations are especially risky. In this case, they may induct smugglers into their clans in the hope of binding them more firmly. This was the case with heroin smuggling, where the volumes and profits involved were too large to keep the operations at arm›s length. Danny figured the fish business transporting stolen goods, probably cigarettes, or money laundering for the Cosa Nostra, was the source of the asylum's problem, and he determined to get to the bottom of it all. This was a Major Crimes issue now.

CHAPTER 4

Jacob Whitesides' next move, late Wednesday night, August 31, 1967

HE WAS NOT PANICKED, BUT Jacob was a bit nervous. He knew that his next grilling would take place the coming Monday, September the fifth. He had to gain the upper hand, and he had to do it *tout suite*. If he did too much, there would be more attention on the asylum itself; and it seemed to him that he would be the most likely suspect. Even though he knew there was no evidence against him, and that motive alone was only rarely enough to convict, he wanted to shift all interest away from himself. He had to add a new conjecture into the suspicions related to missing persons from the asylum. He came up with a useful and believable idea.

He had an insider's piece of information that no one else knew he had. The list from Dr. Driggs' office was going to be the answer to his conundrum. He planned his caper for that night and chose the two Borderline girls on the adolescent ward who were probably going to lie about him to suit the administration's determination to get rid of him.

He suited up, carried his black backpack with his usual paraphernalia, and included a long heavy flashlight. He jimmied the locked entry way as he had done before, and there was enough ambient light to allow him to move along quickly even without using his light. He used his Master Key to enter the adolescent ward, which was asleep, each girl in a separate room. He had left himself plenty of time in order to perform two separate endeavors.

Jacob waited a few minutes to be sure that there was no one entering or leaving a room, no doors open through which he could be seen and identified and checked the night nurse's sleeping room. The door was locked, and he could hear the faint soft whooshing of her ladylike snoring. He walked quietly, ever vigilant, to the first girl's quarters–Mary Anne Patterson. He eased open the door and placed the sleeping girl in a Mata Leão–rear naked choke–and held it until she quietly suffocated and died. He placed a plastic bag over her head and glued it to the skin of the neck to be certain. He stripped her and carefully made sure that he had taken what any runaway girl would take in her travel bag. Second, he went to Petra Sloweski's room and repeated his procedure. The girls were both slight—age 16—and he was able to carry each girl and a carefully and well packed luggage bag out to his car, place it on plastic sheeting, and close the trunk lid. He was hypervigilant throughout this particularly fraught period in his plans. He repeated the exact process with the second girl and stuffed both of the girls' luggage in and then locked the trunk.

His last move at the asylum was to sneak back in the door to the adolescent ward, check all around to remove mistakes, and to double check that no one had reacted to the minimal sounds of his activities so far. When he was absolutely certain that he was alone, and every girl and every member of the staff was deeply asleep, he very quickly kicked out the girls' doors from the inside and broke down the larger exit door, also from the inside out. Then, he threw caution to the wind and sprinted full out back to his car, executed a bootlegger's back-up turn, and raced out the back exit gate and off to Hill Country. He glanced quickly to see if anyone came out of the building, if the building's lights suddenly came on, or if any kind of alarm sounded. He was relieved not to see, hear, or feel, anything.

Back at his farm, Jacob disposed of the two bodies quickly and efficiently, partly owing to his previous experience, and learning to be more proficient in his chosen work. He reasoned with himself that the disposals of the once human beings was necessary for his own and the greater good. He was being ill-used as all Jews had been for all time, and enough was enough. He could not allow them to win again. Not with him.

He thought himself to be in imminent lethal danger, and self-preservation was always warranted, even despite the *Ten Commandments*. Hoping once again to avoid traffic cops, he decided to race back to his apartment and to establish an alibi when he arrived. He pondered on that problem most of the way.

Danny McGraw switched his thought processes to the idea that he was dealing with a major criminal enterprise issue and an incidental possible murder and a very minor escape by a disgruntled and mentally ill adolescent. After his profitable dinner with the two loquacious employees of the obvious Mafia front fish market, he was enlivened with the thought that this could be his chance to get promoted and to achieve yet another major step in his pursuit of the office of the Dallas PD Chief.

He arrived at his Major Crimes office early, before anyone else, and drew up a detailed plan of attack to bring down the Mafia based enterprise and maybe even the Texas Costra Nostra as a domino effect. He had a completed and polished document to submit to the secretaries as soon as they arrived. With that in hand, he went to the Chief of Ds and Police Chief Robert V. Murray and presented his document as an urgent priority.

"Slow down, Danny," Gus Abrams said. "This is too complicated for me when you talk so fast. Give us the overview summary, then get to the details."

Danny took a deep breath and calmed down. He did a workman's good effort to lay out the causes, effects, plans of approach, options, and potential pitfalls and sources of failure. The two chiefs were caught up in his enthusiasm and convinced by his logical approach based on the available evidence. The witnesses he had so carefully interrogated where the clincher.

"Danny, turn everything you've got into this investigation. Let's bring them down. I confess that I want to run for District Attorney next year; Gus will make chief, and I see you as jumping to Chief of Ds with this. Dot all your i's and cross your t's. Go over everything three times if you have to. Pile on the details. This has to be airtight and no way around it. That way everyone wins here," Murray said, his stern face almost breaking into a smile.

"With the possible exception of the Mafia and its goons and collaborators," added Gus.

Monday brought Jacob to the administrator's office five minutes early. He took his seat and opened his brief case to put the required papers in front of him; so, he would look as well prepared as he always was; and so, he could practice relaxing the muscles of his face so that he would not betray anything he should not.

The others entered the room looking confident that this time they had him. Even with the hopefully temporary loss of the lawyer Cranston III and the star witness, the Borderline girl, Abigail Constella, they still had two great witnesses to spring against him today, probably more convincing than Abby had been expected to be.

Dr. Christiansen gave Jacob a smug "gotcha" smile, and Nurse Cantrell offered her usual accusatory grim face as her welcome.

Dr. Driggs walked in and stood in front of them.

"I wish I could say good morning, but I can't," he said abruptly.

He had their full attention.

"Last Wednesday, our two witnesses apparently went AWOL, broke down their room doors and the expensive glass main door in their rush. They took their luggage… like they planned to stay away for a long time. They covered their tracks perfectly, no evidence of how they planned it, nor anything showing how they traveled or to where. We have hunted the buildings on campus, the grounds, and the nearby woods for twenty miles out. Nothing. The Copperas Cove police, Dallas detectives, and the highway patrol have searched everywhere. Again, nothing. I am beginning to think they planned all of this with Abigail Constella, and she likely helped them. We cannot tolerate this. I have locked down the buildings— all of them. The girls are to do homework sitting at their desks where we can see them all day, every day, until we get those girls back. What a terrible humiliation for our Burkheart Asylum, Sanatorium, and Destitute Orphans Home. We are stymied. Dr. Whitesides, you will attend each and every meeting we arrange, despite the setbacks that are occurring. We will have our day with you, mark my words."

Jacob put on as glum a face as everyone else to commiserate his disappointment along with them. He rewarded himself with a trip to the ice-cream store and a brief bout of gluttony before getting into his car and heading back to Copperas Cove, laughing all the way.

CHAPTER 5

Lt. Danny McGraw and the Major Crimes unit goes after the Dallas Mafia, nothing left to chance, September-October, 1967

DANNY WAS ABSOLUTELY DETERMINED ON a personal level to bring down the Dallas Mafia, the blood suckers. He sided wholly with the unfortunate little people who were extorted by the high living low lives, especially the scattered and struggling Italian community. He put his Major Crimes Division on notice that this was either the most important case project or the only one. The locals and their mob bosses were going to see the inside of bars, or he was going to fire them all and get a new crew. The men and women of Major Crimes were convinced of his commitment, and it was infectious.

He gathered them for a strategic planning session—how they were going to start, and how they were going to proceed in this new venture of crime fighting.

"Listen up," he said. "Nothing we say here, do here, or hear here, stays here when we leave here."

Det. 1st Lydia Henepin said, "I get it boss, we are talkin' serious about leaves and trees, heah."

She spread an impish grin around the room which made everyone laugh. They liked it when the boss got a bit of a put-down, especially when it came from the tough beauty and all business detective Henepin.

He gave her a mock scowl, and she did a little curtsey.

"All serious now, you guys. Elaine is passing out a roster with assignments unique to each of you. Do not talk about anything you learn with anyone but your partner. The Mafia is very good at extracting information by extortion or bribery, and they cannot get anything from you that you do not know. Trust no one. Tell no one but me anything; so, I can be the filter and the decider. Tell no one anything about what you are working on, not even your family or mistresses."

The crew members met with their new partners later in the day and began planning their day and night's work. It was obvious that few of them would have any free time out for anything so mundane as garden work, bowling, playing with their kids, or making new babies. This thing they were getting into was going to dominate. Had it not been for their profound respect for Danny McGraw, few of them would have signed up.

Danny teamed himself up with newly promoted Lieutenant Kent Thacker with whom he had carried on a friendly competition for the past few years, ever since the two of them made detective first. They worked well with each other, thought alike, worked hard and efficiently, and communicated well with each other and with perps and commanders. They took the first assignment directly in the fish market and designed an undercover persona for each of them that would seem that they were total strangers who were on the prowl for some dirty money—from the operations of the Grenly Bros Fish Market on Cockrell Avenue in southside Dallas.

He and Kent huddled with the two discontented and frankly afraid Pettigrew girls, Penny and Ruth, and hatched a plan. They would establish phony romantic interests and let them be publicly noted. They were to work independently from each other ostensibly, a means of getting across the men's interest in working in the darker underworld strata of the secretive market. It would be too long and cumbersome to try and make their way from the bottom rungs of the legitimated fish mongering business to the mid to upper rungs of the criminal ladder. They had to start with a leg up in that conspiracy element.

The girls quickly caught on to the excitement and minor danger they were involved in and became active cooperating witnesses and willing coconspirators with the sophisticated police detectives. They devised their own reporting and record keeping system, an actual code to be used by all four of the spies, and found a safe hiding place for the records, including photographs, known only to the four undercover agents.

The girls were not ready for any kind of real romantic involvement, and kept that part of the relationship a definite hands off. The dangers were too great. Danny and Kent could not get into any of that except as an act, lest real emotions and entanglements cloud the issues, including the validity of the evidence obtained.

The introduction work into the fish market community was tedious and was taking too much time, but the detectives knew they had to be patient. The breakthrough came when the market bosses threw a party for a particularly profitable quarter of business. The girls were invited and proved to be popular and on a friendly basis with the bosses, joking and flirting. By then, their relationship to the two scruffy looking thugs they had for boyfriends was an easy part of the social gossip among the employees. There was drinking, laughing, and loosening of tongues, that evening in the underboss's house in Uptown, a neighborhood in Dallas, adjacent to the downtown area.

The underboss, Guiseppe Puglisi, struck up a casual conversation with Danny which—lubricated by alcohol—edged into the forbidden area of the criminal activities.

"Look, Danny," he said, "we're lookin' for some kinda special help around here. Seems like you and your pal… what's his name?…"

"Oh, you mean Kent?"

"Yeah, that one. Anyhows youse guys look like comers, if you take my meanin'."

"Maybe I do, maybe I don't. Look, Guiseppe, we like your place; we like your girls; we need money like the next guy. I gotta say, though, we ain't all that interested in slappin' fish around all day."

Guiseppe laughed, "Me neither. Think youse two might be interested in making some side money, like we say?"

"Might be. We gotta be careful, here, Guiseppe, we kinda have a history if you get me what I'm gettin' at. We need ta keep clear of cops, customs people, and other record keepers. We need to know that there's good people here who can keep things on the down low. You know what *I* mean."

"I do, and alla us in the upper floors do. Mind if we check youse out by our sources to see if youse would be a good fit?"

"Nope... so long as the fuzz don't get involved."

"Look, Danny, we got guys on the take in the county, city, and state, even the feds. We have had a coupla hundred years of doin' secret stuff, and the cops are happy gettin' rich on the side, while givin' us some inside help. Not to worry there, pal."

"Okay, Guiseppe, I got a coupla New York names for ya, and you can look into our kin and their friends in Agrigento province where we made our bones."

He gave Guiseppe a name–one of the turncoat mafiosos in the happy employment of the Dallas Police Department–a man whose very life depended on his full cooperation. He told Guiseppe that Guido was from Agrigento—which was true—but that was about all that was true.

Guiseppe asked with exaggerated casualness, "Danny don't sound like no Agrigento name. What's up with that? That a cop moniker?"

Danny laughed out loud.

"Hey, compadre, ever know of a guy havin' ta make a few changes to get along in the US when he came from the old country?"

"I ain't *baciannicchiu* [Sicilian slang: fool, silly, stupid, idiot], I also wasn't always Guiseppe, but it'll do for my time stayin' with Uncle Sam."

They had a meeting of the minds, and Guido Licato proved to have a wealth of information about the old country and its Sicilian Mafia, including names, dates, places, and events in Agrigento. He was also a highly accomplished liar, fully wedded to the police who kept him alive and his real identity a sacred secret.

CHAPTER 6

Progress going after the Dallas Mafia, September-October, 1967

DANNY'S FIRST INDICATION OF REAL progress came when—two weeks later–Guiseppe Puglisi, the underboss of both the fish business and the dirty business, met Danny in a greasy spoon joint on South Lamar Street near the Southside Ballroom.

"Hey, Paisano," called Guiseppe when Danny walked in the door. "Over here, inna back."

He was shrouded in darkness in a closed booth. The greeting was a good omen, Danny thought.

He sat in the booth across from the mobster, and the waitress came immediately.

"What can I get y'all?" she asked Danny.

Guiseppe was already getting well into a large plate of Bucatini with Sicilian Meatballs, spilling considerable amounts on the plastic bib supplied by the restaurant. He slurped on his large glass of red wine.

"Good to see you Mr. G.," Danny said. "What's up that you called for this meet?"

"A little bidness if you and your compadre are innerested."

"Ya got my curiosity. How can we help?"

"That was a good way to put your question; shows youse ain't lookin' to make capo this week."

He said it with his toothy smile.

"Maybe not," said Danny, "but maybe ready to get our feet inside the back door."

"Let's get to it, then," Guiseppe said, all business now. "Oh, where's my manners, ya want somethin' ta eat?"

"No thanks, Mr. G. I had a big breakfast."

"Awright. The don wants us to have a meet in his office at Grenly Bros. Ya know where his office is?"

"Top floor, I'm guessin'."

"Si, right on. It's the only room at the top. Real swanky. He'll be expectin' us and Kent at ten sharp. He has a coupla heavies—Alceu and Salvatore–at the door; they'll be waitin' to frisk ya and let ya in. They ain't big on talkin'."

"We'll be there."

He and Kent dressed up in dark suits, shirts, and ties, hoping to give the just-right look—respectful but not overly obsequious; neat and well-shaved and groomed, but not enough to remove their native tough look. Danny pronounced them ready for the big show, and they arrived at the door to the godfather's office five minutes early.

Salvatore held up a hand, palm out to have them stand in place.

"Youse Danny and Kent?" he asked.

Danny nodded.

"Be a minute."

The door opened in sixty seconds, and a third goon stood big enough to block all view of the office.

"Don's ready ta see youse now."

He frisked them thoroughly, as good as any experienced cop. They entered and saw the don, Emiliano "Vito" Trapani, sitting at the large and ornate wood desk. They had never known his name before, but it was sitting on a plaque fastened to the front of the desk.

"Come in boys," he said. "Good of you to come and to be punctual. I like that. Want something to drink?"

"How about we have what you're having, Don Emiliano?"

"Call me Vito, everybody does, even cops and judges," he said with a smug laugh.

"Yes, sir, Vito," said Kent.

"Good, I'm glad to see he talks," Vito said with a genuinely friendly smile this time.

As promised, they got right down to business.

"My guys checked you out real thorough. You have the right creds for our operation. You done some time, kept the *omertà*, did your jobs, and could be relied on. I want you two to work as a team to move some product from here to the western states' outlets. It's a big ask; and you get big bucks to do it. There's some risk attached, but you guys seem to be up to it. I remind you that I am a generous man, but also an unforgiving one. *Capiche?*"

They nodded and kept serious looks fixed on their faces.

His bodyguard and consigliere, Liuni—no last name–gave them printed directions for their new jobs, unusual, but they were new. It was incriminating for the don and his organization, but it was a significant indicator that they had been thoroughly vetted, and the DPD and Sicilian authorities had been very helpful—life savingly so. He handed them keys to two large semis and sent them out for their first long trip.

Kenny and Kent communicated with DPD headquarters and got the go-ahead to deliver the heroin and cocaine to twenty-seven destinations throughout the western states. It took them a full three weeks working as hard and as efficiently as they could without breaking speed limits or having conversations with the local pigs/bacons or county mounties. Their trucks were never over-weight, and they were deferential and cooperative at each stop. They stayed in out of the way cheap Patel motels, ate in places decent people avoided like a pestilence, and were careful not to divulge anything to anyone. As a result, they were picking up intelligence as fast as they could write it down.

After six months of combined dedicated cop and robber work, Danny and Kent reported to the Chief of Ds and Chief Murray that they had enough for a case. Both of them had witnessed felonies, including violent ones; and, for the purposes of their case in chief, they were accumulating reams of records of fraud, money laundering, extortion, and corruption—including with law enforcement at local police departments, county sheriff's offices, state troopers, and federal law enforcement agencies. The Pettigrew girls had seen, heard, and understood the implications.

Therein lay the rub. How were the two clean cops going to make their case against the fish market criminals and the Mafia without bringing down law enforcement?

Danny and Kent took the problem to Dallas PD Chief Murray in a secret meeting held in his whitetail deer hunting cabin getaway in Pearsall, South Texas. They met while on one of their runs for Don Emiliano which did not arouse any suspicions.

"Chief," Danny told him, "We have plenty of rock solid evidence to put most of the local Dallas Mafia away for years, including every bad guy in the fish market business. The DA and courts all over the state, and in several other jurisdictions will be busy for years working at it and running trials."

"So, what's the problem, you guys… can't stand a little Success? You'll be famous, and I'll be the DA."

"Or we'll all be dead in a ditch," commented Kent morosely. "We have a tiger by the tail."

"Uh, oh," said Murray.

"Yes, sir. A big 'uh oh'. We have dirty cops all over the place. When this breaks, there will be scandals reaching from bottom to top for as long as we are working. That is not going to sit well with the boys in blue, or tan, in campaign hats, or our friends among the fibbies—at multiple levels in multiple branches," Danny said.

Chief Murray blanched and paused; "how far and wide does this go, boys? Looks like we might be about to stir up a hornet's nest."

"More than one, sir. And we have a lot of witnesses and CIs we will have to protect."

"Involving the marshal's service, right?"

"Very right… along with DEA, ATF, DOJ, ICE, FBI, coast guard, you name it."

"Covers most of the cop alphabet, you guys. Look, either we drop this hot potato now before we get a lot of people—including us three—into a whole lot of trouble, or we start up a major task force, probably run by the FBI. What's your take, Danny… Kent?"

"I'm not the boss here… you are. But, this is a big case that will clean up a lot of cop shops and do a lot of good in the long run to make our profession cleaner and better all up and down the line. I say, let's get it going; but, let's get all our ducks in a row first."

"Like protection of our good cops, arrest files for the bad ones, and jails ready to overfill for cops and robbers both."

Danny said, "And, we need to get on with it, while the iron's hot. This evidence is not going to stay around much longer. Look, Chief, this is above our pay grade; we are convinced of that. Maybe even above yours, but you need to be the start of it all from here on out, if I may be so bold as to suggest."

"Y'all are nothing if not bold, Detective. And now is the time for me to fish or cut bait. Man, do I wish I had never heard about any of this. What a mess! I can probably kiss my future political ambitions goodbye."

"Or get to be president!" the two detectives said at the same time.

The process went just about as Danny and Kent predicted. It was long, messy, angry, and dangerous. Department heads were fired, whole divisions of law enforcement went to prison, nearly a hundred mafiosos went to the same prisons as the cops; that created a nearly impossible conundrum for the departments of correction involved. Danny and Kent became minor cogs within months of revealing their evidence logs. Higherups with greater political ambitions took over, and the two Texas detectives were content to get out of the limelight. Penny and Ruth got name changes, new jobs, and then took up residence who knows where?

There was something that nagged at the back of Danny's mind. This whole thing had started by trying to get to the bottom of a missing person's case in a Texas backwater. He could not shake the idea that he was missing something. And that something was probably multiple murders. He shared his opinions with Kent.

"Look, Kent, we have been missing something right in our own jurisdiction and at our level of function. I have this lingering doubt about that case up in Copperas Cove. Something's fishy in that pond, and we have been missing it. We did all this grand cop work because we could not get at the nut of that problem. I think we have been conned out of investigating some criminal activity at that asylum… even murders, maybe even a serial killer. Partner, whatta you say lets get back to work on that?"

"I think I would be more at ease dealing with this kind of Texas crime, Danny. We speak the language better here. Let's take a bit of a long weekend of R and R, then hit it with all we got on Monday," Kent responded.

CHAPTER 7

Another challenge for Jacob, November, 1967

JACOB HAD SEEN HIMSELF AS an underdog and oppressed since before he entered medical school: always the Jew, always the Communist; always last and least to get picked. His ongoing struggles at Burkheart Asylum, Sanatorium, and Destitute Orphans Home with the crook, Dr. Driggs, and the fake witnesses, brought against him, had soured his outlook on life, his profession, and Texas. He felt as if he were trapped in all of that, and that he was required to defend himself however and whenever necessary. He was becoming ever more bitter, ever more remorseless.

For those reasons, he became an early fan of the Dallas Cowboys NFL franchise in Dallas. They were the victims of the NFL which showed overt prejudice, bias, intolerance, narrow-mindedness, unfairness, inequity, favoritism, and one-sidedness. He was a fan before the franchise even came into being. In the early 1960s, the NFL was late in awarding Dallas the new franchise because its would-be owner–Lamar Hunt was rebuffed in his efforts to acquire an NFL franchise for Dallas, and became part of a group of owners that formed the American Football League; his team was the Texans. In an effort not to cede the South to the AFL, the NFL reluctantly awarded Dallas a franchise as the Dallas Steers, then the Dallas Rangers., but not until after the 1960 college draft had been held. As a result, the NFL's first ever expansion team played its inaugural season without the benefit of a college draft and did—as expected—very poorly. That made Dr. Jacob Whitesides very angry.

Danny and his friends from the DPD were likewise upset by the bad treatment being meted out to the aspiring new team—the Texas team. They attended a peaceful rally in Dealey Plaza at 500 Main Street in the heart of downtown. There was a massive but peaceful crowd who had come to learn what could be done to change the NFL's mind.

The small group of cops were not there in an official capacity, but their obvious presence lent a calming effect. Danny and Kent were standing by a bespectacled man with dark hair, an aquiline nose, and somehow a familiar face. Danny struggled to place the man. He seemed to be decidedly out of place—dressed in an off-the-rack blue serge suit, white shirt, and plain blue tie in a crowd of young faces, scraggly beards, T shirts, shorts, and flip-flops. It bothered him that he could not place the man. He prided himself for having a good memory about faces, but this one was escaping him.

"Recognize the guy next to me, Kent? He's familiar, but I can't quite place him."

"I figured him out a few minutes ago. It's a matter of context. You're seeing him out of place. Remember the doctor at the asylum we interviewed a while back? The one who seemed like he had motive for the disappearances or murders—whichever—but there was no evidence of anything, and we let it be for lack of anything to go on."

"Oh, yeah. That's what has been bothering me. It feels like unfinished business. I don't think he recognizes us. Let's do a little exploring here without flashing our copness."

He sidled up a little closer to the asylum psychiatrist, looking for an opening to talk.

Mr. Hunt [whose goal was to bring professional football to Texas and to acquire an NFL team for the Hunt family] was saying, "As y'all know, originally, the formation of an NFL expansion team in Texas was met with strong opposition by Washington Redskins owner George Preston Marshall, bless his pointy little head, and my poor picked on AFL Texans have got to contend with his brainchild, the Dallas Cowboys. Should be our'n, don't y'all think?"

The crowd had a good laugh; Preston Marshall was the demon in Washington holding Dallas back.

"Despite being located in the nation's capital, Marshall's Redskins have been enjoying a monopoly as the only NFL team to represent the American South for over 20 years since moving from Boston in 1937."

"Ain't fair," a redneck shouted from in front of 411 Elm Street on the northwest corner of Elm and North Houston Streets, the infamous School Book Repository, from which the unpopular Democrat President John F. Kennedy was shot back in 1963.

The crowd booed.

Danny took the opportunity.

"Shame, isn't it, that one WASP from up in DC can hold all that kind of power over us southerners."

Jacob answered, "Most certainly is. I know something about unfairness, and I am going to support our Dallas team… even donate a bit of money."

"Oh, me too. Severala us guys are havin' a little palaver after the suits get done talking. Like to come?"

"Where?"

"Cindy's New York Deli… it's at… let's see… 306 South Houston, if memory serves."

"Hey, I'd like to. Don't want to be a buttinsky…"

"David," Danny answered without hesitation. He was becoming something of a smooth liar.

"Shake on it," he said.

Hunt had yielded the bull horn to the founding investors of the Dallas Cowboys—Clint (Jr.) and John D. Murchison.

"Marshall's not about to give up the Redskins' status as the professional football team of Dixie without a down-in-the-gutter-fight, y'all. No surprise there. We got a little something up our sleeves, and the fight is not over. To ensure the birth of our Dallas expansion team, a couple of us bought the rights to the Redskins fight song, *Hail to the Redskins* and won't let them to play their old song at games. We think that nasty old man just might begin to see reason."

The crowd roared its approval. The rally ended as a party and everyone was upbeat about the possibility that—at long last—the real South would get its team. The new fast friends, "David", Jacob, and Kent, made their way to Cindy's where Jacob swallowed a NY Ruebens and a bowl of matzo ball soup, and the two undercover cops had their usual—cheese burgers, fries, and a beer.

The press of work kept the newly established friends from getting together with any frequency, but it was enough for the DPD and Dr. Whitesides to shell out some donation money along with the oil tycoons, and the likes of the heads of Haggar Slacks, and Lone Star Gas. Jacob could not help feeling his spirits lift as he started to fit in with the upscale crowd of Dallas—the real movers and shakers.

Danny and Kent played their newly hatched undercover hand carefully—moved slowly and avoided overplaying the cards they had been dealt. Jacob was hungry for friendship and accepted whatever he could get without getting his suspicions aroused. Any process of mining information about the asylum or about Jacob himself looked likely to be a slow and frustrating effort. Danny seriously believed that the outcome would be worth the wait and effort.

CHAPTER 8

More work for Jacob, late December, 1967

THE WEATHER STAYED CLEAR AND temperate during December—which was a good thing for Jacob Whitesides—because it turned out that more serious work turned up for him to take care of. Just when it looked like all the unpleasantness was behind him, he began to recognize that—once again—Driggs and his henchmen and women were throwing up impediments for him getting his work done. The psych library was moved to an outbuilding, and a quarter of the most valuable new books turned up missing. Educationally speaking, the institution seemed to be reverting to its old, tried, and false premises of care with which the old-school caregivers were more comfortable. There were more corporal punishments, more lobotomies, isolations, strait jacketings, and humiliations.

Jacob did not like it, and he protested to the administration and to the staff and faculty board at the hospital. The response came as a very unwelcome surprise. Instead of giving him an audience about the shortcomings of the Burkheart Asylum, Sanatorium, and Destitute Orphans Home, he received a summons from the law firm of Pratt, Chevelton, and Loftin, to appear in person at their law offices in Copperas Cove, and with records in hand on Wednesday, December 18—just before Chanukah–for a deposition. It was—at the least by the timing—an ill omen.

> "Greetings," the summons read, "You are hereby summoned to attend a deposition to give testimony in the matter of the disappearance of several staff members and patients of the Burkheart Asylum, Sanatorium, and

Destitute Orphans Home. Bring all pertinent records."
—"Cordially yours, Damon Loftin, Jr., Partner and attorney at law of Pratt, Chevelton, and Loftin, Esqs."

Because of the surprise and short time to prepare, Jacob had to scramble to make his preparations, some of which were not entirely the same as the hospital's or the law firm's. He outlined a plan with priorities in order, and how to get it all done in time as second. First, he set about to learn everything he could about the hospital's new law firm, and particularly about Mr. Loftin, upon whom he centered most of his attention.

Second, he made a rapid and concentrated search for an attorney of his own, looking for an attack dog firm, if he could find one. That proved to be easy since the yellow pages were full of advertising law firms, many of which fit his needs to a T. It took him three in-person interviews to locate the perfect attorney, a hard-bitten middle-aged, Jewish, former communist, woman.

"What can I help you with, Dr. Whitesides?" Asnat Netter-Polonsky asked.

For as hard-bitten as she had sounded on the telephone, the greying attorney had soft hazel eyes, a wrinkled face consisting largely of smile lines. Her complexion was sallow from long hours away from the sun. Her clothing was apparently based on the late-great Golda Meir—ill fitting, simple v neck, light print, and large buttons. Her lace-up shoes were flat heeled, scuffed, and grey, where they once had been black. All utilitarian. He liked her immediately.

"The Aryans are after me, Ms. Netter-Polonsky. I need someone on my side in an upcoming discovery deposition."

"Asnat, please. Can I call you Jacob?"

"Both good, thanks. Now, here's what has been going on."

He gave her a rendition of his troubles at Burkheart Asylum, Sanatorium, and Destitute Orphans Home, his suspicions about the criminality going on in the administration, and the efforts to oust him anyway they could, even going so far as to accuse him of murder.

She checked his files—which were copious, annotated, and in both chronological and topical order. She was impressed but recognized the OCD tendency of her tribe.

"Jacob, it seems to me that we should dispense with the murder suspicion. Tell me again why they would think such a thing."

"Two witnesses and an attorney have disappeared who were going to testify against me, apparently. There is not a scintilla of evidence either that there has been a death, a murder, or any kind of crime. Certainly nothing that points at me. At this point, they lack a crime and a criminal; so, they focus on my so-called "short comings" to get rid of me since they can't get me on a crime. Asnat, I am the traditional scape-goat. To say it is not fair is a huge understatement. I would be framed outright if they could come up with something… anything.

"It's a matter of the pot calling the kettle black. They are just a bunch of corrupt crooks stealing from the till by fraud. I need you and your investigators to bring that out. I need some tough Jews to change the narrative. I grew up in a communist Orthodox Jewish community. They banded together to protect themselves, and I want to achieve the same thing here. That's it."

"I presume the evidence you produced will bear all that out, Jacob."

"It will. I did not exaggerate or bear any false witness. It is possible that there are hidden things I have missed or couldn't get at; but I have faith that you can ferret out the truth, and, hopefully get rid of them… or at least get them to leave me be."

Jacob was less tense about the upcoming deposition he had to face after meeting with the doughty attorney Asnat, but he knew he could not leave anything to chance. His next project—beginning that very day—was to find everything there was to know about the firm of Pratt, Chevelton, and Loftin, and about his primary nemesis there, partner Damon Loftin, Jr.

Several elements of Loftin's life made Jacob's task easier. First, he lived and worked in little Copperas Cove; second, his life was an open-book. Hardly a week passed without his social schedule and frequent foreign travels being high-noted in the local press. He and his wife, Gwendolyn, led lives of interest and excitement that exceeded anything anybody else in the town did or hardly even thought of doing.

That week—for example—Damon and Gwendolyn were hosting a major fundraiser for the Republican candidate for governor, Lincoln

Hunt Crosby, at Hills of Cove Golf Course–an 18-hole facility owned and operated by the City of Copperas Cove. Jacob fixated on the amenity provided by the Hills course of a fleet of 40 golf carts. The anticipated crowd for the weekend was expected to be very large, rowdy, and in alcohol lubricated good Texas-style spirits, guaranteeing anonymity for an interloper.

Jacob dressed the part: tall white Stetson cowboy hat, Besteel western cowboy natural tiger eye leather-slide necktie, new Tecovas rattlesnake skin cowboy boots, and floral graphic print turndown yellow red-purple 3D long sleeve print button-down snap button cowboy shirt, and 19th century striped grey dress trousers. He laughed when he saw himself in his full-length mirror but found himself fitting in without attracting attention in the similarly dressed dandies flashing their Texasness. He went about his plan in a concentrated working manner.

He circled Loftin and his wife multiple times, staying out of their view. He took pains to vary his route, to change hats, and to put on some facial disguises from time to time: several beards, eyeglasses, dark glasses, even a fake nose. No one paid him any attention. The golf course is green and ornamented with bright and beautiful weed-free flower beds. The buildings are adobe hacienda style. However, the setting beyond the course proper is hilly, and the hills are fairly bare except for clumps of six-feet tall rounded White Mistflower/Shrubby Boneset bushes and Texas sage—the state bush. He expropriated a new Club Car golf cart.

In the early part of the decade, golf carts were seen primarily as utility vehicles, designed to serve a functional purpose, which was what Jacob really needed. Technological advancements had begun to play a pivotal role in shaping the golf carts of the 1960s. Batteries became more efficient, allowing for longer rides without the need for frequent recharges. The carts' designs began to incorporate more comfortable seating—double seating in Jacob's Club Car–better suspension systems because golfing had become a luxury sport. The large, durable vehicle was perfect for Jacob's brief need.

Jacob drove to a particularly dense patch of Boneset and set up a working site for his project. His original plan was to take just Damon and to make him disappear. However, Gwendolyn was constantly at his side and holding his hand. Jacob had to adjust. His opportunity came after a full day of patiently waiting in his chosen bushes. The host couple wearied of the madding crowds and took a brief sunset stroll. They walked on a well-worn dirt trail that had once led from one extra golf hole to another, which had the advantage for them of being out of sight of the rest of the festivities and crowds. It was to Jacob's advantage as well.

He saw it something like God using Joshua and Caleb—two Israelite men who were spies–and helped them in their cause. That was because their focus was not on the giants the feared but on their God and His purpose. Their hearts were not divided between the past and the promise. They trusted just as Jacob was doing, that his efforts were sanctified because one of his Chosen was in need of protection and assistance. Like Joshua and Caleb, Jacob trusted in the Lord because of his faithful commitment to him and His purposes.

The happy couple was more than a little inebriated, tired, and absorbed in each other. Jacob moved silently in behind them, directly at the man's back. He waited until Gwendolyn rounded a curve in front of Damon, then pounced. Damon went down and off to the side with a perfectly directed karate chop to the back of his neck. Jacob ignored him and moved up close to Gwendolyn. She chatted amiably with the man behind her whom she believed to be her husband.

"Looks like a complete success, Damon," she was saying. "I think the funding we generate tonight for Lincoln could easily be enough to get you the attorney general slot, maybe even the lieutenant governorship. What do you think?"

Those were her last words. A plastic bag over her head stunned and silenced the beautiful woman. It was glued to her neck; and, after five minutes of futile struggle, she was dead. Jacob walked in the shadows back to Damon and administered the same coup de grâce. He slid the two bodies into his covering Boneset bushes and set to the work of beginning to make them disappear from the world below and at large.

He now had the procedures down pat. He wrapped them in plastic sheeting, put them on his nice fancy golf cart and carried them to his waiting truck and loaded them into the waiting bed. He ditched the cart on a well-traveled resort path and motored on in his truck. He stopped by a garbage dump on the way back into town where he found constant fires eating away at the accumulated trash. His gaudy cowboy gear disappeared into one particularly intense fire pit; he changed into his Hill Country work clothes and began his now entirely familiar drive to his farm and to accomplish the tasks necessary for the bodies to become a thick sludge of ash and to sink pleasingly into his pond, which was beginning to be a busy repository.

Saturday evening—even though he was fairly tired from his Hill Country labors—Jacob kept his date with his new friends from the Dallas Cowboys funding group, "David" and Kent, at Sunny Brian's Smokehouse for barbecue and beer. They learned about the ongoing efforts to bring the new NFL franchise to Dallas.

Kent was the info guy. He shared his newest update.

"The team organization has just announced that the official team name is the Cowboys—which everyone already new–to avoid confusion with the American Association Dallas Rangers baseball team. Hunt and the Murchisons have developed some new minority shareholders–Toddie Lee, Bedford Wynne, and Bill Hawn. The new owners are about to hire CBS Sports executive and former Los Angeles Rams general manager Tex Schramm as president and general manager, San Francisco 49ers scout Gil Brandt as player personnel director, and New York Giants defensive coordinator Tom Landry as head coach."

The group chorused their pleasure and had a few more beers.

"David" used the opportunity to make the request for a round of funds. Jacob was feeling upbeat from his week's successes; so, he put two-hundred bucks in the kitty, more than he could afford, but it kept him on something of a par with the big spenders.

Danny chatted up Jacob about his job, the asylum, the drought in the Hill Country, and the Eagles.

"David, my friend, our Eagles played at Burnett Field from 1951 and just set an attendance record of nearly 54,000 for a Texas League game at the Cotton Bowl. Things are looking up for professional baseball. There's a rumor that the Texas League plans to revive the franchise in 1965 as the Dallas-Fort Worth Spurs. That'll mean bigger crowds, more income, better players, and a longer future for baseball in the twin cities. Things are looking up all over my friend."

"And, I'm glad to be part of all that," Jacob responded, feeling an unusual sense of warmth for his chosen place to live and his new friends.

After the meet and eat, Kent showed Danny a spread sheet of Jacob Whitesides' finances—which was unrevealing and pretty tame stuff. However, the information about Dr. Driggs and his Burkheart Asylum, Sanatorium, and Destitute Orphans Home was more than productive. For it to receive full attention, the world had to wait for the cliffhanger Viet Nam Tet offensive of January, 1968 to pass; but the work they did was inexorable and led to an inescapable conclusion.

Kent summed up his presentation with the comment, "It is as phony as a three-dollar bill."

CHAPTER 9

Trouble all around, February, 1968

JACOB PREPARED FOR THE MONDAY meeting by introducing a pro-
phylactic note. He made an anonymous call to the *Copperas Cove Leader
Press* letting the paper and the people of that part of Texas know a scoop
regarding the prominent and well-traveled couple, Damon and Gwendo-
lyn Loftin.

> "Damon and Gwendolyn, our famous gadabouts and
> hunters, recently had an enormous success fund raising
> for the next governor, Lincoln Hunt Crosby. To celebrate,
> they rewarded themselves with a hunting safari to South
> Africa, following the route traveled by the late, great Teddy
> Roosevelt. They expect to be gone for three months, per-
> haps even more. We will miss them."

He decided on a brazen move. He scouted out Loftin's law offices,
broke in during Sunday night, and left a note to Damon's secretary,
Hermione Wentworth, to forward to his partners.

> "Sorry Grant and Homer, I have to go on a safari—tough
> work, but someone has to do it—to schmooze with some of
> Lincoln's oil pals. Should help us in the long run. Be gone
> a good three maybe even four months. Take care of my cli-
> ents, like the good partners you are. I'll make it up to you."
> –Damon

On Monday, at one o'clock in the afternoon, Jacob slipped into the administration office and took his seat at the conference table without anyone seeing him enter. He spread the papers from his brief case in front of him, locked his fingers behind his head, and took a brief nap. Ten minutes later, Drs. Driggs and Christiansen walked in followed by secretary Gywneth P. Rogers and a court recorder who was new to Jacob. None of the people in the room said "hello", "good afternoon" or otherwise acknowledged the presence of any other person there.

By one-thirty, it was evident that the deposition was going to have a late start at best, and the tension in the room was becoming awkward. Jacob determined fiercely to keep his trap shut and the expression on his face as devoid of emotion and information as a slice of Velveeta Cheese, and less attractive. Dr. Driggs fidgeted; Gywneth wiped her brow, and the court recorder checked her schedule and made a few adjustments on her Stentura 400 SRT Stenograph Court Reporting Machine with Case & Try-Pod for the third time. It was still functioning properly and ready for use.

Time dragged. Jacob was the most comfortable of all because he knew more than the rest of them and could simply wait for the script to work its way to conclusion. At one-fifty, a knock came on the conference door. Gywneth was glad for the opportunity to move around and opened the door.

A very attractive, buxom, well-dressed—Neiman Marcus, ivory brocade suit dress with rhinestone buttons and Vinnie 100 Dorsey high heel pumps, all in the ivory/egg shell color that currently all the rage— outfit walked in following Gywneth. She smiled nervously.

"I am the bearer of bad news, I regret to say… My employer, Attorney Damon Loftin is unavoidably detained. An important matter of business has called him away; out of the country actually. I am also obliged to tell you that it will be more than three months before he can reschedule. He sends his regrets. It is also important for me to let you know that neither of the other partners or senior associates will be available until after the Spring rush."

She was chagrined, angry at having drawn the black bean and being subjected to this humiliation. Dr. Driggs was livid; Dr. Christiansen ground his teeth audibly; Gywneth glared daggers at the innocent secretary.

Everyone ignored Dr. Whitesides and the fact that the other witness, a girl from the adolescent ward was also absent. Jacob concentrated on keeping all hints of a smile away from his lips and eyes. Inside, he was laughing out loud.

Finally, Dr. Driggs heaved a small sigh and deigned to take notice of Jacob.

"Well, sir," he said, "it seems that once again our purposes are thwarted. Once again, we will have to postpone our meeting. Once again, we will fail to get to the information we wish to convey and which we wish to obtain from you. Thank you for attending, but the meeting is adjourned indefinitely. One day, we will come to a reckoning, young Jacob."

Jacob showed his empathy and concern with a bit of faked facial sadness. He would have shed crocodile tears if he thought it would have been helpful. He shrugged his shoulders, shuffled his papers, put them back in his briefcase, and left the room without having ever uttered a word.

Kent's information presented to the Major Crimes unit about the asylum's shady activities was almost as exciting as when the unit had came to realize that they had the Mafiosos by the short hairs.

"The spread sheet tells it all, and speaks volumes," Kent said to a rapt audience.

"We have brought in the department's forensic accountancy team to make the information as clear as possible and to get to you guys as fast as we can; so, we can get the investigation formally underway."

They had two long tables, and Lyle Sharma (from Uttar Pradesh)—the forensic accountant–spread several dozen sheets of paper around their periphery.

"All right, a little careful definition so it would be apparent to you that there have been felonies. As I talk, I'll point out on the sheets where the evidence is sitting." Lyle said.

"There are a couple of simple and flagrant tells, both of which are present here. Two sets of books is the most obvious, and then there is obvious smurfing. That's structuring deposits. That method involves breaking up large amounts of money into smaller, less-suspicious amounts.

In the United States, the smaller amount has to be below $10,000. That is the dollar amount at which US banks have to report the transaction to the government. The money is then deposited into one or more bank accounts either by multiple people [smurfs] or by a single person over an extended period of time which is sometimes harder to detect, but it does take longer for the perps.

"Then the money has to be cleaned, which is where the laundering term comes from. "Cleaning" money obtained illegally to erase its connection to criminal activity. Money laundering is a relatively simple process. It works by finding a place to house the dirty money, leveraging performative bookkeeping to make it appear as if the money came from legitimate transactions and then returning the clean money for use in the financial system.

"The money—usually cash money—originates from certain crimes, such as extortion, insider trading, drug trafficking, human trafficking, and illegal gambling. It is—by legal definition, felonious—"dirty" and needs to appear to have been derived from legal activities, so that banks and other financial institutions will deal with it without suspicion or else it might as well be Chinese New Year money for all it is worth. So, money laundering is the process of illegally concealing the origin of money and converting the funds into a seemingly legitimate source, usually through a front organization like we are dealing with here. As I said, money laundering—at its simplest—is the act of making money that comes from Source A look like it comes from Source B."

He pointed to yellow high-lighted items on pages 6-14.

"Terrorists and organized criminals seriously need good laundering systems because they deal almost exclusively in cash," pointing that out on pages 15 and 16.

Money laundering can take several forms, although most methodologies can be categorized into one of a few types. These include bank methods—smurfing [also known as structuring], currency exchanges, and double-invoicing. Not only does cash draw the attention of law-enforcement officials, but it's also really heavy. Not to brag, but most of you and even CPAs are not familiar enough to see the evidence in accounting documents. I can, and here they are."

Pages 17-22.

"And then, there are Overseas banks: Money launderers often send money through various offshore accounts in countries that have bank secrecy laws, meaning that for all intents and purposes, those countries allow anonymous banking. A complex scheme can involve hundreds of bank transfers to and from offshore banks. According to the International Monetary Fund, 'major offshore centers' include the Bahamas, Bahrain, the Cayman Islands, Hong Kong, Vanuatu, Panama, and Singapore. Just seeing a bank account number from one of those countries is a major tipoff.

Pages 23-25.

"Another tipoff is for an accountant to find underground/alternative banking. Some countries in Asia have well-established, legal alternative banking systems that allow for undocumented deposits, withdrawals, and transfers. These are trust-based systems, often with ancient roots, that leave no paper trail and operate outside of government control. This includes the *hawala* system in Pakistan and India and the *fie chen* system in China. We are nowhere near being able to crack those systems, but it is a work in progress.

Page 26.

"Shell companies are fake entities that exist for no other reason than to launder money. They take in dirty money recorded as "payment" for supposed goods or services but actually provide neither; they simply create the appearance of legitimate transactions through fake invoices and balance sheets. It is elaborate and requires serious work on our part to track down the fakes. The Burkheart Asylum, Sanatorium, and Destitute Orphans Home is the poster boy for that. There are fifty shell companies on their roster, some are thirty and forty years old.

Pages 27-41

"Today's crooks are neither stupid nor ignorant. Illegal businesses are not all that hard for us to find; so, the Mafia and terrorist groups have taken to investing in legitimate businesses. For us and the public the view becomes somewhat grey. Launderers may use large businesses like brokerage firms or casinos that deal in so much money it's easy for the dirty stuff to blend in, or they may use small, cash-intensive businesses like bars, car washes, strip clubs, check-cashing stores, and even pizza parlors, especially chains. These businesses become front companies that actually do provide a good or service but whose real purpose is to clean the launderers' money.

"This method typically works in one of two ways: The launderer can combine his dirty money with the company's clean revenues; then the apparently legit company reports higher revenues from its legitimate business than it is really earning—and it is in hard-to-trace and quickly moved cash; or the launderer can simply hide his dirty money in the company's legitimate bank accounts in the hopes that authorities won't compare the bank balance to the company's financial statements. That's naive, but with so many companies around to check, it can go on for a long time.

Page 42-50.

"Most money-laundering schemes involve some combination of these methods. I'll give you one example which should suffice. The Asylum Gang (our term) appeared to invest heavily in the Black Market Peso–a one-stop-shopping system once someone smuggles the cash to the peso broker. The Asylum Gang had one man who was ostensibly a psych tech, whose sole job was to deliver dollars changed to pesos to Peru and the gang's safe banks.

"That market, and many others create headaches for his white-hat workers. The variety of tools available to launderers makes this a difficult crime to stop. However, we caught up with Pedro Lopez-Juarez after his forty-fifth entry and exit from Peru's Jorge Chávez International Airport in Lima. He was on his way in and had two 100 pound bags full of pesos. He had paid the overweight charges quite willingly. He had a family to feed, and he did not want to go to jail in Peru ever. He became the best singer in our choir, and is still pumping out great info to us fibbies."

Page 51-53

"There's more, but let me tell you about the coup de grâce for your friends at the "healthcare center". They got caught having two sets of account books—the sine qua non—of guilt. Once we find them–or significantly altered books–it's all over for the banditos. Knowledge of the second set of books was above tech Nicolás Torres' paygrade. However, Nic was ambitious and curious, and something of a philanderer. He seduced nice secretary Gywneth P. Rogers… yes, that Gywneth—the apparent pillar of ice—into a long term torrid affair. She let down her guard; he took advantage; and presto-chango, he found the second account book; and—industrious as he is—he made a Xerox copy, which he presented us as his get-out-of-jail card.

Pages 54-70.

"It is all packed, wrapped in Christmas paper and tied with a bow. All you have to do is to skedaddle out there to Copperas Cove and make arrests. You're welcome."

The entire room erupted into a cathartic joyous laughter. Several burly cops hoisted light-weight Lyle Sharma above their heads with arms outstretched and paraded him around the room. Afterwards they shared too much champagne provided by Chief Robert V. Murray.

CHAPTER 10

It hits the fan, March, 1968

THE ARRESTS AT BURKHEART ASYLUM, Sanatorium, and Destitute Orphans Home, were perfunctory, quiet, and went the way Danny and the arrest team planned, with one exception. Somehow, from somewhere, Dr. Lyman Christiansen caught wind of something being up, decided that he might be looking at real trouble; so, he fled. He was sought by dozens of law enforcement agencies from around the world and put on a permanent Red Notice by INTERPOL. There were sightings reported to the FBI, CIA, Mossad, Scotland Yard, and MI-6; but none of them panned out. Several of the offshore accounts were cleaned out, but the money was never traced. It was presumed that he was somewhere in the Caribbean sipping mint juleps or Mastiha Sours in the Aegean.

The administrators and their corrupt underlings of the asylum quickly became minor players in the overall scheme of things. MOCGs [mobile organized crime groups] in the EU, Mafia dons, banking CEOs, real estate moguls, managers of healthcare systems, check cashing enterprises, and several members of ISIS, the Taliban, Hezbollah, Hamas, and their strange bedfellows–heads of Israeli gangs–the Abergils, the Dumranis, Zeev Rosenstein syndicates, the Shirazis, AlHanatsheh Cartel, the Amir Molnar—and the Arab Jarushi family, and several chieftains of the Russian mafia in Israel were all identified.

The Asylum Gangsters faced a 77-page, 82-count, federal indictment that alleged murder, massive embezzlement, money laundering, racketeering, money laundering, drug and gun running, and controlling a large Los

Angeles-based ecstasy ring. The US federal, state, and local, courts; the EU court system, Israeli, Iraqi, South Korean, Indian, Argentinian, and Brazilian court systems, were occupied for five years as they processed the data and prosecuted the crimes which emerged from the major bust.

Things went badly all around for the criminals. With minor exceptions, it was a good period for law enforcement and the good guys. There were severe penalties under the RICO statutes, ongoing criminal enterprise rulings, and life sentences for incidentals like murder, rape, torture, extortion, corrupt influence crimes, and the "Three Strikes and You're Out" law. Billions of dollars in fines, confiscations, and ill-gotten gains, hundreds of years of prison time, and the dissolution of hundreds of criminal enterprises resulted.

Back in Dallas, Danny McGraw and his Major Crimes unit had a time to bask in the sunshine of jobs well done and being the original good guys in the process. However, there still remained one nagging matter for Danny.

He finally arrived at the conclusion that someone, somewhere, somehow, was getting away with murder right in his back yard. Six people—that he knew of–had disappeared without a trace. The most recent disappearances were Damon and Gwendolyn Loftin, the well-known and respected attorney and his socialite wife from Copperas Cove. There was no explaining their disappearance away; they disappeared one night from their fundraising event at the golf course. They never boarded a plane, traveled to Africa, were seen in any foreign country; and they were never seen again. Unlike the disappeared ones at the asylum, that was noticed; and they were missed.

Danny called the entire staff of the Major Crimes unit, even the secretaries and janitors for a confab about the perplexing disappearances, he now routinely referred to as "unsolved murders."

"Look," he said, "it bugs me no end that we have been sitting on at least six murders for years now. I don't wanna hear any more talk about "disappearances", "lost souls", and "crazies". We will now investigate full out everyone of them as presumed murders. No exceptions. I think they are all related, but that remains to be seen."

"What's the plan, Boss? " Det. 2 Nielson asked.

She was the unit's computer whiz.

"Give me a little time, Ingrid. I want to hear from everybody else first."

Kent spoke up next, "Ya know, Boss, we have all been taught that when cases get cold, it is time to start over from the very beginning and check every jot and tittle of the investigation so far, nothing left out."

"I agree; and yes, it's fundamental."

Analyst Conrad Gertsch [D1] offered a reason for a plan and the plan itself. It was the best received suggestion of the day.

"Look, we have circled around on set of facts since all of this began. Every time we go out to the asylum, the name of Jacob Whitesides pops up. I checked out the situations, and they are definitely similar. He gets accused of some malfeasance—or more commonly of some sexual molestation of one of the teenage girls; that girl is identified by name, and a hearing is scheduled to delve into the charges. Then, one after the other, the girls fail to show; they are never heard from again; and they are written off as being squirrelly or runaways. End of story. I think it is time posthumous to look seriously into the almost invisible young psychiatrist."

"Conrad, that is so obvious that we have all just ignored it. The man disappears into the background of our thinking and is ignored. That may well be exactly what he wants. I am convinced you are onto something here. I have had niggling thoughts creep into my mind occasionally; and for some reason, I have always gotten distracted. It is time to change that and come to a definitive conclusion one way or the other about him. Since you brought it up, give us a plan of action."

Nothing could have pleased the usually ignored desk jockey more.

"I just so happen to have given it some thought," he said.

"Let's divide up into units. One set to review everything. Another set to search out every little or big thing about Jacob Whitesides, as if he were the main person of interest, or the only person of interest, until something else pops up. The third unit works on the ground. Interview everyone who ever worked with or had to do with the man. Women, men, children, neighbors, fellow doctors, nurses, psych techs, grounds people, where he lives and why, what he does in his spare time, etc. etc."

"Write it up. I'll make the assignments today, and we will come alive. People… this is now a homicide investigation. Gear up and put on your best thinking caps. I will get everything you need; I happen to be in the good graces of the grand poohbahs lately. I will take every advantage of that," Danny said. "And, we'll submit what we have when we get it with central control here. I want Ingrid to be the central controller and collator. She's got the logical mind for it. Conrad, you get out into the field and dig. Find something."

He was his old self, hot to trot and ready to roar. It was the Boss Danny they all respected and liked. Murder investigations were not fun, but this was getting to be close to that.

Danny and Kent wanted to play it cagey, leaving the face-to-face with Whitesides until they had more to go on. They went to the primary intake prisoner facility to have their investigatory interviews. first. Most of the local felons were housed in Huntsville State Penitentiary and were going to be imprisoned for the rest of their natural lives. The 93 acre James "Jay" H. Byrd Jr. Unit (DU) is the Texas Department of Criminal Justice prison for men located in Huntsville, Texas one mile north of downtown Huntsville on Farm to Market Road 247.

Danny got full cooperation from Warden George John Beto. The warden believed the Asylum Gang had gotten a soft deal; so, he wanted to see them squirm a bit or at least contribute to the next part of the Texas crime investigation and punishments. Beto provided them a work room in the third story education/library building of the Walls Unit. Warden Beto chatted with them over a meal of chicken dumplings, steamed rice, sliced bread, black-eyed peas, and iced tea with quiet Tex-Mex music in the background. The prison had a long and sometimes turbulent history. The Huntsville Penitentiary was the only prison in the eleven Confederate states still standing at the end of the Civil War.

Danny wanted cooperation; so, he and Kent visited with the Asylum Gang in their cells—two men to a cell. They had quickly gained trustee status, and the warden allowed them to take the DPD detectives on a little excursion around the sprawling prison. That allowed some breaking of the ice and a chance to speak fairly freely.

Quentin Driggs kept up a chatter most of the way, and Danny gave him free reign; so, he could feel safe and unthreatened by the two tough looking police officers.

"We landed pretty well, you know. Beto has done a lot of improving here: established weekly worship services with choir presentations and Bible study like my wife and I enjoyed together. It's not home, but there are vestiges. He initiated night classes that offered the rudiments of a basic education and offered to let me teach some psychology and psychiatric treatment classes. The previous two wardens set up a library of several thousand volumes."

"Do you get the chance to work... I mean physical work, Quentin?"

"Yeah, I find it relieves some of the stress. It's not like the old ball-and-chain gang sweat labor of before. Prisoners work on state-owned farms in the coastal areas of the state, where their labor earns greater revenues than come from the sale of goods produced in the prison shops. There's a plant to manufacture license plates. Maybe half of the inmates have some kind of work... passes the time, and apparently has made things safer in the cell blocks and the yard. Less violence."

Back on the cell block, the four men sat around a table which was fixed securely to the floor and talked about the disappearances at the asylum and the possibility... even probability, that the missing were murder victims.

"I know you came to question us about the missing girls and the lawyer. No problems for us; it isn't like we were ratting on anybody inside or in one of the prison gangs. I can tell you that we had our suspicions since the very first girl did not show up to give testimony about Dr. Whitesides... what was her name, Tom?"

"Don't remember for sure, but it was one of the four trouble maker Borderline Personality girls: Abigail Constella, Mary Anne Patterson, Petra Sloweski, or Ingrid Pettersdotter."

Driggs templed his fingers on the bridge of his nose and thought a moment. "I really think it was Abby Constella who was first. We had it on good reliability that Whitesides gave her bosum a naughty squeeze."

"Right, and the next three left the place... or were killed off down the line just about every time we scheduled a meeting. Whitesides came every time. Sat there like a sphinx and had nothing to say. He certainly never admitted to anything hinky."

Danny asked both inmates, "Did Whitesides have a reputation?"

"You mean besides being a Jew and a commie? Yeah, I heard that he got a girl to sneak off to the storeroom or into his office and close the door every once in a while."

"Any proof?"

"Not really, but you know about those city Jews. They can't leave the Christian girls alone. I am as sure as my name is Quentin that the man played the slap-and-tickle game with more than one of them."

"Any claims of violence?"

"Lots of them. Went after some of the garden staff with a switch blade like those *Rassenschandes* [Nazi term for racial disgrace] do, ya know. Two or three nurses and a tech or three got scared off by him when he had a temper tantrum. He was very prone to that, and I told him to get into anger management. He never obeyed any order I ever gave him, as I recall."

Tom raised one questioning eyebrow as his former boss gave those pieces of "information".

The talks with the principal criminals from asylum for another hour produced 15-20 pages of accusatory notes, none of which had any backup evidence behind them. Danny and Kent then went to the second cell block where the lesser members of the Asylum were housed.

It was a waste of time. There were litanies of self-excusing, self-pitying, rationalizations:

"I need to do it from my team and my family."

"I wanted the dream to keep on going."

"I didn't want to disappoint the people who believed in me."

"It is better to tweak the numbers one time than to leave people without bonuses."

"I was instructed to do it."

"Everybody does it."

"You would have done the same thing if you were in my shoes."

"It was outside of my control; I just didn't have a choice."

"Since so many people were aware, it couldn't have been that bad."

"My contribution was so small that—relative to everyone else and what they did—what I did didn't matter."

"I'm a victim of circumstances."

"It was the auditors' job to catch this. It's their fault."

"No one will ever notice."

"I'll pay it back."

"It's not a big deal… material… doesn't really matter in the big scheme of business."

"I was just leveling the field."

"You know, technically, everything was within the GAAP [Generally Accepted Accounting Principles]."

"They deserved it."

"They owe me this."

"They don't pay me enough."

"They passed me over for my promotion."

"It was just a case of me or them."

"Look, it's their duty to exercise proper due diligence."

"Shareholders aren't real people, you know that."

"It's just transactional capitalism and quid quo politics; what's the big deal?"

"It was just a temporary loan."

"It was just a timing difference."

"A lot of people were worse than me. This isn't fair."

"It was nothing, maybe a few off-the-sheet items… we didn't amortize, so what?… creation of separate subsidiaries, so what? Everybody does it. Everybody does it. Everybody does it…"

CHAPTER 11

Laser focus on Jacob Whitesides, late April, 1968

THE APRIL MEETING OF DANNY McGraw's Major Crimes unit produced working material sufficient to convince the detectives and analysts that they were definitely on the right track. The assiduous forensic accounting effort served only to prove that Jacob Whitesides was not a white-collared crook and had nothing to do with the ongoing criminal enterprise of the Asylum Gang. The intensive canvass of every employee of the Burkheart Asylum, Sanatorium, and Destitute Orphans Home since Jacob arrived on the scene produced a picture of a man dedicated to his work, who protected, not molested the girls, and who was being wrongfully persecuted for some reason.

The most important data came from now D2 Analyst Conrad Gertsch's prodigious work on Jacob Whitesides' troubled background. He uncovered Jacob's life in Brooklyn Heights, Los Angeles and exposed the leitmotiv of his life which was his being regularly discriminated against for being Jewish and the severe costs and impediments that produced for the ambitious young professional. He read the entire transcript of the House Subcommittee on UnAmerican Activities and the phony accusations against the unfortunate witnesses. Jacob Whitesides was tarred with the same brush.

"I think it poisoned his whole life and way of looking at things. He wanted to get his education in California near his family and friends. Instead, he had to settle for Texas. He wanted to be a surgeon. He had to settle for becoming a psychiatrist. He wanted to pursue a rewarding academic career. Instead, he had to settle for becoming stuck in a dead-end job in the middle of nowhere.

"There is ample evidence to support the statement that Jacob Whitesides was again the victim of outright prejudice and discrimination. Evidence against him was faked. Witnesses—such as they were—were inveigled or coerced into memorizing scripts showing him as a molester, a violator of the most sacred contracts between patients and doctors. He was almost—but not totally friendless. It is not surprising that our man became very defensive, even paranoid. He lost all trust in the justice system, even as operated in academia and the asylum where he ended up trying to do his best to help people.

"That, my good colleagues, is the basis of a different—but potent motive, one that was entirely logical to Whitesides, because it was self-protective. I have copies of the notes written by Dr. Driggs and the others about how the plan was hatched to destroy the new man's reputation and to get rid of him.

"Why did they do that? Because he was the only honest one of the bunch, the only guy not part of their very lucrative criminal industry, and the only person likely to become a whistleblower. He knew that, and he fought back. Thus, the murders."

Danny asked D2 Ingrid Nielson to present next. She had been assigned to be the controller which sounded like a desk job. Ingrid was— at heart—a field agent. The third unit worked on the ground interviewing everyone who ever worked with or had to do with the man. Women, men, children, neighbors, fellow doctors, nurses, psych techs, grounds people, where Whitesides lives and why, what he does in his spare time. Ingrid went at that like a dynamo machine—one that turned mechanical energy into the electricity of proof. She went everywhere, saw and interviewed everyone who mattered, and put two and two together to come up with the correct and rather simple answer.

"Thanks for letting me talk. This data has been crunching around in my pointy little head for too long. We started at the beginning and worked to the present day, but I am going to present the evidence and conclusions by starting at the end, the last two people who disappeared.

"Damon and Gwendolyn Loftin's disappearance attracted the most attention, although not at first. It seemed to me that they were so important and recognizable that somebody had to have seen at least a minor something. Our star witness was Alfred "Stumpy" Jones, a homeless man who camped in the bushes above the Hills of Cove Golf Course in Copperas Cove. He is a vet of the Viet Nam war with serious PTSD which has pushed him to withdraw from society. He is actually well educated, intelligent, curious, and observant.

"Stumpy—so named because he lost his left lower leg to an IED in country—was altogether willing to talk; and he talked volumes, about the night the couple disappeared. He had been an army ranger who put in four tours of duty; so, he was a master of camouflage, escape and evade, and not being detected. He watched Whitesides drive a Club Car golf cart—which he described in full detail—into a clump of tall boneset bushes and settle in for a stake out of sorts.

"Apparently, Whitesides knew something nobody else knew—nobody but Stumpy—which was that the Loftins like to get away from the cloying crowds and take moonlight walks. He and Whitesides knew the exact trail. Whitesides ambushed the Loftins and killed them on the spot. Stumpy witnessed it all, and he is willing to testify in court. His affidavit is probably the best I have ever encountered. I am pleased to announce that we have our killer dead to rights with full detail.

"And there is more. Until we pushed the envelope some more, we were left with a probable motive, a definite murder, but still no body or bodies. We hashed it over and came to several conclusions. First, no one had seen Whitesides doing anything suspicious in or around the asylum that suggested hiding a corpse. Second, he seems to have no social life and no activities in Copperas Cove other than his work at the asylum. Third, he must have another place, one where he feels safe. So, we set out to find such a place.

"Modern technology is marvelous. His Mazda Eunos Cosmo car has a GPS tracker system. Presumably, he does not even know about it. We got a warrant to search the car, took it to our shop when he was asleep, and traced its entire history. We have that in an evidence document. We tracked him to a little place in the Hill Country, near Lost Maples State Park and the towns of Kerrville and Vanderpool."

There was rapt attention in the room. Det. 2 Nielson was laying out what appeared to be the entire case against the heretofore completely invisible murderer.

"So, we went to the Hill Country and began poking around. Not that many folks there. We flashed Whitesides photo around, and after a couple of weeks of flatfoot work, we turned up or first lead—an old farmer named Jimmy West. Seems he sold our perp his farm, lock, stock, and barrel. He described the place, and it seems perfect for a corpse hider, but that remains to be seen.

"Our search led us to a nice old lady, Cynthia Pluxen. She had a nephew on her brother's side who she believed had worked for Whitesides. We traced him—one Lemuel Pluxen–to New Orleans, found him; and he gave us almost everything else we needed to make our case."

"Like... ?" Danny asked.

"A bunch of stuff for hiding bodies and information about where we can find it. I am thinking that we might find a lot of trace DNA at the site, but we haven't been able to get to there yet. It's next on the do list."

Danny had all he needed.

"Absolutely great work, Ingrid. Don't believe anything the locals here say about you," he said with an affectionate smile.

She stuck her tongue out at him, maybe a centimeter of its length and laughed. She knew that being put down as small joke from the boss was the equivalent of a New York ticker tape parade. She had a glow on when they loaded up the whole army and all its equipment the next morning and began the expedition towards Vanderpool.

They spent an entire week scouring the property and found nothing suspicious, certainly no equipment of desecration. Danny had a brain flash and went back into town and got Jimmy West to come out to the farm to lend a hand in the search.

When he saw where they had been looking, Jimmie laughed, showing his rotting three tooth dentition.

"Betcha a beer I can find his spot in less than an hour," Jimmie said to Danny and Ingrid.

"You're on."

It took the old man less than fifteen minutes. First, he found Jacob's well-hidden new road and followed its serpentine path to Jacob's hard fought for clearing in the very north east corner by the Guadalupe River. Everyone was in a fast trot by the time they passed the roads first curve. Five minutes later, they were looking at Jacob Whiteside's master work for human body desecration.

"Nobody touch a thing," Danny shouted, and everyone stopped in their tracks. "Trace DNA is going to be critical; and as of now, this place belongs to the lab."

Painstaking would not aptly describe the ensuing process; excruciatingly tedious came closer. The lab rats worked during daylight every day for a full week before bringing their preliminary results the boss, Kent, and Ingrid.

"Whitesides is very smart and extremely thorough about cleaning. But… we are smarter, and even more thorough; besides we have been at our jobs a lot longer. I won't say we never make mistakes, but I can say with conviction that Dr. Whitesides made at least one more than we did, and it was a doozy."

"Out with it," Ingrid said, her taut nerves pushing her adrenaline level to the top of the measure.

"Right on," Analyst D2 Conrad Gertsch and Irena Gottschalk-Polonski, CCSA [Certified Crime Scene Analyst] said together, already bursting with enthusiasm to fire their final information bomb.

"You have to hand it to the man. He did everything imaginable to get rid of any evidence, especially DNA. He hosed out the wood chipper with a fire hose; he scrubbed everything down with Clorox and burned what remained with a gasoline fire. Seeing the equipment he had, he had to have incinerated the remains, let it soak in two separate solutions—potassium hydroxide, then hydrochloric acid–and carted off the ash-sludge-inert mass somehow. We're still working on that part. Don't expect anything anywhere near like an intact human corpse.

"And we don't need it. He was not as thorough as us professional OCD masters are. He missed an entire ring of highly usable DNA, almost fresh, under the lip of the chipper. What we got will make the case. He is a goner."

"What do you have so far?"

"Fifteen, maybe more, separate sets of DNA."

"Any of it animal tissue or blood?"

"No, that much is clear. He bought the thing new, and this appears to be the first time it was used. The paint is still shiny. It will take a full week to get this all sorted out and identified by the FBI DNA lab in Quantico. But when we do, we will have a locked down case like you have never seen before."

"Break out the champagne time, Boss?" asked Ingrid.

"Not yet. I want that guy behind bars before we wrench a muscle clapping ourselves on the back."

"I suggest we go after him right now. No time like the present."

"Okay, let's get cleaned up and bring in the apprehension squad. I do not any kind of mistake to ruin this party."

It took them forty-five minutes to clean up and another two hours to get back to Copperas Cove where they expected to find Jacob Whitesides hard and work with his patients and completely oblivious to the mountain that was about to land on his head.

CHAPTER 12

Swooping in on Jacob Whitesides, late April, 1968, late that same afternoon

AFTER THE SLOW START GETTING away from the Hill Country, things began to move in a rapidly changing kaleidoscope. Danny left Kent and Ingrid at the farm in case Whitesides came back. The race was on; Danny could feel it in his bones. He called ahead to the DA's office. The law enforcement motorcade entered Copperas Cove and drove to the 6th red light, turned right on Robertson Avenue and went to the 4 way stop. They were across the street to the left. Corner of Main St. and Robertson in front of the municipal court house/city hall on 602 S. Main Street. They left their motors running, and Danny rushed into the building and up the stairs three at a time. He paused for a second to catch his breath, then burst into DA Owen C. Brightell's private office on the second floor.

Brightell was as excited as Danny; he said, "You got him, really got him ?!"

"And a ton of the best circumstantial evidence you will ever see."

"Here's the arrest warrant, signed by Judge Gabler. Get outta here!"

The ready-to-go motorcade roared full throttle through the quiet streets of Copperas Cove, lights and sirens at maximum. Motorists and pedestrians on busy Creek Street hurried out of the way to safety. The motorcade skidded left at the corner of Bowen Avenue and again at KLM street and into the cul-de-sac were Whitesides kept his apartment.

The levels of adrenaline and testosterone were revved up beyond the healthy upper limits of normal. The posse swept out of the vehicles and surrounded the apartment building with the precision and earnestness of D-Day.

Danny yelled into his coms, "Don't shoot the guy unless you absolutely have to. We came here to bring down a perp and to get the man to jail. I want just the arrest unit to come with me."

They did not bother knocking on either the main apartment house door or the door to Whitesides. The DPD SWAT team bashed in both doors, and the unit swept in crouched behind tall rectangular anti-riot shields, the phalanx bristling like a forest of firearms. It was a small, neat, two-bedroom-one-bathroom place with a kitchenette and sitting TV room. The table, counters, TV top, and bedside table/chest of drawers were clean, neat, and disappointing. The draws were empty everywhere; so, were the new trash bins. The carpet had been recently cleaned professionally, and the floors beneath were spotless and shiny.

The words, "clear", "clear", and "clear" echoed throughout the empty apartment.

"Cleaned out professionally," Danny said. "I'll bet we don't find a print or DNA sample anywhere."

"You'ed likely win," responded the head of the CIS team, "but we'll go through the drill anyway.

His response was as morose as Danny's.

In the end, they were both right. They got nothing, nada, nil. The walls blistered blue with the language of the discouraged coppers and crime scene analysts.

Within ten minutes of that disappointing entrance, a massive manhunt got underway. Over the coming days, weeks, and months, it turned from a local to a statewide to a federal dragnet and spilled over to most of the civilized countries still on speaking terms with the United States. Copperas Cove patrolmen, Texas Highway patrol, Texas State CID units, the FBI, CIA, military investigators, MI-6, Mossad, Scotland Yard, Europol, INTERPOL, European Union Police Mission, GCCPOL [Gulf Cooperaton Council Police], SELEC [Southeast European Law Center], and friendly police from Africa—even Eritrea–Egypt, Greece, Australia, New Zealand, and a host of places and police units Danny had never heard of before this worldwide hunt with him as the ostensible boss. After two years of complete futility at a cost of hundreds of thousands of dollars and manhours, the search was put on pause.

DA Brightell made a decision and informed all the law enforcement agencies and the DOJ that he intended to hold a trial-in-absentia; so, at least something would come out of the massive effort. It became the main subject of breaking news for that five-day cycle, then dropped off the interest list in favor of the opinion "news" of a new election silly season.

Brightell and his friends among Texas constitutional lawyers studied constitutional and case law for several months. For more than 100 years, courts in the United States have held that the United States Constitution protects a criminal defendant's right to appear in person at their trial, as a matter of due process, under the Fifth, Sixth, and Fourteenth, Amendments. However, Brightell et.al. found the following exceptions are included in the "Rule":

- the defendant waives his or her right to be present if he or she voluntarily leaves the trial after it has commenced,
- if he or she persists in disruptive conduct after being warned that such conduct will cause him or her to be removed from the courtroom,
- in prosecutions for misdemeanors, the court may permit arraignment, plea, trial, and imposition of sentence in the defendant's absence with his or her written consent, and
- the defendant need not be present at a conference or argument upon a question of law or at a reduction of sentence under Rule 35 of the Federal Rules of Criminal Procedure.

Indeed, several SCOTUS decisions have recognized that a defendant may forfeit the right to be present at trial after several unsuccessful attempts to capture or kill him if society has a legitimate interest in the resolution of criminal cases, which it does. One way to avoid these negative consequences is a trial in absentia because it helps to prevent the defendants from manipulating the judicial system by deciding with their presence whether or not a case can be tried. Next, it will explain the content of this "public necessity".

The federal courts of appeal moved forward to the possibility of trying a person in absentia even though he had been absent from the beginning of the trial. In United States v. Tortora, it was found that there was no element to justify his failure to appear. It was without question that his absence was voluntary and knowing which helped to determine and classify what has been considered sufficient "public interest" to justify a trial in absentia. It was deemed—at most levels of the justice system—that the public interest in an orderly system of justice and conservation of judicial resources warranted commencement and continuation with the Whitesides trial.

In United States v. Muzevsky, the court extended the public necessity prong to single defendant cases affirming that these cases did not compel a per se rule that single defendant trials cannot proceed in a defendant's absence.

Crosby v. US The court concluded that he—and by extension, Whitesides–had voluntarily waived his right, and the public interest in proceeding with the trial in his absence outweighed his interest in being present during the proceedings.

Although the legal haggling took months, the trial in absentia of Jacob Roth Whitesides only used up four days of judicial time from voir dire and seating of the jury to the presentation of the mountains of evidence—abbreviated by a panel of judges in the interest of judicial efficiency and the capacity of the jury to deal with such volume—to the attorneys' summations, to jury deliberation and decision, and to verdict, lasted just an hour less that four days. The verdict was guilty; the sentence was life imprisonment without the chance of obtaining parole. It might well have been a capital crime, except that Texas's execution law was still in abeyance.

The issue of public necessity was presented in court in order for it to be promulgated abroad even to foreign countries, thereby exhausting every avenue of communication with the defendant who had been convicted in absentia. For the court, the burden lay in difficulties in rescheduling the trial for several reasons that all courts face, but in the Whitesides case, because there was no time in sight when he would be arrested and brought to trial. Time was of the essence to comply with the constitutional rights to a speedy trial. In that case, the likelihood that the trial could take place soon with defendant's presence was nil.

In Crosby, and again in Whitesides, the constitutional possibility to try someone who has never appeared at his trial because he wanted to prevent the proceedings from continuing requires performance that is possible for the court to accomplish. In the Supreme Court US v. Whitesides case involving trial in absentia the majority ruling was that the Constitution grants the defendant *only* the opportunity to confront the witnesses against him, but if he refuses that privilege, he cannot insist on it later. As long as this chance is sufficiently guaranteed, there is no necessity under the Constitution to give any different protection based upon absconding either at the commencement of the trial or during it. In the end, SCOTUS ruled that worldwide repeated public notice met the requirements sufficiently.

Due diligence to inform the defendant throughout the world's information avenues was set in motion. That was based on the premise that the defendant knows that the verdict will go against him prior to the beginning of the trial proceedings since the defendant knows the evidence against him before entering the courtroom. Nothing in the *Constitution* prohibits a trial from being commenced in the defendant's absence as long as the defendant knowingly and voluntarily waives his right to be present. The well educated fugitive could not have been wholly ignorant of his rights; so, further communication was no longer indicated; it was even impossible. The *Constitution* does not require the defendant's presence during a trial. It is possible to try him without his presence, either when he is absent from the beginning of the trial or when he fails to appear on a subsequent day. In other words, it would continue only under extraordinary circumstances; in this case in absentia.

One legal tool that defendants have to manipulate their trials is by absconding before the commencement, because the federal rule and the case law forbid continuing with a trial if the defendant was not present at the beginning. On the other hand, the *United States Constitution* does not go that far and only requires the possibility that the defendant confront the witnesses against him. This right can be waived as long as it was a voluntary and knowing waiver. Whitesides' implied waiver was the fact that he put himself knowingly into absentia.

An abuse of trials without the defendant's presence or an arbitrary application of the trial in absentia can also undermine the principles supposedly safeguarded by a trial in absentia–the confidence of the people in the judicial system. For this reason, it was considered advisable to consider the "balancing test" which, in addition to a defendant's voluntary and knowing waiver of his right to be present. In this unusual case, SCOTUS took into account the "public interest" to continue with the proceedings of the trial.

Jacob Roth Whitesides had planned for this time for two full years and had left no stone unturned to become invisible and unfindable. To get money, he successfully robbed two Canadian banks—enough to fund him until he could get settled with a new name, new face, and new credentials, in a new place, where no one knew the quiet new guy in the neighborhoods, which changed with frequency.

Danny McGraw refused to give up. He kept doggedly on, accepting failures as the natural cost.

CHAPTER 13

The denouement, late April, 1969, afternoon

THE MAN SAT PLACIDLY IN a beach lounge seldom moving. Occasionally, he stood to cast his heavy line into the surging surf weighted by a heavy triangular lead sinker. His line sailed out beyond the excited large waves and undertow to where the water was calmer and over seven feet deep. It was a beautiful azure blue color of the sky on a clear day with a tint of 5BG Munsell green. Rarely, he brought in a reasonable sized Blackchin tilapia, Kingklip, or Red Snapper, which went into his plastic bucket. He stared at the ocean in the mean time, not interfering with his reverie by reading, listening to music, or talking to the occasional passer-by.

The coastal sea breeze was soothing; his sporadic tugs on his long-necked bottle of pale lager chicha required no concentration on his part, and he appeared to be oblivious to his surroundings otherwise, especially what was behind him.

His watcher took note of the man's shoulder length black hair, heavily tanned skin, and his rude fisherman's canvas cloth shirt and beach shorts. His feet were bare. At his side was a small metal lunch pail, from which he withdrew what appeared to be a fish taco and chewed on it lazily every now and again.

Finally, the watcher was satisfied. He stood up and stretched his muscles sore from sitting on a hard block of construction concrete. He walked across the myriad footprints in the sand of the beach to stand immediately behind the man he had been scrutinizing for over an hour.

He said in an authoritative baritone voice, "Dr. Whitesides, I presume."

Danny McGraw felt the man's body become rigid. Otherwise, he did not move.

"How... how did you find me?" Jacob finally managed.

He did not try to turn around, to face Danny, or to protest. Danny presumed that he knew that the jig was up finally.

"I'm a detective. I find out things, and I am very persistent. In your case, we found about you the old fashion way; we had a snitch."

"Really... who? I hardly have any acquaintances let alone friends. I mean, who could know that kind of stuff about me?"

"Think a minute, Jacob. Have a girl friend... somebody who is the only one to know something no one else knows, despite how close-mouthed you have been your whole life?"

He tugged at his neckline as if it were too tight.

"Ah, Dina Cantrell ?"

"Not a chance. She hates your guts. Try again."

"Detective, you got me. Tell me that little bit... please."

"How about someone like Dr. Gladys Y. Jefferson, the expert on adolescent personality disorders, Jacob? Hmmh?"

He put his face into the palms of his hands and began to cry.

"I can't believe that," between his sobs and gulping to try and regain his composure.

"I now truly believe that no one can ever really trust anyone else. We had a serious, behind the scenes, loving relationship born from the mind, not the endocrine system. How could she?"

"Don't blame Dr. Jefferson over much. I have to take some of the blame, or credit, as the case may be. We found her number on your cell phone, one of only three. There were not even numbers for your immediate family. We got her address, account numbers, e-mail address from our patient search of her phone use. The main way that police can track your phone is by working with your mobile carrier. Carriers keep a record of what cell towers your device has connected to and the associated signal strength. The police can use this information to triangulate your location both historically and in real time. We also used reverse phone lookup. We found several bits of intel that were easy and highly useful. In a matter of days, we knew where you were and could keep track of your changes of address and phones. Dr. Jefferson referred you to a colleague, a plastic surgeon. He referred you to an ENT cosmetologist. She referred you to some shady friends for a price, and they made illegal documents for you: driver licenses, passports, birth certificates, school graduations… the whole magillah.

"Probably the most useful of all the data was the call she made to you day before yesterday. That was the first time we knew about your neat little pied a terre here in remote Samara Beach, Guanacaste province, Costa Rica. Nice place here. All I had to do was to look for the place I thought I'd like if I was a secret fugitive on the lam. Here we are on this very long crescent shaped beach where you can see trouble coming for miles. You are protected by a coral reef so the water is very warm all year round and big fast police boats can't come at you from the open ocean."

"But, you didn't any idea what I look like now. How did you know you were looking at Jacob Whitesides and not Moishe Goldblum, proprietor of the beach's most successful jewelry emporium?"

"Almost dumb luck, Jacob. I guessed that you would revert back to your Jewishness where you felt comfortable, not so much faking it all the time. I poked around with the local gendarmes and learned who came in about the same time as Dr. Jefferson said you had moved here."

"How did you force her to help you?"

"Gave her some clearcut choices. Prison or rat on you. Took her less than ten minutes to cave in. Full immunity bought everything she ever knew or would know about you. It was like finding a long lost neighbor down the street—telephone numbers, names of doctors, dentists, grocers, preferences—everything we needed to know."

"But, I had all that cosmetic surgery; it wasn't cheap, you know. And it was private HIPAA [The Health Insurance Portability and Accountability Act rules and all that."

"That was just plain greed and bribery, Jacob, old fashion stuff. Marilyn Bell Geddes, secretary of Dr. Guido Lopez, premier facial artist, etc. etc. She likes money and the good life. We helped her get her share of all of that. She was so happy to help that she even provided before and after photographs… nice work. I had a copy of your face on my phone and had a good idea of what the back of your head looks like now that you have grown out your hair so extravagantly. Not a good look, Jacob; but it is easy to spot. I looked at you for a good hour and compared. It was you all right. I had struck the Holy Grail."

He sighed. It was over. He knew all about the trial in absentia and the sentence of life inside for the rest of his years. He knew there was no chance of bribing this poster boy cop or getting leniency.

He said, "Detective McGraw, how about we share a last supper together, my treat?"

Danny smiled, put the cuffs on Jacob's wrists, and together they went to Soda la Peria for a splendid dinner of ceviche, Chilean crab—which they shared family style—and Casado [the combo plate]. It cost a whopping 4000 colones (or $8 USD for two). He kept one cuff on Jacob and one on himself during the meal, throughout the night, and on the 1,780 mile four and a half hour flight to Dallas and Jacob Roth Whitesides final denouncement and comeuppance.

— THE END —